# HOW STATES PAY FOR WARS

# HOW STATES PAY FOR WARS

Rosella Cappella Zielinski

CORNELL UNIVERSITY PRESS ITHACA AND LONDON

Cornell University Press gratefully acknowledges receipt of a subvention from Boston University, which aided in the publication of this book.



First published 2016 by Cornell University Press
Printed in the United States of America

**Library of Congress Cataloging-in-Publication Data**

Names: Cappella Zielinski, Rosella, author.
Title: How states pay for wars / Rosella Cappella Zielinski.
Description: Ithaca : Cornell University Press, 2016. | Includes bibliographical references and index.
Identifiers: LCCN 2016003676 | ISBN 9781501702495 (cloth : alk. paper)
Subjects: LCSH: War finance—Political aspects. | War finance—History—19th century. | War finance—History—20th century.
Classification: LCC HB195 .C28 2016 | DDC 355.6/22—dc23
LC record available at http://lccn.loc.gov/2016003676

Cornell University Press strives to use environmentally responsible suppliers and materials to the fullest extent possible in the publishing of its books. Such materials include vegetable-based, low-VOC inks and acid-free papers that are recycled, totally chlorine-free, or partly composed of nonwood fibers. For further information, visit our website at www.cornellpress.cornell.edu.

Cloth printing 10 9 8 7 6 5 4 3 2 1

*For Michael and Rosa Cappella*

**If we can go on giving the army what they want longer than the Germans can do this to theirs, we may appear to win by military prowess. But we shall really have won by financial prowess.**

—John Maynard Keynes, 1916

# Contents

# Illustrations

## Figures



## Tables

# Preface

I began work on what would become this book about war finance in 2008–2009. At that time, the United States was in the midst of two wars: the 2007 "surge" in Iraq was ending and the 2009 "surge" in Afghanistan was beginning. The American economy was plunging into a recession that has since been dubbed the worst financial crisis since the Great Depression. The strength of American military and economic power was coming into question.

It was against this backdrop that this project was conceived. This American landscape sparked three questions for me: How and why was the United States paying for two wars without a tax increase? What does the state of the American economy mean for America's ability to project its military power? Do the horrific consequences of war also mean economic ruin for a state? In pursuing the answers to these questions, the puzzles of this book emerged: What explains the variation in how states finance war? Why does taxation finance some wars while others are paid for via domestic debt, external funding, or printing?

As I started to explore war finance, I found state and military power to be not what I thought they were. I had thought military power generally reflected the size of a state's economy—more money, more guns. Instead, I found that mobilizing resources for war was a wholly different ball game from "military power," broadly defined. First, I was mistaken to think a state's resources were bound by its economy. States can tax, print money, borrow from their domestic population, borrow from abroad, and plunder. Second, I was mistaken to think war finance was a simple tax-versus-debt tradeoff. This dichotomy obscures the various forms of taxation—sales taxes, income taxes, excess profit taxes, and tariffs, to name a few—and various forms of debt—floated at fixed or market rates, purchased by individuals or banks, a targeted bond campaign, or issued to society at large—all of which have different political and economic costs for leaders and citizens. Third, I had a go-it-alone attitude. I thought states could finance wars domestically if the state had the capacity to raise taxes or float debt. Regardless of domestic economic might, however, when states are constrained by their currency reserves when purchasing inputs for the war effort from abroad, they are forced to rely on external third parties. Fourth, I thought war trumps all. That is, when fighting a war, leaders are concerned with the war effort above all else. Leaders, however, often use war finance policy to meet other domestic goals, that is, the redistribution of wealth, beyond the war effort. Finally, it was confirmed for me that to study guns separately from money is a mistake. If we as scholars and policymakers are ever to truly understand state power—our own, an ally's, or an adversary's—we need to understand how money affects guns and vice versa.

This book has a vast mandate. Given that scholars have largely ignored the nature of war finance, it was necessary to go beyond one country's experience or war finance in the post–World War II era. Hence the book explores two hundred years of war finance from 1800 to 2003. Beyond empirical breath, the project provides theoretical depth. It invests in concept building: What is war finance? What do we mean by cost of war? What are the various attributes of war finance? It is only after investing in concept building that I could begin to answer the question of what explains the variation in war finance. In brief, I argue that war finance is a function of political decision making as leaders attempt to control the costs of war as well as the capacity of the state to extract resources from its citizens and abroad.

While the mandate for the book is large, it is designed in such a way that the reader can pick and choose the aspects in which he or she is interested. The Introduction and chapter 1 of the book examine the study of war finance thus far, present various war finance concepts, and theorize the manner in which states pay for wars. Chapters 2 through 5 provide the empirical analysis of my theory using six case studies in a theoretical (versus chronological) order. Chapters 2 and 3, Truman's financing of the Korean War and Johnson's financing of the Vietnam War, explore how war finance policy is affected by a leader's attempt to control the political costs of war via fear of inflation and public support. Chapters 4 and 5 investigate how leaders' attempts to control the political costs of war are constrained by state capacity. Chapter 4 explores British war finance in the face of balance of payments constraints during World War II and in the absence of those constrains during the Crimean War. Chapter 5 explores a state's extractive tax capacity as well as the need for currency reserves by comparing Russian and Japanese financing of the Russo-Japanese War. The empirical section of the book closes with a bird's eye view of war finance. Using a novel data set of interstate war finance from 1823–2003, chapter 6 provides descriptive statistics of how wars have been financed during this period. I conclude the book with a discussion of future research on war finance.

In an era when states are facing ballooning deficits, economic austerity, and increased financial globalization, understanding war finance is more important than ever. How a state finances war has implications for the outcome of the war, the economic health of the state (particularly regarding debt accumulation, inflation, and the redistribution of wealth), state autonomy, and leadership survival. Thus, as economies contract and states cut spending to balance their budgets, the source of war finance is at the forefront of contemporary debates regarding future economic growth, political stability, and national security.

# Acknowledgments

It takes a village. This project, supported by various people and institutions, took a village, and I am forever grateful for their support.

This book began at the University of Pennsylvania under the advisement of Edward Mansfield, Avery Goldstein, Michael Horowitz, and Alex Weisiger. Together, these four scholars provided the intellectual and emotional support that allowed me to embark on a relatively understudied subject area with boldness and confidence. It certainly helped that they are wonderful people who made me laugh along the way. The support received at the University of Pennsylvania extended beyond my committee members. This project could not have been written without the insights and merriment of Justin Bolker; Ryan Grauer; Ellen Kennedy; Matthew Levendusky; Ian Lustick; Rogers Smith; Rudy Sil and Eileen Doherty-Sil and their children Anna, Analyn, and Aiden; Matthew Tubin; and Pablo Yanguas. I also thank Jennifer Bottomly, Pat Kozak, and Naya Sanders for always making the administrative process pleasant and easy. I also consider myself lucky to have shared my graduate student journey with three amazing and talented women: Barbara Elias, Allison Evans, and Meredith Wooten.

Beyond the University of Pennsylvania, I was fortunate to have enjoyed the financial and scholarly support of the John Sloan Dickey Center for International Understanding at Dartmouth College. I owe thanks to Stephen Brooks, William Wohlforth, and Christianne Hardy Wohlforth, who helped get this project ready for publication and shared with me their love of the great outdoors. I thank Michael Beckley for great conversations and letting me have the desk with the view. My time at Dartmouth could not have been completed without the generous hospitality of the Seale family.

My current intellectual home, Boston University, has provided me the support and encouragement to bring this process to completion. Cathie Jo Martin, David Mayers, and Graham Wilson have been wonderful mentors. I have appreciated the thoughtful words of encouragement from Ivan Arreguín-Toft and William Grimes. I could also not be more grateful for the friendship and intellectual camaraderie of Kaija Schilde and her family.

The research in this book could not have been done without the support of various institutions. I owe a debt of gratitude to the Harry S. Truman Presidential Library for the generous financial support that allowed me to spend a week in the archives. I thank the Christopher H. Browne Center at the University of

Pennsylvania for support that allowed me to attend various conferences at early stages of this project as well as a visit to the LBJ Presidential Library. The Earnhardt Foundation and the Boston University Political Science Department supported a visit to the British National Archives as well as the Rothschild Archive. I also want to thank the generous support of the Boston University Center for Finance, Law, and Policy and its director Cornelius Hurley for a grant to support the expansion of the data set. Finally, I want to thank the various archivists who took the time to help me navigate their collections.

I also want to acknowledge insights from colleagues I have gathered along the way, two anonymous reviewers, and Roger Haydon of Cornell University Press. As the book has come to fruition, it was influenced by insightful conversations with Adriana Lins de Albuquerque, Jonathan Caverley, Benjamin Cohen, Benjamin Fordham, Erik Gartzke, Jarrod Hayes, Sarah Kreps, Paul Poast, and Hugh Rockoff. The comments that the two reviewers provided were illuminating and the process of responding to them improved the project beyond my expectations. I have read many book acknowledgments thanking Roger Haydon, and now I understand why. His sense of humor coupled with his professionalism makes him a delight to work with.

The motivation for this project began when I was an undergraduate at the University of Southern California. I thank John Odell and Peter Rosendorff, who encouraged me to pursue my research. Every Christmas when I came home to Los Angeles to visit my family, I always looked forward to stopping by John's lovely home in Pasadena to share my tales of academia. In addition, the School of International Relations and the Center for International Studies fostered my early research projects with grants to conduct field research in Geneva, Switzerland.

Writing a book is an isolating experience. I owe particular thanks to my friends and family. My sister, Roxy Cappella, endured many phone calls as I pined for California sunshine. My best friend of countless years, Janna Velasquez, kept me grounded. Richard Agron is a force of laughter like no other. My stepchildren, Owen and Grace, whom I met while editing this book, have taught me a whole new level of love. Thank you for your patience while I wrote. My husband, John Cappella Zielinski, is my ultimate confidant. Not only did he graciously read multiple drafts, his ability to know just what to say (or not to say) always provided the best emotional support. He is truly my favorite person to spend time in nature with.

Finally, I thank my parents, Michael and Rosa Cappella. Growing up as the daughter of two public high school teachers in Los Angeles, I learned to value education at an early age. My mother, an immigrant from El Salvador, and my father, a child of a Sicilian immigrant and an Irish mother, instilled in me that life is hard and while we should always be trying to better ourselves, it is important to help others along the way. I hope that the lessons from this work make life a little easier for others and I will continue to do my best. This work is dedicated to them.

# HOW STATES PAY FOR WARS

Introduction

# MAKING MONEY, MAKING WAR

John Maynard Keynes predicted World War I would not last more than a year. An extensive international conflict was economically unsustainable. The world, he believed, was wealthy, yet because its wealth consisted primarily of capital equipment, it could not be converted into cash and goods for war purposes. As soon as cash funds were used up, warring states would have to negotiate. Keynes was wrong. World War I lasted four years and imposed enormous human and financial costs, with daily war expenditures for the primary belligerents averaging more than $30 million.[1]

World War I was not the only war in which national financial conditions were expected to influence duration or outcome. During the Russo-Turkish War (1877–1878), Ottoman Turkey was dismissed as unable to fight a long war because of its economic disarray. A British military observer wrote, "A total financial collapse had been predicted for months, and yet large bodies of troops were moved about, and the provisioning of the huge armies in the fields went on without interruption."[2] Similarly, during the First Balkan War, the *Wall Street Journal* wrote, "Lack of funds will probably put an end to the new Balkan war. All of the states in the Balkan League—Bulgaria, Serbia, Greece, and Montenegro—are close to bankruptcy. The powers are expected to refuse any more loans, in order to compel the cessation of hostilities."[3] Yet in both conflicts, insufficient funds did not force a cessation of hostilities.

Each of these states found ways to avoid capitulating or negotiating with their enemies due to financial constraints, but their strategies for mobilizing resources varied in interesting ways. For example, despite the near equal cost for all primary belligerents, each state paid for World War I differently. The United States and Britain were the only countries that paid for a significant percentage of the war by taxation, 30 percent and 25 percent, respectively.[4] France raised taxes but was unable to meet any of the cost with the increased revenue. Britain, France, and Russia borrowed both domestically and from allies abroad. The United States, on the other hand, did not engage in any foreign debt. Finally, while the war was inflationary for all states, Russia and Germany printed money most frequently. When faced with military emergencies, states find creative solutions to pay for war.

This book clarifies several critical yet chronically underexamined dynamics lying at the nexus of financial and military policy. For millennia, ruling groups have had to acquire resources to support their war efforts. Leaders must decide where to get money. Do they raise money domestically or borrow from abroad? If the sources are domestic, who should pay? Should the state levy taxes, incur debt, or print money? If leaders look outside their borders for finance, where should they look?

Each war-financing alternative—taxation, domestic debt, printing money, and external funding—has distinct political and economic costs and benefits. Borrowing compounds the cost of war through high interest rates, printing can result in disastrous inflation, taxation combats inflation yet can be politically damaging, and garnering money from abroad invites outside influence and fosters dependency. What explains the variation in war finance policy chosen?

These are important questions, as military power stems from an economic base. Without wealth, soldiers cannot be paid, weapons cannot be procured, and food cannot be bought. States, however, do not act in a vacuum. They are constrained by domestic and international politics. Understanding how states finance war is essential to understanding the extent to which state capacity and leaders' preferences affect a state's ability to meet its foreign policy goals via military and economic power as well as its pursuit of domestic macroeconomic stability.

## The Study of War Finance

It is only recently that social scientists began to explore how states finance war. The contemporary origins of this literature can be traced back to Charles Tilly's 1975 edited volume, *The Formation of National States in Western Europe*. Tilly and participating scholars looked to war finance as a key variable to explain the rise of the modern state, as exemplified by Gabriel Ardant and his contribution, "Financial Policy and Economic Infrastructure of Modern States in Europe."[5]

While these works emphasize the effects of war finance, they ignore how leaders choose a particular war finance policy.

Around the same time, international relations scholars were beginning to link financial and military power.[6] Knorr, Organski and Kugler, and Kugler and Domke argued that the ability to extract resources from society, particularly tax revenue, was essential for projecting military power.[7] Paul Kennedy and Karen Rasler and William Thompson emphasized the role of credit to sustain and fight great power rivalries as well as the effect of amassing large amounts of war debt to explain power decline.[8] Continuing this theme of scholarship, Kenneth Schultz and Barry Weingast argued states that have better access to credit, specifically democracies, are more likely to win long-standing rivalries.[9] While these works emphasize the importance of war finance and their effects, they also do not address how war finance policy is chosen.

Economists have a more varied history with the study of war finance. Early political economists, such as David Hume, Adam Smith, David Ricardo, Alexander Hamilton, and Francis Hirst, framed early Western debates on war finance.[10] These works, written around the time of war, were policy oriented and normative in nature.[11] During the 1980s, economists attempting to understand the optimal policy to finance government expenditures began to tackle war finance in a more systematic manner. The concept of tax smoothing emerged from this line of thought.[12] Tax smoothing proponents argued when a government faces an exogenous expenditure, tax rates should not necessarily adjust to achieve a balanced budget because extreme tax increases distort microeconomic incentives.[13] Thus states should borrow to pay for costly wars.

A general consensus emerged from these works—how a war is financed has lasting effects on state capacity, can fundamentally alter the relationship between state and society, and sustained periods of particular forms of war finance can account for balance of power shifts in the international system. Perhaps more significantly, what also emerged was the consensus that regime type and debt dominate war finance. Wars are financed by debt, and democracies are better able to float said debt.

These studies, indispensable for drawing attention to the importance of war finance, almost always put the proverbial cart before the horse, as they focused on the effects of the finance policy chosen and ignored how the policy came to be. Moreover, these theories too willingly assumed static preferences of state leaders as well as insufficiently addressed variation in state capacity. Through assuming static preferences, these works disregard the role of the war in shaping decision making and state capacity. That is, the tides of war affect leaders' preferences for war finance and the ability of the state to raise taxes and float debt. By failing to take war into account, these theories ignore the costs and trade-offs of decision making by leaders.

Furthermore, these works overemphasize the role of regime type. Schultz and Weingast's work is excellent at drawing our attention to the importance of credit.[14] However, the study makes an assumption that regime type matters to creditors. It also assumes that elected officials, fearful of political fallout, worry about the political cost of default. Michael Tomz, for example, found that creditors value reputation formed by the repeated successful repayment of debt, not necessarily regime type.[15]

Moreover, studies that assume that creditors look to regime type when extending loans ignore the political aspects of war debt. The Cold War is a prime example. The United States and Soviet Union extended vast amounts of war debt to myriad "nonliberal" regimes with bad credit for geopolitical reasons. The Japanese and Russian experience during the Russo-Japanese war serves as another

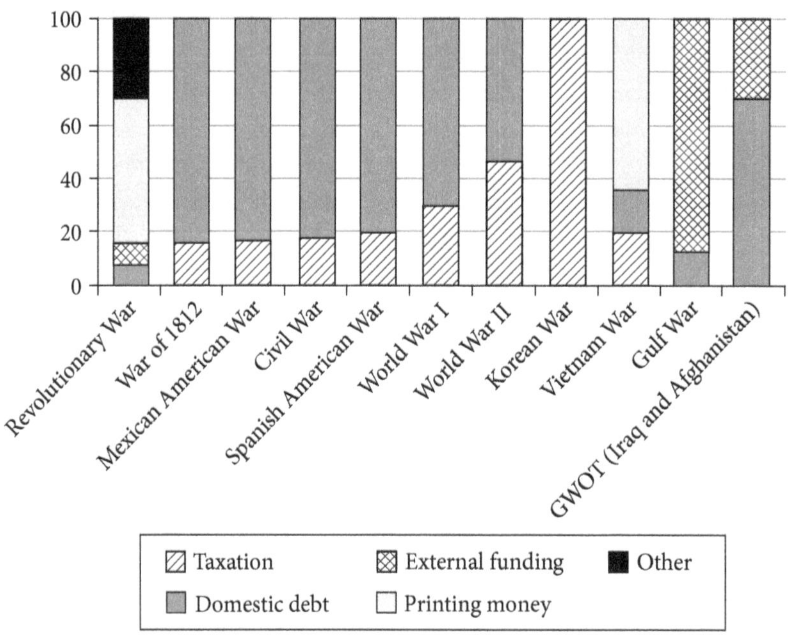


**FIGURE I.1** Variation in US war finance

*Sources:* What constitutes a tax, domestic debt, external funding, and printing are discussed in chapter 3. For US financing of the War of 1812 to the Korean War, see Paul Studenski and Herman Kroos's *Financial History of the United States* (New York: McGraw-Hill Book Company, 1952). For US financing of the Vietnam War, see Tom Riddell, *A Political Economy of the American War in Indo-China: Its Costs and Consequences* (Washington, DC: American University, 1975). For Gulf War finance, see US Department of Defense, "Conduct of the Persian Gulf War: Final Report," US Congressional Report (1992), appendix P. In the Revolutionary War column, "other" is referring to plunder and the selling of land for money.

counterexample. Both nations were able to secure credit despite being nondemocratic. Russia's credit, provided by France and Germany, wavered with battlefield success and not with political cost to elected representatives. Furthermore, worried investors found confidence not in Russia's institutions but in Russia's gold reserves and the state's perceived ability to pay.[16] Japan's credit, provided by England and the United States, continued to be extended as Japan advanced successfully in battle.[17]

In addition to the inability to capture preferences, these theories connecting regime type to resource extraction do not capture important variation within democracies.[18] Consider the variation in US war finance presented in figure I.1. None of the aforementioned theories can explain why the United States chose to finance World War II by 50 percent taxation and the Korean War entirely by taxation, whereas the wars in Iraq and Afghanistan have been financed by domestic and foreign debt.

Finally, as made apparent in figure I.1, war finance-related theories do not advance beyond the tax-versus-debt dichotomy and thus cannot account for the complexity of leaders' decisions. As mentioned previously, leaders can also engage in external extraction as well as printing. Moreover, treating taxation and debt as unitary concepts ignores variation in types of taxation and debt, each with different political and economic costs.

## Argument in Brief

I build on previous theories and discussions of war finance and account for the variation in war finance policy options, the dynamics of the war, and leaders' preferences. First, I invest in concept building. War finance has been studied in a piecemeal fashion, and therefore, scholars who study it are at risk of talking past each other.[19] Thus I address what is meant by the cost of war, the various war finance policy options, the difference between what I term short- and long-term war finance, and introduce the concept of war finance strategy.

I argue that the various means of war finance lie on a continuum characterized by direct resource extraction at one end, indirect resource extraction in the middle, and external extraction at the other end. Where a war finance policy lies on the continuum is contingent on the ability of citizens or groups within society to opt out of the government's claim on resources and the extent to which citizens are aware of war finance policy. Direct resource extraction, such as forced labor or an income tax, is compulsory and, therefore, results in a high level of citizen awareness. In contrast, indirect resource extraction, such a borrowing, only requests citizens to interact with the war finance policy. Thus, citizens may (or may not) interact with the policy, resulting in some awareness. Finally, when the government engages in external resource extraction, it asks nothing from society. Thus citizens do not interact with the policy, resulting in low awareness.

Second, I argue that leaders, attempting to maximize their power at home and state power abroad, are in a constant balancing act, attempting to win the war and remain in office. Thus they prefer war finance policies that meet the needs of the war effort and are the least politically costly. Political costs, shaped by public support for the war, dictate leaders' preference for direct or indirect resource extraction or an external war finance policy to avoid the citizenry entirely via procuring resources from abroad.

Leaders' attempts to maximize power, however, are constrained by the capacity of the state to extract revenue as well as secure currency reserves when purchasing war inputs from abroad. If state capacity limits the ability to extract revenue via direct means and leaders desire to continue the war effort, they will have to engage in indirect revenue extraction or external war finance. In addition, if the state needs currency to pay for goods purchased from abroad, it will need to engage in external war finance.

It is through this lens of constrained decision making that I derive three hypotheses of war finance. Leaders are more likely to engage in direct resource extraction to finance a war when they fear inflation, when public support for the war is high, and when the state has the capacity to extract revenue. Indirect resource extraction and external war finance are more likely when the fear of inflation or public support for the war is low or when the state does not have extraction capacity. External funding becomes a necessary component of war finance when the state has to purchase inputs for the war from abroad and does not have the currency to pay for it. I also derive a corollary hypothesis. When fear of inflation and public support for the war are both high but the state does not have the initial capacity to raise revenue, the state invests in state building. That is to say, it is only under these conditions—high inflation fear and public support—when the Tilly "war makes states" notion is realized.[20]

## The Importance of War Finance

The study of war finance is critical to understanding the relationship between international relations and domestic politics.[21] How and under what circumstances will domestic factors impede states from pursuing the types of strategies predicted by balance of power theory? How do states go about extracting and mobilizing resources necessary to implement foreign and security policies? How does domestic mobilization for foreign policy objectives affect the relationship between the citizen and the state? How are domestic institutions changed as a result of economic mobilization for national security purposes? The following paragraphs discuss this work's contribution to these questions.

Primacy in the international system is subject to domestic political institutional constraints. Extractive and mobilization capacity is a crucial intervening variable between systemic imperatives and the actual foreign and defense policies states pursue.[22] Historians and military scholars tend to attribute victories of war to variables ranging from military leadership to tactics, strategy, and technological superiority. Yet states fight wars. To focus solely on armies is to dismiss the broader story of victory and defeat. Soldiers need to eat, be paid, and be supplied with military equipment. Where does the state acquire the money to meet these costs? Military logisticians have a saying: "Good logistics alone can't win a war, bad logistics alone can lose."[23] War financers should have an equivalent. The manner in which war is financed may not result in certain victory, but it may make defeat more likely. Inadequate war finance can result in the inability to secure adequate supplies and pay soldiers, and also bankrupt the state.

While there is no study of the relationship between war finance and war outcome, there are many examples highlighting the vital role war finance plays in war. The extension of Lend-Lease aid from the United States to Great Britain during World War II is one illustration. Ponder the outcome of World War II had the United States decided not to extend a $30 billion loan to the British to purchase badly needed war supplies after the loss at Dunkirk. German war production was rapidly outpacing British production in the early years of the war. With the evacuation of Dunkirk in May 1940, the British lost all recently produced equipment that had been delivered and incorporated in the field. The only way the British could compensate for this loss was to purchase supplies from abroad, specifically the United States. Unable to finance the dollars needed for these purchases domestically, the British had to resort to external war finance if they wanted to continue fighting the war.

Another example is American financing and war outcome during the Revolutionary War. Throughout the war, General Washington as well as others feared the war effort would fail because of a lack of funds. As Washington lamented in 1778, "Can *we* carry on the War much longer? Certainly NO, unless some measure can be devised and speedily to restore the credit of the currency. . . . Without these can be effected, what funds can stand the present expenses of the Army?"[24] The lack of funds did not just threaten the American war effort through lack of soldier pay and supplies; it also threatened support from Canada. Inadequate financing prevented Americans from being able to pay Canadian creditors and turned plundering locals against the rebel army.[25]

War finance not only has implications for war outcome but also for democratic accountability and the relationship between citizens and war. When a state is fighting a war, only a fraction of its citizens are mobilized as soldiers and participants in the war industry. The manner in which the war is financed may be the only direct link between all members of society and the war. When a war is paid for by taxation, society becomes conscious of the war, allowing citizens to evaluate their leader's foreign policy choices and sanction that leader if they disagree. If a leader chooses to finance a war by printing or funding from abroad, the direct connection between citizens and the war is lost. Leaders, consequently, are able to shield their policy choices, lowering the political cost of fighting war. This implies that how leaders finance war not only has an effect on the democratic process but also on a leader's tenure in office.

How a state finances a war also has implications for understanding state autonomy. While a state may be fighting a war to protect its sovereignty, the manner of war finance may also undermine it. As the cost of war rises, leaders need to raise large sums of money. As the amount of money garnered increases, so can the leverage the lenders have over the state. The state may also become beholden to individuals and institutions at home or abroad. David Hume, in his essay *Of Public Credit*, feared that, "as foreigners possess a great share of our national funds, they render the public, in a manner, tributary to them, and may in time occasion the transport of our people and our industry."[26] During the Crimean War, the [London] *Times* summed up this sentiment in England as war loans went to the Rothschilds: "We certainly were under the impression that we lived in an age of competition. . . . Now we are at the mercy of a few great contractors."[27]

War finance can also have redistributive effects within a society, either regressively or progressively.[28] Financing by the United States of the Civil War and World War I provides an example. During the Civil War, taxation was regressive as government revenues came from excise taxes and customs duties. Thus the cost of the war was passed on to the consumer in the form of higher prices and fell most heavily on those at the bottom of the income scale. In addition, government borrowing was also regressive, as it was restricted to banks and financial elites, leaving the interest to be reaped by elites and paid by the masses. In contrast, during World War I, because of the extraordinary increase in income taxes, the burden fell most heavily on those in the upper income brackets. Individuals in the lower income groups were much heavier buyers of bonds. It was estimated that 30 percent of all Liberty Bonds were bought by people with incomes of two thousand dollars or less.[29] These examples, not unique to the United States, demonstrate how the decisions of war finance have large repercussions on the distribution of wealth within a society.

How a state finances a war also affects the economic and, consequently, political stability of the state. Wars are inflationary. Wars cause the supply of available goods to decrease as goods are either shifted toward the war effort or events of the war curtail the ability to produce and deliver goods. Simultaneously, when fighting a war, the demand for goods increases as the government purchases inputs for the war effort. How a state finances war can exacerbate or mitigate a war's inflationary effects. The hyperinflation experienced in Germany during the interwar years that peaked in 1923 is a prime example. During the financing of World War I, the German Reichsbank issued new notes, *Darlehnskassenscheine*, which were not legal tender but receivable at face value at all public offices. The consequence of this policy was a soaring increase of money in circulation. The Reichsbank's reserve ratio rule, requiring a cash reserve of 33 1/3 percent, was down to 3 percent by December 31, 1919.[30] The result was one of the worst bouts of inflation in world history, the extent of which is illustrated by the artistic depictions of the time: children making houses using stacks of notes and people transporting money in wheelbarrows and using notes to paper walls.[31]

Understanding how states finance wars is necessary to advance the scholarly literature on the study of war, leadership survival, state autonomy, the creation and destruction of economic structures within a state, the distribution of wealth within a society, and the redistribution of power within the international system. Given the importance of war finance, the following chapters present the first cross-national systemic study of the subject.

1

# HOW STATES PAY FOR WARS

In 1749, English poet Samuel Johnson wrote, "Yet Reason frowns on War's unequal game, / Where wasted nations raise a single name, / And mortgaged states their grandsires wreaths regret, / From age to age in everlasting debt."[1] A quarter century later, Adam Smith, writing about war taxation in *Wealth of Nations*, stated, "When a nation is already over burdened with taxes, nothing but the necessities of a new war, nothing but either the animosity of national vengeance, or the anxiety for national security, can induce the people to submit, with tolerable patience, to a new tax."[2] How does one reconcile these two notions that wars result in such vast sums of debt that they bankrupt the state, while at the same time, they are the only means to which the state can raise taxes avoiding said debt? Why are some wars financed via direct resource extraction from a state's citizenry and others via indirect means or from foreign sources, bypassing a state's resources entirely? This chapter provides a framework for understanding the tension between Johnson's poem and Smith's claim. Part I provides a foundation for the study of war finance, while Part II provides a theory to account for war finance policies chosen.

## Part I: Key Concepts and Definitions

### The Costs of War

This work strives to explain how states confront the costs of fighting a war. Before scholars can understand war finance, what is being financed needs to be addressed, for the costs of war can mean several different things.[3] This work concerns itself with what I term the *budgetary cost of the war*: the direct financial outlays to pursue military objectives.[4] This definition echoes what Seligman refers to as the narrow cost of war, "the actual money outlay, or expenditure in dollars and cents, directly involved in prosecuting the war."[5] It should be noted that financing allies who are aiding in the war effort is also included in the budgetary costs of war. For example, during World War I, almost 30 percent of the gross cost of the US war effort went to advances to allies.[6] This cost, while eventually repaid, was borne by the US government during the war.

This narrower conception of the cost of war excludes many pertinent expenses as well as human costs in life and suffering. This definition excludes prewar armament programs, demobilization, postwar occupation, or arms races. It also omits indirect or long-term costs to society such as veterans' benefits, the effect of loss of life on a state's economy, or interest payments on debt accumulated to pay for the war.[7] While preparation, postwar occupation, demobilization, and indirect costs are all expensive proceedings, this project is concerned with understanding the financial and political dynamics during conflict. While a broader conceptualization of cost may be useful for other purposes, such as policy debates or long-term analyses of the consequences of war, the focus of this work, like that of leaders themselves, is procuring money for specific military operations within a specific theater and for a specific duration.

## Paying for War

*War finance* is the means by which the state meets the costs of executing the war effort. It is the manner by which the state redirects or procures monetary resources to meet government outlays to continue the war. There are various means of war finance. Wars can be financed by direct or indirect resource extraction from the state's citizens or from resources outside the state.[8] Taken together, these three forms of procuring resources for war create a war finance continuum. Where a war finance policy lies on the continuum is contingent on the ability of citizens or groups within society to opt out of the government's claim on resources and, correspondingly, citizen awareness of the war finance policy chosen.

*Direct resource extraction* lies on one end of the continuum. It refers to resources paid to the state directly by citizens within society. This method of extraction is imposed on individuals or groups. That is to say, one cannot opt out of the extraction policy or transfer the labor burden or monetary costs of said policy to others. Thus, given the effect on them, citizens are highly aware of this policy. There are three forms of direct resource extraction: forced labor, forced savings plans, and direct taxation.

Forced labor occurs when a state forces its citizens into service for the war effort that is exacted under the threat of penalty and for which said people have not offered themselves voluntarily.[9] Hence, citizens cannot opt out of a forced labor policy and are aware said policy is taking place as the government confiscates their autonomy.[10] Forced savings plans occur when the government mandates individuals to set aside a portion of their income to invest in the war effort.[11] While the notion that citizens will be paid back is implied, payback does not negate the compulsory nature of this war finance policy.

The most common form of direct resource extraction is direct taxation. Taxation refers to the sum of revenue raised from war taxes and the existing tax structure that is funneled toward the war effort.[12] While there are various forms of taxes, direct taxes are paid to the state directly by citizens and groups, that is, firms, within society.[13] These include income, corporate, property, and payroll taxes. Direct taxation, like forced labor and savings, results in high citizen awareness as the state seizes its citizens' income.[14]

*Indirect resource extraction* refers to resources indirectly transferred from citizens or groups within society to the state. When an indirect resource extraction policy is implemented, the government procures resources by asking nothing from citizens initially or provides citizens a choice of either opting out of the policy or transferring the costs. Thus, whereas direct resource extraction is compulsory and citizens are highly aware of government policy, indirect resource extraction leaves citizens relatively less aware of the government's war finance policy. Forms of indirect resource extraction include indirect taxation, domestic debt, printing, austerity measures, and the use of existing coffers.

Unlike direct taxes, intermediaries collect indirect taxes, such as sales, value-added, excise, and customs taxes.[15] Moreover, citizens can opt out of these taxes if they choose not to engage in the taxed transaction. For example, during the Spanish-American War, the Revenue Bill of June 1898 affected a broad spectrum of items such as beer, tobacco and cigars, and proprietors of theaters and circuses, as well as bankers' capital, pawnbrokers, and commercial brokers. In addition, an excise tax was placed on sugar and petroleum refiners and a federal tax on inheritances. Citizens could choose not to purchase these goods. Furthermore, when taxes are collected at the source, that is, the manufacturer, the burden of the tax can be passed to the consumer discreetly in the form of higher prices.

Another form of indirect resource extraction is domestic debt. Domestic debt refers to money lent to the government from its citizens or institutions within the country with the explicit understanding that it will be paid back over time.[16] Domestic debt is voluntary, as citizens choose whether or not they would like to purchase it. It should be noted that while it would appear taxation and debt are interchangeable, as citizens have to pay for the war either from their current or future income, they are not. Individuals do not treat the two sums equally.[17] Under a public-loan scheme, the individual retains "control" over a capital value, which, even though fully offset by the liability stemming from the capitalized value of future taxes, remains desirable. Because of this "control" over assets, the individual prefers to pay the tax in perpetuity.[18] Simply put, citizens prefer debt to taxation.

There are various forms of domestic debt, each with varying degrees of citizen awareness. Domestic debt may be in the form of a war bond campaign or general floated debt. When a government engages in a war bond campaign, citizens are aware of the policy as the government promotes bond purchases via posters, newspaper ads, and television commercials. Domestic debt may also be in the form of general public debt. Unlike war bonds, citizens' interaction with general floated debt may be minimized as citizens may or may not be aware of the government issued war debt. Thus, while both general floated debt and bond campaigns are indirect forms of war finance, bond campaigns interact with society more than the issue of general public debt.

Indirect resource extraction can also take the form of printing money. Printing, unlike taxation and domestic debt, does not use money already circulating within the state, and it does not extract revenue from society. In the words of Buchanan, "Public debt embodies an obligation to make interest payments in periods of time subsequent to issue. Currency involves no such obligation and, for this reason, its issue becomes a distinctly different fiscal operation."[19] Thus the initial interaction between printing as a war finance policy and citizens is low, as the government pays for the war effort without demanding anything from society. The citizens may become aware of a printing policy, however, when the inflationary consequences of printing become evident.[20] Hence printing is often referred to as an "indirect tax" on the population.

Other forms of indirect revenue extraction include austerity measures and the use of existing coffers. Austerity measures refer to the curtailment of government spending on non-war-related policies in order to use those funds for the war effort. The extent to which citizens interact with said policy is contingent on the nature, size, and scope of government spending cuts on non-war-related funding. Existing coffers, particularly excess currency reserves, ask nothing from society, as the war is paid for via preexisting revenue surplus.

In sum, indirect revenue extraction comprises the largest portion of the war finance continuum, as it includes indirect taxation, war bonds, general domestic debt, printing, austerity measures, and use of existing coffers. Unlike direct resource extraction these indirect means of revenue extraction are either voluntary, allow the citizen to transfer costs, or initially ask nothing of the citizenry. All three characteristics result in relatively low citizen awareness.

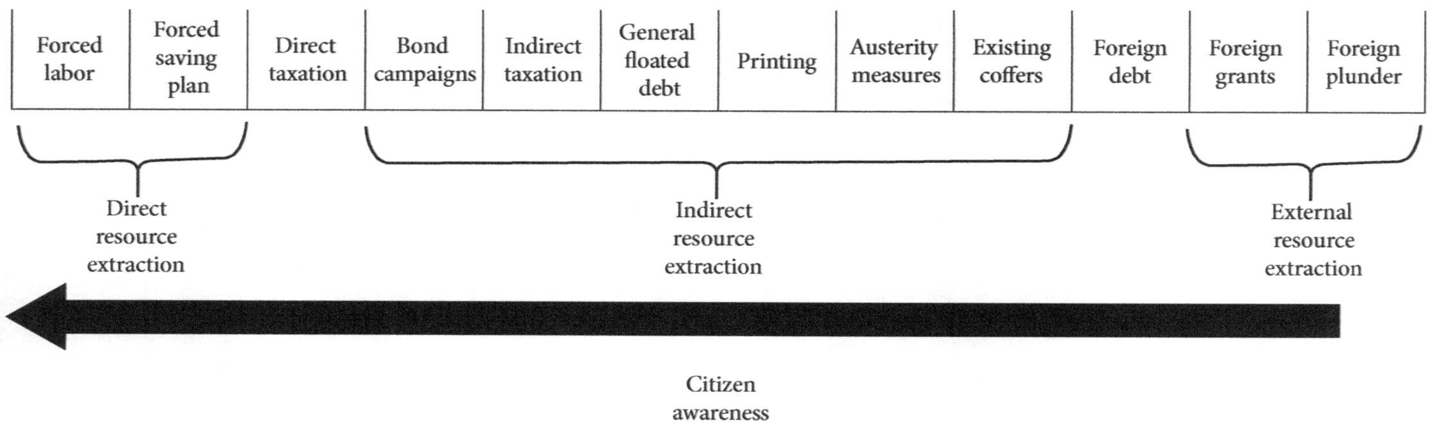


**FIGURE 1.1** War finance continuum

*External resource extraction* refers to resources procured from abroad that can be used to achieve domestic objectives.[21] External funding is a broad category that includes securities floated on foreign markets, interstate or sovereign-to-sovereign loans, grants, plunder, and diaspora remittances. Similar to some forms of indirect resource extraction, when a state engages in external resource extraction, it does not initially ask anything from society. However, unlike indirect resource extraction, external extraction further removes the citizen from interacting with the state's war finance policy. Foreign grants or plunder, for example, do not need to be paid back, resulting in no financial interaction with society. Hence citizens may or may not be aware of these war finance policies.

As shown in figure 1.1, the various means of war finance can be combined to create a war finance continuum reflecting the extent to which the chosen policy interacts with society. Direct resource extration results in high citizen awarness, indirect resource extraction less so, and external resource extraction even less so or not at all.

It should be noted that states often do not resort to only one type of war finance, that is, financing a war entirely by taxation or entirely by direct resource extraction. Generally, states resort to multiple methods.[22] For example, during World War II, the United States paid for the war domestically through a combination of taxation and domestic debt, about 50 percent of each,[23] whereas Britain during World War II financed their war though a combination of domestic and external means—25 percent taxation, 50 percent domestic debt, and 25 percent external funding.[24] Thus I introduce the concept *war finance strategy.* War finance strategy is the combination of methods and sources of resource extraction used to pay for war.

## War Duration and the Dynamics of War Finance: Long versus Short Wars

War finance has a temporal component. The duration of a war affects the means of war financing available to leaders as well as their time horizons. The war finance decisions made by the various belligerents of the 1967 Arab-Israeli Six Day War, for example, are not comparable to the belligerents during World War II. During the Six Day War, belligerents were bound by the amount of revenue that could be collected in six days.[25] Furthermore, given the duration of the war, leaders were unlikely to have given much thought to the political and economic costs of their war finance decisions, let alone their ability to implement their decisions once the war started. In contrast, during World War II, once belligerents emptied existing coffers and there was no end to the war in sight, they needed a sustainable war finance plan. The war finance policy had to take into account the need to continuously fund a war in which the duration was indeterminate as well as the political and economic costs of their policies. Moreover, these leaders had all the war finance means at their disposal. In order to delineate between these war finance experiences, I introduce the concept of short- and long-war finance. Short- or long-war finance is contingent on the war's actual duration and the leader's perception of how long the war will last.[26] In the following paragraphs, I discuss the time-dependent nature of various forms of revenue extraction as well as leaders' actual and perceived time horizons.

First, short wars come with a limited war finance tool kit. Certain forms of revenue are available immediately while others are not. For example, in regards to taxation, the expediency by which tax revenue can flow into state coffers is a function of the type of tax to be raised and the size of the revenue administration needed. A tax on imports or exports provides the fastest means of generating revenue. Revenue can be collected at the point of state entry and exit and takes little effort for the revenue administration. Customs agents at each border crossings are sufficient. In addition, as tariffs, sales, or value-added taxes are collected onsite, their revenue flows immediately to the state. Moreover, the feasibility of monitoring and collecting imported and exported goods allows the state to easily change the tax rate. Income taxes lie at the opposite end of the spectrum, as their implementation and collection is a daunting task. The state has to audit, collect, and process the means of all members of society.[27] Thus states fighting short wars are unable to raise large sums of revenue by direct taxation.

Borrowing either from home or abroad, while faster, also takes time. The parameters of the debt need to be negotiated: these include choosing loan underwriters and location of debt placement, and determining interest rate, issue price, timing of debt flotation, and collateral. Even when contracts are successfully negotiated, they take time to execute. Financial intermediaries must float the debt, which may or may not be purchased by creditors, or lending states must transfer resources to the belligerent. During World War II, there was a lengthy gap between President Roosevelt's announcement of Lend-Lease in early 1941, the subsequent Anglo-American loan, and the actual extending of resources in 1942.[28]

The most expedient forms of revenue are printing and taking from existing coffers. In contrast to taxation or debt, these forms of revenue are not bound by the state's bureaucracies to implement, collect, and process revenue. These funds are available immediately. Hence, short wars are often likely to be funded via these means.

Second, long wars have different revenue needs. Short wars are expenditure bursts. Leaders want to win the war. Thus once a war begins they want to avoid instant defeat. Therefore, their primary focus is to ensure that the military is outfitted as best as possible as fast as possible. Consequently, the initial needs of the war must be met using money that is immediately available, either using existing coffers, printing, or in some cases, debt. Once a short war turns into a long war, the needs of the state change. Under long-war finance, the leader becomes concerned with maintaining a winning war effort while simultaneously protecting the state's economy from the negative effects of economic mobilization for a long war. The state needs renewable sources of revenue that have the least disastrous effect on its economy.

In addition to actual war duration, leadership perception about the war's duration affects the choice of war finance policy. When a war begins, leaders finance the war they think that they are going to fight, engaging in either short- or long-war finance.[29] When a leader commences the war with a short-war finance policy and the war duration exceeds the initial duration perception, the leader will shift to a long-war finance policy.[30] What matters here is that when a state switches policies from the expenditure-burst financing method of short wars to long-war finance, leaders have to adapt the war financing strategy to the new reality.[31]

Thus war finance is not a static process. States often attempt one finance strategy at the beginning of a war and adjust as the war unfolds. In addition, a revised war finance strategy may depend on the first attempt. Hence war finance may become both learning- and path-dependent processes. Union financing of the American Civil War provides an excellent example. United States treasury secretary Salmon P. Chase believed the war would be over in a few months. Instead of pressuring Congress to increase taxes or improve on the existing bureaucratic capacity and collect income taxes, Chase issued short-term debt. After the Battle of Bull Run in July 1861, leaders and creditors realized that the war was not going to be short. Chase was left with a large amount of short-term debt that needed to be repaid, poor credit because of recent military events, and meager tax revenue. As a result, by 1862, there was a shift in war finance strategy away from short-term debt bought by banks to direct taxation and a public bond campaign. By 1863, the nation's first income tax was imposed along with the creation of the tax-collecting agency, Bureau of Internal Revenue.[32]

Short and long wars are subject to different revenue options as well as different time horizons that affect leadership decision making. It is for these reasons that financing short wars should be treated separately from financing long wars. The rest of this study concerns itself with long-war finance. Long wars provide the richest insight into how the dynamics of war affect the ability of the state to extract resources from society, leadership preferences for extraction, and due to lengthy mobilization duration, how the various means of mobilization affect institutions within the state.

## Part II: Hypothesizing War Finance

The following section presents my theory of long-war finance for interstate wars. First, I discuss the importance of understanding leaders' preferences as well as how those preferences are formed. When a leader is deciding how to pay for the state's war effort, his or her decision making is shaped by his or her desire to stay in power.[33] Thus leaders prefer a war finance strategy that both wins the war and avoids economic ruin. In order to maximize power at home, leaders take into account public support for the war effort and inflation. I argue that when public support for the war and fear of inflation are low, leaders prefer a war finance policy characterized by low citizen awareness, either indirect or external resource extraction. In contrast, when fear of inflation or support for the war is high, leaders prefer direct resource extraction.

Second, I discuss state capacity. Regardless of leaders' preferences, states must have the capacity to implement a leader's war finance selection. I address how leaders are constrained by the state's ability to extract revenue as well as to cope with low currency reserves when purchasing war inputs from abroad. I argue that in spite of the desire to finance the war via direct resource extraction, when state capacity is low, the state will engage in indirect or external resource extraction. Furthermore, external resource extraction will become part of a state's war finance strategy when a state needs currency from abroad to fund its war effort. Finally, while a leader may be bound by state capacity to raise revenue, they are able to invest in state capacity throughout the war effort if so inclined. Thus, when a leader invests in state capacity, a larger percentage of the war will be financed via direct resource extraction, particularly taxation.

### The Importance of Preferences

To understand war finance, we must first understand leader's preferences. Preferences are important for three reasons. First, as aforementioned, at war's onset, policymakers have limited information on the length, cost, or ultimate economic impact of the conflict. When policymakers meet to discuss how costs should be met, they bring to the table their beliefs on taxation, debt, and society's relationship with the war effort. Such beliefs define the early war finance effort. Thus they base their initial war finance strategy on their preferences, and these preferences are updated as policymakers begin to understand what is needed for the conflict.

For example, during the War of 1812, American war finance was initially defined by Jeffersonian ideals and a preference for low taxation. In 1807, Jefferson's treasury secretary, Albert Gallatin, presented his principles of war finance to

Congress. He argued that the "losses and privations caused by the war should not be aggravated by taxes beyond what is strictly necessary," and despite his aversion to public debts, he favored borrowing from banks to cover the expenditures of the war itself.[34] Eventually Gallatin's preferences changed as the war became more costly and revenue yields were inadequate to meet war costs. Consequently, taxes became a larger portion of American's war finance strategy, and in July 1813, Congress enacted an internal revenue system requested by Gallatin.[35]

Second, leaders are only somewhat knowledgeable about the state's capacity to extract revenue, as extracting revenue may prove more difficult in war than in peacetime. For example, the war may be fought on the state's territory, which in turn affects its ability to collect revenue. Or the state may increase taxes expecting high revenue yields, yet the dynamics of the war, for instance, a blockade, could hurt the domestic economy, decreasing revenue yields. China during the Third Sino-Japanese War (1937–1945) provides an illustration. Chinese leaders favored a tax-based war finance strategy, attempting to raise taxes immediately before and during the war to pay for it. In 1936, the government first introduced direct taxes, and an income tax subsequently followed in 1938. However, the course of the war affected state capacity to raise revenue. Indiscriminate Japanese bombing behind the lines added confusion to tax collection. Moreover, when the government was driven from Nanking to Hankow and then to Chungking, many experienced administrators could not follow. Thus the ability to collect taxes decreased greatly.[36] Understanding leaders' preferences provides insight into how leaders adjust their war finance strategy to such diminished state capacity.

Third, when a state is characterized by high bureaucratic capacity to extract revenue, it does not necessarily follow that taxation will be a dominant component of a state's war finance strategy. The US financing of the wars in Iraq and Afghanistan is a prime example. The United States had the tax capacity to finance the two wars by taxation, yet these two wars were financed through a combination of domestic and foreign debt.[37] Thus we need to understand leaders' preferences as well as state capacity in order to fully comprehend why states finance wars in the manner they do.

## Public Support for the War

Conventional wisdom suggests it is politically costly for leaders to raise revenue.[38] By wresting money from individuals and households, leaders are taking the means of livelihood from the population. Not only do citizens prefer to not surrender their income to the state, they expect something in return: to surrender revenue to the government is to contribute to the provision of general public goods.[39] During peacetime, it is difficult for citizens to evaluate the public goods for which their revenue is paying. The complexity of the federal budget makes detailed examination impracticable and unfeasible.[40]

In contrast, revenue for the war effort is directly tied to a policy outcome, the articulated goals of the war. Leaders are not only aware of the costly effects of extracting revenue, but they are also aware of the effect of support for the war on their tenure. The field of international relations is rife with literature suggesting that the dynamics of war can negatively affect public opinion[41] and the endurance of regimes and leaders.[42] Thus, to preserve their tenure, leaders attempt to control the political costs of war. They do so by reducing the ability of citizens to evaluate the policy their revenue is paying for by shielding citizens from the war effort.

Behavioral public finance literature suggests citizen awareness of revenue extraction is conditional on the form of extraction and, thus, governments design revenue policy accordingly. James Buchanan, in his 1967 work *Public Finance in Democratic Process*, referred to the actions taken by leaders to shield the public from extracting revenue as the "fiscal illusion."[43] Buchanan argued that citizens associate government services, in this case the war effort, with revenue extraction.[44] It follows that leaders attempt to minimize citizen resistance, especially when the policy being financed is unpopular given the level of revenues collected.[45] Leaders minimize citizen resistance by creating the perception that revenue extraction is less burdensome than it actually is, resorting to indirect and external resource extraction.

In regards to taxation, behavioral public finance literature suggests that individuals not only respond to tax visibility when making purchasing decisions, but more important, politicians are aware of the individuals' response.[46] Consequently, politicians attempt to design the tax system to minimize the perceived burden of any given amount of tax collection.[47] This situation favors indirect taxes, as the tax is nominally included in the price of the good or service. Here the individual adjusts his or her purchases so that the price, including the tax, stands in the same proportion to any other price as the ratio of the relative marginal utilities of two private goods.[48] No explicit recognition of the payment for a public good or service enters into the individual's adjustment here. Hence, the individual is likely to be ignorant of the amount of tax that is paid and, in some cases, is unaware of the tax altogether.[49]

Relative to indirect taxation, general domestic debt and printing further shield the public from the war effort, as they are less visible forms of war finance. Non-tax revenue is less likely to provoke resistance than tax revenue. These forms of revenue enable policymakers to commence a policy without having the public confront the immediate costs. Adam Smith articulated this logic:

> The ordinary expence [*sic*] of the greater part of modern governments in time of peace being equal or nearly equal to their ordinary revenue, when war comes they are both unwilling and unable to increase their revenue proportion to the increase of their expence [*sic*]. They are unwilling, for fear of offending the people, who by so great and so sudden an increase of taxes, would soon be disgusted with the war. . . . The facility of borrowing delivers them from the embarrassment which this fear and inability would otherwise occasion.[50]

Thus, if the war becomes increasingly expensive or drawn out, the public will be less frustrated when not directly sacrificing to pay for an ailing policy. Finally, leaders can avoid their citizenry altogether and procure resources from outside the state.

Wars, however, are not always unpopular. Leaders may not face negative political consequences of adverse public opinion vis-à-vis the war effort. As the quote from Adam Smith at the beginning of this chapter posits, some wars are so "popular" that they may be the only means by which people submit to new taxes or more direct forms of resource extraction.[51] Thus high support in favor of the conflict reduces the political costs to leaders to engage in more direct forms of resource extraction.

Leaders prefer the least politically costly war finance policy. They control political costs via the source of resource extration. When support for the war is low, leaders prefer a war finance policy that does not draw further attention to the war effort—either indirect or external resource extraction. Conversely, high support in favor of the conflict reduces the political costs to leaders to engage in direct resource extraction. Hence, when support for the war is high, we should expect to see direct resource extraction comprise a larger percentage of the state's war finance strategy than it would when support for the war is low.

## Fearing Inflation

The political costs of war extend beyond public support. Unfortunately for leaders who want to stay in power, wars are inflationary. To fight a war, especially a protracted one, the state becomes a dominant player in the market, procuring supplies and labor to confront the enemy. The inflationary effects of the state's actions are twofold. First, the state is removing goods and labor from the market, decreasing the supply accessible to the private sector. This decrease in supply creates an upward pressure on prices as the private sector competes for now-scarce resources. Second, the state is increasing the money supply as it purchases inputs for the war effort. Citizens now have more income to spend, increasing demand for now scarce goods. This scarcity may be further aggravated during wartime if there is a significant decrease in trade or citizens fearing inflation begin to hoard goods.[52]

Wartime inflation is common. Since 1800, the average change in prices from the consumer price index taken a year before war onset to the peak consumer price change experienced during the war is an almost 30 percent increase for primary belligerents fighting wars over six months long.[53] Of these belligerents, 41 percent experienced at least a 10 percent increase in prices. An excellent example of wartime inflation occurred in Russia during the Crimean War. Regions nearest the fighting experienced the highest rates of inflation. In the southern and western provinces (Kursk, Chernigov, Volyn) the price of flour increased nearly 200 percent, whereas the northern, eastern, and central regions (Viatka, Perm, Volgda, and St. Petersburg) experienced only about a 10 percent to 20 percent increase.[54] These figures do not capture the inflationary effects of war finance that arise after the war is over. In 1914 Germany, for example, the mark was valued at 4.2 marks to the dollar. In 1924, partially due to the financing of World War I, post war inflation resulted in mark depreciation to 4.2 trillion marks to the dollar.[55]

High inflation can cripple a state's economy and a leader's tenure. Inflation has been shown to inhibit economic growth,[56] exacerbate inefficiencies in the tax system,[57] lead to greater price variability,[58] and redistribute income among both individuals and groups within a society benefitting debtors at the expense of creditors.[59] As Keynes passionately wrote, "As inflation proceeds and the real value of the currency fluctuates wildly from month to month, all permanent relations between debtors and creditors . . . becomes so utterly disordered as to be almost meaningless; and the process of wealth-getting degenerates into a gamble and a lottery."[60] These negative effects on the economy and, therefore, the livelihood of citizens can damage a leader's, a political party's, and a regime's hold on power. American politics scholars have found that good macroeconomic conditions benefit the incumbent president and his or her party at the polls, and voters base their assessment of an administration on inflation.[61] In addition, comparative politics scholars have found that inflation has often been associated with regime change.[62]

How a state finances its war effort can mitigate or compound the effect of war inflation. Direct revenue extraction, specifically direct taxation and forced saving campaigns, decrease the amount of money in the economy. By removing money from citizens, the government limits their spending power.[63] In contrast to direct taxation and loan campaigns, indirect revenue extraction such as printing and general domestic debt, as well as external war finance, exacerbate the effects of war inflation. Indirect war finance policies not only compound the amount of money in the economy; they do nothing to reduce the spending power of the consumer. Thus they place an upward pressure on prices. Returning to the example of the Russian economy during the Crimean War, inflation was exacerbated by Russian war finance. Russia financed the majority of its war effort via printing.[64] Consequently, the amount of notes in circulation during the war more than doubled.

While war inflation is common, not all leaders or citizens fear inflation. A number of economists have found that the relationship between inflation and economic growth is nonlinear.[65] Inflation has a neutral or even positive relationship on economic growth below a certain threshold, particularly for advancing countries.[66] Moreover, even in advanced economies, leaders may welcome increased spending and expanding the state's money supply to counteract recessions or sluggish economies.[67] Thus when war inflation is not feared or is even welcome, leaders will prefer a war financed via indirect resource extraction to increase the money supply.

In sum, when policymakers are concerned about war inflation, they will attempt to mitigate its effects via direct revenue extraction. However, some leaders may welcome an expansion of the money supply caused by spending on the war effort to improve the state's economy. Here, leaders are not concerned about the effects of inflation, and they will therefore be more likely to implement indirect resource or external extraction policies.

## Leader's Preferences Are Bound by State Capacity

International relations and comparative politics scholars have long acknowledged that the state must draw from its society and domestic economy for material resources when in pursuit of foreign policy objectives.[68] An intervening variable between these foreign policy ends and resource means is state institutions. When financing a war, leaders' preferences are bound by the ability of the state's institutions to implement them. As Harvard finance professor Oliver Sprague aptly noted during World War I, "A war finance policy based on taxation presupposes that a country must have established and in operation a highly developed income-tax machinery in time of peace."[69]

The following sections explore the effect of state capacity and the ability of state institutions to effectively implement the various war finance options. I discuss the role of bureaucratic capacity and the ability of the state to develop, fund, and carry out revenue extraction policies.[70] I argue that the capacity needed to implement a state's war finance policy becomes increasingly complex as one moves from external to direct resource extraction on the war finance continuum.

Given that states are bound by their administrative capacity to extract resources, if they do not have capable institutions (i.e., income tax machinery), they will have to resort to less complex forms of war finance.

I then argue that states are also bound by the source of inputs for the war effort and the ability to secure currency reserves to purchase inputs for the war from abroad. If a state needs to purchase goods from abroad to continue its war efforts, it will need the supplier state's currency. If a state's currency reserves fall below the level needed to make purchases, the state will need to engage in external extraction—either a foreign loan or grant—to continue with the war effort.

## Bureaucratic Capacity

States are bound by the capacity of their bureaucratic institutions to raise revenue. Yet not all forms of revenue require the same institutional capacity. Some forms of revenue require large and complex bureaucratic institutions for extraction while others do not. The size and complexity of institutions needed is contingent on the amount of citizens from which the state extracts resources.[71] The more citizens subjected to the state's policies, the more interactions the state institutions need to have. I refer to each citizen-state interaction as a collection point. For each collection point, the state needs to identify, locate, access, and collect the source of revenue as well as process it for state use.[72] As the number of collection points increase, so does the complexity needed to effectively extract revenue.[73]

Direct extraction is characterized by more collection points than indirect extraction, whereas external extraction, which bypasses the citizenry all together, is characterized by no collection points. In regards to direct taxation, the state needs to interact with every (taxable) citizen in society. Thus, to assess the tax base, information is needed on a larger segment of society that is geographically dispersed, and a larger institutional structure is needed to collect and process revenue.[74] In contrast, indirect taxes, such as customs revenue or tariffs, are levied on a smaller, more concentrated segment of the population. Therefore, they require a lower volume of information and smaller supporting institutions to collect and process revenue. Tariffs, for example, tend to be collected at ports and on narrow bands of the economy.[75] Thus, if a state wants to finance a war via direct revenue or bond campaigns, it will need a developed and complex bureaucracy to carry out its war finance policies. To finance a war via indirect taxation requires a lower level of state capacity.

Similar to indirect taxation, borrowing requires a relatively low level of state capacity. Unlike taxation, there are relatively fewer collection points and the institutions necessary to facilitate government debt are less complex. In order to finance war, a state may borrow from one or a group of individuals or banks or from society at large. There is no prerequisite number of collection points. The institutions required to facilitate the transactions may be public or private (e.g., the Bank of England at its founding before becoming a public entity).[76] Thus relatively little capacity is required at the simplest level of debt extraction. That said, as collection points increase, that is, money is taken from a larger percentage of the population, so does the complexity of supporting institutions.

Low extractive capacity does not necessarily mean surrender or defeat. Low-capacity states often engage in long wars. They must turn to other means, however, of financing. The Mexican war effort during the Mexican-American War (1846–1848) is one such example. An already-weak revenue administration was further weakened by the war, resulting in extremely low extractive capacity. "During the war with the United States, expenditures were more than double income. With her ports blockaded and a vast portion of the country overrun, Mexico could not even depend on the normal sources of revenue."[77] The state turned to other sources of war finance, borrowing from the church and the British as well as plunder.[78] Thus, if governments do not have the capacity to tax or borrow, they will be forced to resort to means farther down on the war finance continuum—printing or external war finance. These war finance means do not directly engage with citizens as there are no collection points that need supporting state institutions.

In addition to other forms of war finance that require less complex bureaucratic capacity, the state may be able to enhance its capacity to extract revenue by investing in state building. The US financing of the Civil War is a clear example. At the onset of the war, taxes were confined to tariffs and customs duties.[79] Like Mexico during the Mexican-American War, the outbreak of war brought about a sharp curtailment in foreign trade and resulted in much lower revenue collections than expected.[80] Consequently, the state had to look elsewhere for revenue. Eventually, the state chose to invest in state building, resulting in the nation's first income tax.[81] More important, during the course of the war, the country's extractive capacity expanded to collect and process the increase in levels and kinds of taxation.[82] Thus, as can be seen in table 1.1, the percentage of the war expenses financed by taxation increased dramatically, practically tripling during the course of the war.

In sum, states characterized by a low bureaucratic capacity to extract revenues will be confined to indirect or external revenue extraction. If so inclined, these states may also engage in state building during the war effort, allowing higher levels of direct revenue extraction over time than would be otherwise available. At the other end of the spectrum, high-capacity states will be able to implement high revenue-yielding taxes, such as corporate and income taxes, that

**TABLE 1.1** United States Civil War finance, 1861–1865 (in millions of dollars)

| | WAR YEAR | | | | |
|---|---|---|---|---|---|
| **SOURCES OF REVENUE** | **1861** | **1862** | **1863** | **1864** | **1865** |
| Receipts: | | | | | |
| Customs | $39.6 | $49.1 | $69.1 | $102.3 | $84.9 |
| Income tax | | | 2.7 | 20.3 | 61.0 |
| Direct tax | | 1.8 | 1.5 | 0.5 | 1.2 |
| Excise | | | 34.9 | 89.4 | 148.5 |
| Spirits and liquor | | | 6.8 | 32.6 | 22.5 |
| Tobacco | | | 3.1 | 8.6 | 11.4 |
| Manufactures | | | 16.5 | 36.2 | 73.3 |
| Stamps | | | 4.1 | 5.9 | 11.2 |
| License | | | 4.8 | 5.2 | 9.8 |
| Gross receipts | | | 1.7 | 3.4 | 9.9 |
| Other | | | 1.3 | 4.9 | 12.0 |
| Sale of public lands | 0.9 | 0.2 | 0.2 | 0.6 | 1.0 |
| Miscellaneous | 1.0 | 0.9 | 3.7 | 30.3 | 25.4 |
| Premiums on gold sales | | 0.1 | 0.6 | 21.2 | 11.7 |
| Totals | $41.5 | $52.0 | $112.7 | $264.6 | $333.7 |
| Percent of tax revenue composed of income taxes | 0 | 0 | 2.4% | 7.7% | 18.3% |
| War expenditure* | $24.4 | $431.8 | $666.6 | $776.2 | $1,143.3 |
| Total government expenditure | $66.6 | $469.6 | $718.7 | $865.0 | $1,296.8 |
| Percent of war financed by taxation** | | **11.1%** | **15.7%** | **30.6%** | **25.7%** |

*Source:* Adapted from Studenski and Krooss, *Financial History of the United States.*

* The figures for war expenditure are comprised of expenditures of the War and Navy departments. Consistent with my definition of the budgetary cost of war, I exclude the rising cost of pensions and interest on government debt.

**Since I am unable to parse out what and how much of each tax went to the war effort, I take the percent of total government expenditure financed by taxation. Because war expenditure comprised such a large percentage of total government expenditure—almost 90 percent from 1862 onward—my estimates of the percentage of war financed by taxation are only minimally distorted. However, I exclude 1861, as only 36.6 percent of government expenditure was war expenditure.

are more elastic to policy change and yield higher revenue. Thus revenue from direct extraction may comprise a larger percentage of a high-capacity state's war finance strategy.

## Currency Reserves and Foreign War Finance

When leaders prefer to shield the public from the costs of war or a state has low extractive capacity, it may engage in external war finance. Under what other conditions do leaders turn to foreign war finance? Regardless of the state's capacity to extract domestic revenue or war finance preferences, if a state is unable to procure enough currency reserves to purchase war inputs from abroad, it will have to incorporate external war finance into its war finance strategy.

Leaders have three ways of acquiring inputs for war: seize them, make them, or buy them.[83] Inputs for war include manpower, equipment (typically reflected via a defense industry or a civilian industry that is convertible to purchase inputs for war coupled with raw materials), foodstuffs, and transportation assets.[84] When a state can supply its entire war effort via domestic inputs, it negates the need to purchase inputs from abroad and, thus, the need to obtain a currency loan pay for them. However, when a state is unable to supply its war effort domestically, it will need to look outside its borders. In order to purchase inputs for the war effort from abroad, the state needs either gold or the currency of the supplier state. A problem arises when the necessary currency diminishes to critical levels while the belligerent state needs to continue to purchase goods to maintain its war effort.

The problem of low currency reserves may be compounded due to wartime circumstances. During wartime, exports, a primary mechanism through which states garner currencies, often become severely limited through decreased trade. A state may encourage exports, prompting the flow of currency into the country, or reduce imports, keeping needed currency from flowing out of the country to redress the imbalance. War, however, decreases a state's ability to trade, as trading partners are hurt by the war, states enact blockades or sanctions, or states need industries that normally are export oriented for the war effort. Simultaneously, the need to import goods increases, as the state needs to supplement goods that it is no longer able to produce to supply the armed forces. The decrease in exports results in a decrease of reserve currency, while the increase in imports increases the need for it. The need for reserve currency further increases when a state maintains forward operating bases or is fighting abroad and purchasing goods in theater.

Under these circumstances, the only way for the state to continue paying for needed imported inputs for the war effort is to engage in external resource extraction. Here, external extraction may be in the form of foreign loans, grants, or plunder.

## War Finance Strategy

Akin to Weber's ideal type, the war finance continuum is a heuristic device that allows scholars to better understand the political costs and state capacity limits to each method of war finance. Figure 1.2 synthesizes the theory laid out in the chapter. It provides a schematic of how preferences and capacity interact with the various variables to create a war finance strategy.

States often resort to multiple means of war finance. They engage in multiple forms of extraction simultaneously and/or sequentially as leaders' preferences

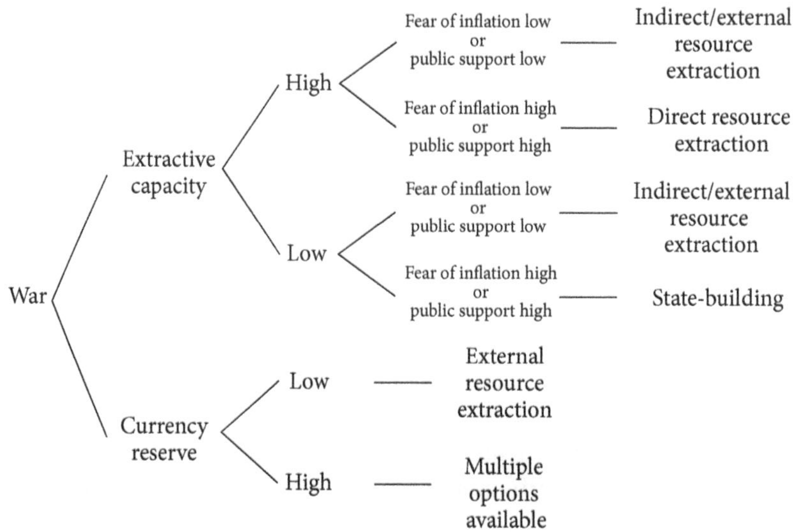


**FIGURE 1.2** War finance strategy model

or state capacity change. For example, a war finance strategy may be characterized as comprising of direct, indirect, and external resource extraction. Chapters 2 and 3, the study of American financing of the Korean and Vietnam Wars, respectively, are characterized by within-case variation that provides the reader insight into how the various war finance means coexist and change over time. As the fear of inflation and public support varied throughout the Korean and Vietnam wars, Truman and Johnson adjusted the percentage of the war financed by direct and indirect taxation. State capacity also varies in wartime, affecting a state's war finance strategy. In chapter 4, for example, I discuss British currency reserve capacity throughout World War II. As Britain's capacity decreased, external resource extraction comprised a larger percentage of the state's war finance strategy. In chapter 5, I discuss how Japan invested in state building during the Russo-Japanese war, whereas Russia was constrained by its state's capacity.

This chapter provided a framework for understanding how states finance wars. In doing so, it refines the concepts of cost of war; war finance; war finance strategy; and direct, indirect, and external resource extraction. It also provides boundaries for the study of war finance. Short wars have different revenue dynamics than long wars. Finally, it provides a framework that explains when and why states resort to the various war finance means available.

# 2

# TRUMAN AND THE KOREAN WAR

The US war efforts in Korea and Vietnam could not have been financed more differently. The Korean War effort was paid for by direct resource extraction (taxation), with a minimal reliance on indirect extraction (austerity). Vietnam, on the other hand, was paid for by indirect resource extraction (general public debt), with a minimal reliance on direct extraction (taxation). This difference is surprising given the similar political and economic context in which they were financed. Both wars required aid to a small Asian country struggling against a communist enemy backed by the Soviet Union and China. They were also limited wars fought in the shadow of the Cold War that resulted in a similar number of American casualties.[1] In regards to cost, the Korean War was only a modest amount more than Vietnam. At its peak in 1952, the Korean War cost 4.2 percent of American GDP in comparison to a peak cost of 3.2 percent of GDP in 1968 for Vietnam.[2]

In addition, these two cases hold a wide range of domestic variables constant. The bureaucratic capacity to extract revenue is similar across the two cases. In the United States, the administrative machinery to collect taxes and float debt had been put in place by the end of World War I.[3] In addition to capacity, both wars were initiated and primarily fought under Democratic presidents with legislative agendas to expand societal welfare—Truman's Fair Deal and Johnson's Great Society. Moreover, the Democratic Party held the majority in both the Eighty-First and Eighty-Ninth congresses, when each of the wars began. Finally, both wars took place in the era of the Bretton Woods system. Thus a system of capital controls was in effect, giving Truman and Johnson more freedom in their macroeconomic policy.[4]

Given the extent of political and economic similarities, how did these two wars come to be financed so differently? The variation in these cases can be explained by differing leadership preferences vis-à-vis fear of inflation and public support for the war. When the Korean War began, the United States had just emerged from a period of postwar inflation, and both the Truman administration and the American public were afraid of repeating the high levels of inflation they linked to the financing of World War II. Moreover, the hoarding of goods by fearful citizens drove up prices in the early months of the war. Simultaneously, public support in favor of the war lowered the political costs for the Truman administration to implement anti-inflationary war taxes.

The financing of the Vietnam War was the antithesis of Korean War finance. When troops entered Vietnam en masse in 1965, the Johnson administration had just cut taxes to combat a recession. There was no fear of inflation and, therefore, no desire to raise taxes to fund the war effort. When prices began to rise in 1966, the administration viewed the rise as temporary. It was not until 1967 that a fear of inflation began to materialize. This fear prompted an attempt to raise taxes. Low levels of public support for the war, however, raised the political cost of asking for more revenue, limiting the Johnson administration's ability to implement a war tax. The result was a war effort financed primarily by domestic debt with only a minimal reliance on taxation.[5]

This chapter focuses specifically on the financing of the Korean War and its within-case variation. Korean War finance can be divided into two periods, from June 1950 to mid-1951 and from mid-1951 to the end of the war. During the first period, both the fear of inflation and support for the war effort were high. As a result, the Revenue Act of 1950, eliminating an excise tax reduction and increasing both corporate and individual income taxes, and the Excess Profit Tax Law of 1950 were swiftly signed into law.

During the second period of Korean War finance, the political-economic landscape changed. Prices began to stabilize, reducing the public's fear of inflation. The public no longer believed it was necessary to raise taxes to fight inflation. In addition, a bloody stalemate that began in mid-1951 diminished public support for the war, increasing the political cost of implementing additional taxes to fund the war effort. Thus, when Truman asked to raise revenue one more time, he only got half of what he requested, reflected in the Revenue Act of 1951.

## Background

The Korean War began on June 25, 1950, and by July 7, the United States was designated commander of all UN forces and President Truman authorized General

Douglas MacArthur to send US ground forces to Korea.[6] In two weeks' time, the US military establishment, with an actual strength of about 1,460,000 men in June 1950, went from a planned 1951 end strength of 1.5 million to an approved figure of slightly more than 2.1 million, an increase of 41 percent.[7] By the end of the war, 5,720,000 troops served worldwide during the war and 1,789,000 served in-theater.[8]

To appreciate the Truman administration's ability to raise enough tax revenue to finance the war effort, one has to understand the political and economic environment of 1950. First, the United States was not prepared for a full-scale conventional war. When the Korean War began, the Truman administration was in the process of decreasing the budget and the size of the armed forces. President Truman, determined to maintain a balanced budget, imposed a budget ceiling on the Pentagon, cutting defense by about a third to $10 billion per year and leaving the armed forces ill equipped to fight a large-scale conventional war.[9] In addition to the cut in troops, equipment was in poor shape. Stockpiles of material left over from World War II were deteriorating, and budget cuts had retarded both research and development and the procurement of new equipment.[10] Thus a huge renewed investment in the armed forces had to take place in order to meet the needs of the Korean War.

Second, the United States was not just ill prepared for a full-scale conventional war; it was ill prepared to rally against communism. In addition to the cost of the Korean War, there was an acceleration of military spending for the Cold War.[11] In Truman's first speech to Congress regarding the situation in Korea on July 19, 1950, he stated, "The attack upon the Republic of Korea makes it plain beyond all doubt that the international communist movement is prepared to use armed invasion to conquer independent nations. We must therefore recognize the possibility that armed aggression may take place in other areas."[12] Truman directed that the US forces in support of the Philippines be strengthened and that military assistance to the Philippine government, to the Associated States of Indo-China, and to the forces of France in Indochina be sped up. He also ordered the US Seventh Fleet to prevent any attack on Formosa. Truman did not limit anticommunist policy to the Pacific, increasing economic and military aid to other "free" nations such as Greece, Turkey, and Iran.

Third, adding to this enormous increase in military spending, the United States also paid for allied participation in the Korean War. The Korean War was fought under the United Nations but paid for almost entirely by the United States. The South Korean government attempted to pay for its own war effort. It increased taxes, borrowed from its people, and printed money. However, given that the war was being fought on its own soil, self-sufficiency was impossible.[13] In addition, the United States provided large amounts of aid to other allied forces during the war. For example, while the Commonwealth countries—Britain, Canada, Australia, New Zealand—committed troops and basic equipment, they relied on the American supply system as well as any special equipment and logistics. Given the immediacy and urgency of the war, the United States provided said support before a basis for reimbursement was negotiated. The matter was not resolved until February 1964.[14]

Fourth, at the onset of the war, there was a strong movement in Congress to lower taxes. At the end of World War II, Truman signed the Revenue Act of 1945, revoking the excess profits tax and lowering individual and corporate tax rates. Congress wanted another large tax cut in 1947, proposing a further reduction in individual income taxes and increased personal exception.[15] Truman felt otherwise and vetoed the bill.[16] Congress, insistent on rolling back World War II tax hikes, overrode the veto. Consequently, the Revenue Act of 1948 reduced individual income tax rates by 5–13 percent.

In spite of these political and economic hurdles, the Truman administration was able to pay for the war outright. To understand the events that shaped Korean War finance, I emphasize the executive branch, as it is the primary location of war finance policy. Hence I focus on the Truman administration, specifically, his Council of Economic Advisors (CEA)—Chairman Edwin Norse (1946–1949), Chairman Leon Keyserling (1949–1953), John D. Clark, and Roy Blough—as well as Treasury Secretary John Snyder and L. Laszlo Ecker-Racz, director of the Tax Advisory staff in the Department of the Treasury.[17] Other notable figures and agencies include Truman's budget director Frederick Lawton, Secretary of Defense George C. Marshall, and the Bureau of the Budget. While I stress the executive, it is also necessary to examine the role of Congress, in particular, the House Ways and Means Committee, whose chairman was Robert Doughton (D-NC), and the Senate Finance Committee, chaired by Walter George (D-GA). Last, I include the role of the public and the relationship between public opinion and war finance policy.[18]

## Korean War Finance, Phase I: 1950 to Mid-1951

### Fear of Inflation

The fear of inflation for President Truman, members of his administration, and the public began prior to the onset of the war. The fears originated with the rise in prices experienced after World War II. Between June 1947 and January 1948, wholesale prices rose at an annual rate of 20 percent and consumer prices at an annual rate of 12 percent.[19] Even though prices began to decrease and stabilize in the fall of 1948, there was still a fear that inflation would return. On February 4, 1949, CEA chairman Edwin Norse wrote to Truman cautioning the president that inflationary pressures were developing. He argued that national income and the disposable income of consumers was at new peak levels, creating a "great buying power that is being supplemented by growing expenditures of federal, state and local governments." Business investment was high and "market demand was so strong that the wholesale price index had been steadily trending upward." He concluded by noting this economic environment was "not the performance of a softening economy."[20]

The Truman administration was not the only party scarred by the financing of the previous war; so was the American public. Once the Korean War began, citizens were reminded of the shortages experienced during World War II and, consequently, began hoarding goods. The first spurt in retail sales lasted two months. This occurred immediately after the onset of hostilities. Sales then declined for several months as the UN forces advanced northward in Korea, only to spurt once again after the Chinese Communists entered the war and the retreat from the Yalu began.[21]

The result of hording was demand-pull inflation.[22] Both wholesale and consumer prices began to rise in July 1950. Between June and December 1950, the consumer price index increased by 47 percent, while the index of wholesale prices rose by 10.4 percent.[23] Polling surveys reflected the public's awareness of increasing prices. In a Gallup Poll survey in October 1950, 68 percent of adults polled believed that prices would be higher in six months.[24] This belief that prices would continue to rise remained consistent until May 1951.

The Truman administration believed that the best way to counter inflation was a direct resource extraction policy. Postwar inflation was so severe that even before the Korean War began, a war finance plan was already in place dictating that higher levels of taxation should finance the next war. This thinking was evident in a memo written to Assistant Treasury Secretary John Graham in 1948, in which it was "assumed that the Government would . . . finance a major part of the [next] war's cost out of taxes."[25]

Once the war started, a reliance on direct taxation to mitigate the effects of inflation was paramount. L. Laszlo Ecker-Racz, director of the Tax Advisory staff in the Department of the Treasury, argued to President Truman that the financing of Korea should be different from that of World War II. Current war finance policy should avoid direct controls to fight inflation and rely more heavily on taxation.

> In comparison, preparation for the last war [World War II] can be regarded as a sprint, and the economic measures that carried the country

> though it will not necessarily be appropriate at the present time. In particular, for a sustained effort we cannot hope to rely as heavily as we did then on a comprehensive system of direct controls to secure resources necessary for the defense program and at the same time avoid inflation. Although the control system during the last war worked better than many had expected, we feel reasonably confident that, had it been continued much longer, the US economy would have been exposed to the well-known weaknesses of a policy of suppressed inflation. This time, we must rely much more heavily than before on tax policy and credit policy.[26]

Similarly, when attempting to secure a tax increase in 1951, Secretary of the Treasury John Snyder, in a letter to Robert Doughton, chairman of House Ways and Means, stated that the large amount of deficit financing that was seen in World War II should be avoided.[27]

The public, like the Truman administration, also believed that the best way to fight inflation was with taxation. Survey data, telegrams to the White House, and petitions to Congress indicate that the public supported a tax increase to fund the war. In a Gallup Poll Survey in July 1950, 70 percent of respondents stated that they would be "willing to pay more money in taxes to support a larger army." A month later, 51 percent of participants agreed that "federal income taxes must be increased immediately to pay for the present war in Korea and to re-arm the United States." In October 1950, about two months into the war, 51 percent of people surveyed stated that they would prefer increased taxes to pay for the war versus 26 percent who preferred to borrow.[28] Truman, aware of the public's fear of inflation, invoked it in a speech to Congress when outlining his war finance policy: "During World War II, taxes were not high enough, and the government was forced to borrow too much. As a result, when controls were taken off after the war, prices skyrocketed and we paid in inflation for our failure to tax enough. The value of people's savings was cut down by the higher prices they had to pay."[29]

Economists also believed that the primary means to finance the war should be taxation. On November 30, 1950, more than four hundred economists from thirty institutions sent a letter to Congress asking for anti-inflation measures to be implemented. Specifically, they recommended that the government raise tax revenues faster than the growth of defense spending to achieve and maintain a cash surplus: "If the inflationary pressure is to be removed, taxes must take out of private money incomes not only as much as Government spending contributes to them but also a part of the increase of private incomes resulting from increased private spending of idle balances and newly borrowed money."[30] Thus to merely balance the budget was not enough.

The first year of the war was characterized by inflation fears shared by both the Truman administration and the American public. These fears originated by the experiences surrounding the economy of World War II and postwar inflation. When the war began, citizens acted on these fear by hoarding goods. Hoarding only served to further increase prices and compounded existing fears. The Truman administration, the public, and economists were all overwhelmingly in favor of a policy that privileged taxation over deficit spending in order to alleviate rising prices.

## Public Support for the War

When war broke out on the Korean Peninsula, there were two dominant sentiments among US citizens: the public was in support of the war effort and they believed that the United States was now engaged in World War III.[31] These two positions, in conjunction with fear of inflation, lowered the political cost of increased fiscal sacrifice, making it easier for the Truman administration to raise taxes. As a result, the Truman administration was able to pass the Revenue Act and the Excess Profits Tax Law of 1950 without delay.

Public opinion polls conducted at various points during the war gauge support for the war effort.[32] An Elmo Roper survey taken just after the outbreak of hostilities revealed that 75 percent of the people supported Truman's decision to commit US forces to Korea.[33] In November 1950, a Gallup poll survey indicated that 66 percent of Americans believed the country should stay and defend South Korea, even if it meant world war.[34] Not only was the public in favor of the war effort, it was perceived by many that the United States was engaged in a world war. According to a Gallup Poll in July 1950, 57 percent of people believed that the United States was "now actually in World War III."[35] In October 1950, this figure decreased to 45 percent only to rise to 50 percent in November, following Chinese intervention into the conflict.

The belief that the United States was engaged in World War III with communists made controlling inflation imperative. Many policymakers believed that a price increase was exactly what the communists wanted. A report prepared for the Joint Economic Committee argued that if the US government did not raise taxes to fight inflation, the country would drift "into that debauchery of the currency which Lenin and Stalin have favored for decades as the most powerful and most subtle sixth column propelling capitalistic countries toward communism."[36] This report was followed by another titled "Inflation and Communism," which reviewed works by Lenin and other Soviet authors who pointed out that inflation is "both a symptom of economic crises and of a progressive decay of the capitalist system."[37] Moreover, the belief that the United States was in World War III brought with it a sense of complete mobilization, which included a strong economic base. At the start of the war, Truman stated that American strength was not to be measured in military terms alone, "Our power to join in a common defense of peace rests fundamentally on the productive capacity and energies of our people. In all that we do, therefore, we must make sure that the economic strength which is at the base of our security is not impaired, but continues to grow."[38]

## Direct Resource Extraction

Inflation was the primary concern for the Truman administration when concocting the Korean War finance strategy. When President Truman addressed Congress on July 19, 1950, to ask for an increase in defense appropriations, he also asked for a tax increase to pay for it. He explicitly stated that defense spending would have an inflationary effect on the economy and taxation would be the best means to combat it.

> The dollars spent now for military purposes will have a magnified effect upon the economy as a whole, since they will be added to the high level of current civilian demand. These increased pressures, if neglected, could drive us into a general inflationary situation. . . . We must make every effort to finance the greatest possible amount of needed expenditures by taxation. The increase of taxes is our basic weapon in offsetting the inflationary pressures exerted by enlarged government expenditures.[39]

For the rest of 1950 through 1951, the Truman administration pushed for increased taxation.

To raise tax revenue, Truman emphasized direct taxation. Before the war started, Congress was in the process of reducing World War II taxes. The House of Representatives had H.R. 8920 under consideration, a tax bill that would reduce certain excise taxes, close some long-standing tax loopholes, and increase corporate income tax rates.[40] In order to raise tax revenue for the war effort, Truman proposed to (a) eliminate the excise tax reduction and other revenue-losing provisions, (b) adjust the revised corporate rate structure contained in the pending bill by increasing the corporate rate from 21 to 25 percent, and (c) increase individual income tax rates to the "tentative" levels adopted in 1945 by removing the reductions from those levels made in 1945 and 1948.[41] The result of the adjustment to the pending tax bill was estimated by the Truman administration to increase government revenue by about $5 billion.

The Truman administration knew that $5 billion would not be enough money to pay for the war outright. Moreover, they felt that an excess profits tax (EPT) would be necessary to fight inflation. However, they were worried about the difficulty of getting an excess profits tax through Congress.[42] The main source of the controversy was what the EPT would look like and not whether one should be implemented.[43] The administration was focused on speed; to fight inflation, they needed to pull money out of the economy as quickly as possible.[44] Thus, in order to avoid a lengthy debate in Congress, the Truman administration tabled the EPT until after the election. With the EPT tabled, passage of the Revenue Act of 1950 took less than forty-five days for congressional approval.

As soon as Congress reconvened for a lame-duck session, work to enact an EPT began with the mandate to pass a bill before the end of the present session. On November 14, 1950, President Truman asked Congress to enact an EPT retroactively, effective July 1, 1950, to produce additional annual revenue of $4 billion dollars.[45] The EPT was quickly approved: on November 30, the committee reported H.R. 9827 (the EPT Act of 1950), and it passed the House on December 4 by a vote of 378 to 20.[46] The Senate followed close behind and passed a final version two weeks later.[47]

## Alternative Means to Combat Inflation—Price Controls and Monetary Policy

It is important to note that inflation was not just fought on the tax front. Government expenditures unrelated to the war were reduced, price and wage controls were put in place, and monetary policy was tightened.[48] However, fiscal policy was seen as the only real, effective means to control inflation.

To mitigate the effects of inflation, President Truman stopped pursuing many programs that were part of his Fair Deal agenda.[49] The Fair Deal included a repeal of the Taft-Hartley Act, a higher minimum wage, a farm program, expansion of social security, national medical insurance, housing, civil rights, and federal aid to education.[50] However, given that the Fair Deal was not yet fully implemented, savings from the aborted program would have had only a minimal effect on the economy.[51]

To administer price and wage controls, the Office of Price Stabilization was created, and on January 26, 1951, Truman issued a mandatory wage and price freeze.[52] Controls alone, however, were deemed inefficient at taming inflation. The Truman administration believed that controls would take a long time to implement. During that time, prices would rise unchecked. Taxation, on the other hand, had an immediate effect.[53] In July 1950, the CEA wrote to President Truman, "In a situation such as the present, a prompt tax increase can perform a strategically important function. It can compensate for the fact that it takes a relatively long time to develop, and make effective, direct controls such as rationing and price control. A simple program for higher taxes can be put into effect quickly. . . . If taxes are not imposed promptly, inflation becomes an accomplished act."[54] Moreover, controls were unattractive as they were difficult to implement, created a large bureaucracy, and hindered individual choice.[55]

Like price and wage controls, monetary policy did not play a central role in fighting Korean War inflation. The volume of World War II debt inhibited the Federal Reserve's ability to tighten credit in order to keep inflation under control. To finance World War II, financial institutions and investors bought large quantities of government securities carrying relative low interest rates. Debt management in the postwar period aimed at preserving an orderly market for those securities without substantial increase in the interest charges, essentially pegging the rates.[56] Thus the Federal Reserve's policy of market support rendered traditional tools to combat inflation ineffective as market support required the Fed to be ready to buy at predetermined prices whatever securities were offered in the market.[57]

In addition to open market policies, the rediscount rate was also ineffective at combating inflation. The stabilized rate for short-term government debt was below the rediscount rate. Thus when banks needed funds they found it cheaper to sell short-term securities to the Fed than to borrow from the Fed and pay the rediscount rate. Moreover, since banks were holding large amounts of short-term securities, they were hoping to follow this procedure without any inconvenience. Reserve requirements were also deemed ineffective. At the time of the Korean War, there was such large liquidity due to World War II debt that it made the increase in reserve requirements imposed by the Fed largely ineffective.[58]

One report described the latter half of 1950 as a period of frustration for the Federal Reserve Board because of these roadblocks in its use of these traditional control mechanisms over mounting credit.[59]

> The present problem of restraining the expansion of credit must be attacked under conditions differing vastly in degree, if not in kind, from those of any other inflationary period in the nation's history. The distinctive environment in which credit controls must function is fashioned in part of the elements from the past—the tremendous accumulation of public debt during World War II, and the policy of supporting the market for that debt.[60]

Thus, although the Federal Reserve System is the chief government agency charged with controlling inflation and the only agency that has specific authority to combat inflation through monetary measures, the anti-inflation tools traditionally available to it were either unavailable or ineffective.

In addition to limiting the tools at the Fed's disposal, World War II debt altered decision making in the Truman administration. Because the debt was so large, maintaining the market for government securities was considered a primary objective for the administration as well. In November 1950, the CEA expressed its commitment to maintaining the nation's debt in a letter to Joseph O'Mahoney, chairman of the Joint Economic Committee.

> A vital requirement is that the credit of the Government be preserved against doubt, and that the confidence of present holders of Government bonds and of potential investors must not be shaken by the sight of falling market prices induced by raises in interest rates through Federal Reserve action. . . . This kind of [tight] monetary policy, at a time when the existing pattern of interest rates could easily be supported is not justified in our opinion if its positive contribution to an anti-inflation program is as dubious and as imponderable as advocates of the policy say it is, particularly when other measures are available which act more positively and which have fewer undesirable consequences.[61]

Moreover, the Truman administration believed that it could procure the same outcome—stabilizing prices—through fiscal policy and avoid the costly side effects of adjusting monetary policy.[62]

The administration also believed that inhibiting credit expansion would be ineffective at targeting the type of inflation characterizing the American economy. According to the Committee on Fiscal and Monetary Policy, the type of inflation experienced after July 1950 was due to a hoarding psychology, not rapid credit expansion.[63] Moreover, tightening credit would not inhibit plant expansion or inventory accumulation as the means of finance for business came from internal sources.[64] Finally, the Truman administration felt that monetary policy and credit controls were too narrow in scope, placing too much emphasis on businesses. Taxes, on the other hand, were more positive, more widely distributed, subject to better control, and less likely to restrict production.[65]

The bottom line for the Truman administration was that these other means to fight inflation were ineffective. An interdepartmental fiscal committee meeting in August 1950—which included the chairmen and representatives from the Treasury, the Federal Reserve, the Budget Bureau, the National Security Resources Board, and the Council of Economic Advisors—concluded that at best controls on credit could serve as an interim device during the period before the power of taxation fully took hold.[66] Taxation was the only viable anti-inflationary tool.

## An Initial War Finance Success Story

The first six months of the war were a financial success for the Truman administration. A budget surplus began in mid-December 1950 and continued to grow. It reached a climax in March 1951 with a surplus of $4 billion, far exceeding that of any month in history.[67] The Truman administration even raised federal receipts enough to reduce the gross federal debt at the end of the 1951 fiscal year.[68] Truman's war finance plan worked, and in early 1951 prices began to stabilize.

## Phase II: Mid-1951 to October 20, 1951

Truman's war finance success story changed abruptly. In February 1951, he asked Congress to further increase taxes. Unlike the previous two requests, Truman received only half of what he asked for. First, Truman did too good of a job on the economic front. By garnering a surplus in revenue and stabilizing prices, he removed the fear of inflation from the public. Second, public support for the war drastically declined, increasing the political cost of asking the public to sacrifice financially. In the spring of 1951, the public began to perceive the war as an unwinnable battle that was not destined to become World War III. Thus, when Truman asked for more tax revenue, instead of Congress pushing through a bill in record speed and acquiescing to all of Truman's demands, there was congressional delay, and the Revenue Act of 1951 was to yield $5.4 billion in additional annual revenue instead of the $10 billion requested.

### Phase II: Fear of Inflation

By mid-1951, a budget surplus and decreasing prices caused the public's fear of inflation to ebb.[69] Perhaps more important than the actual stabilization of prices was the public perception of price change. By mid-1951 the public perceived prices were falling and, therefore, the fear of inflation was abating. In October 1950, 67 percent of Americans believed that prices would be higher in six months. By May 1951, this figure fell to 51 percent, dropping to 50 percent in July. As the perception of rising prices began to change, so did the desire to raise further taxes for the war effort. As seen in figure 2.1, the percentage of Americans who felt that taxes should be increased declined dramatically.[70]

The Truman administration felt differently. When prices began to slow down in early 1951, the CEA thought it was a perfect moment to continue their fight against inflation before the next surge that they were sure was coming. The CEA Quarterly Report in April stated, "The immediate inflationary pressures seem somewhat abated, thus providing an ideal period in which to act firmly before the next upsurge."[71] On June 8, 1951, Truman received a letter from his CEA stating, "Inflationary pressures in the months and year ahead will be stronger than any yet confronted since the initial Korean outbreak." The CEA then advised "that

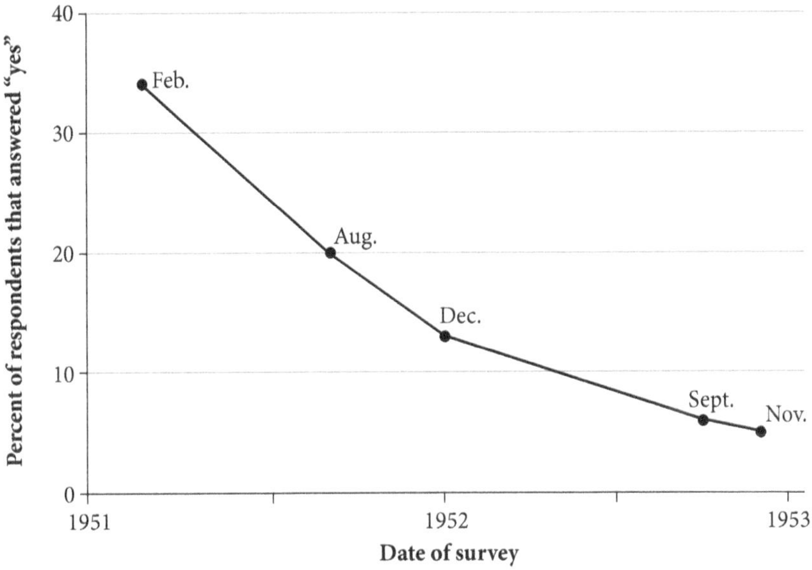


**FIGURE 2.1** Public support for a tax increase, 1951–1953: Percentage of Americans who believe taxes should be increased

an even stronger anti-inflationary program" would be needed to contain rising prices.[72]

The Truman administration quickly realized that the public did not share the same fear. Moreover, the administration was acutely aware that one of the reasons it was unable to pass legislation successfully was because of the public's new sentiment. In a memo to the president, CEA member John D. Clark argued that Americans were not in support of a tax increase because of the current economic climate of stable prices. Moreover, the American people would not support a tax increase unless prices would continue to rise, renewing their inflation fear. "Events in the second and third quarters [of 1951]," Clark wrote, "should disclose whether the phenomenon of 1951 was due to temporary causes or may be counted upon to continue, and those events may reactivate the inflationary movement so vigorously that the American people will eagerly support productive measures, including tax increases, which in the present quiet situation they are not disposed to accept."[73]

In an attempt to reverse the public's now-complacent attitude toward inflation, Truman and his staff went on a campaign to educate the public and Congress of the next wave of inflation they believed was on the horizon. On June 7, 1951, Truman held a press conference. He reminded the public that the US economy was operating at almost full capacity, the defense program was still rapidly expanding, the budgetary surplus of recent months was going to be replaced by a growing deficit, and incomes were still rising.[74] Truman then went to Congress with the same message:

> These recent developments have led some people to think that the inflationary trend is ended. This is a dangerous assumption. . . . If taxes and savings are not sufficiently increased; there would thus be a growing disparity between the incomes which people would desire to spend and the supply of consumer goods. This disparity represents the inflationary gap. If controls were to be relaxed, the inflationary gap would be greater—probably very much greater. The price-wage spiral would again be set in motion. Winning the battle against inflation is an essential element in our struggle for peace.[75]

Truman even invoked the fears of World War II postwar inflation that was so prevalent in 1950. In his annual economic report to Congress, he stated, "We contained inflation, under more difficult circumstances, during World War II, although we did not do a good enough job of forestalling postwar inflation. We must learn from past mistakes as well as from past successes."[76]

The attempts of Truman and his administration were in vain. The public no longer feared inflation and firmly opposed a tax increase to pay for the war.

## Phase II: Public Support for the War

The spring and early summer of 1951 were difficult times for the Truman tax campaign. Not only was the rationale for a tax increase gone, the political cost of extracting more revenue had also risen due to lackluster support for the war effort. The bloody stalemate that ensued after the Fifth Chinese Offensive drastically changed the public's attitude about the war as well as about the president. More important, the perception that the United States was fighting World War III had abated. The political climate to raise taxes was made even worse with an unpopular president, as the firing of General MacArthur caused Truman's approval ratings to hit a new low.

In February and March of 1951, the United States led two offensives—Operation Killer and Ripper. The purpose of these operations was to restore the Eighth Army's line extending east from Yanpyong to Hoensgong, to trap and kill all enemy that had penetrated that sector, and to disrupt Chinese plans for another offensive.[77] The operations had mixed results. The success of Operation Killer was hampered by poor weather and logistical difficulties. Few enemy soldiers were killed or captured. Yet, Hoensgong was recaptured and the territory south of the Han River was reoccupied. Operation Ripper, however, was slightly more successful and resulted in the recapturing of Seoul. The two operations were followed by a Chinese and North Korean offensive that resulted in heavy American casualties. On May 24, Omar Bradley revealed in congressional testimony that there were 69,276 American battle casualties and 72,679 nonbattle casualties.[78] From this time onward, although fighting continued, little territory would change hands.

Public opinion in support of the war dwindled as a result of the high casualty stalemate. In July 1950, a Gallup poll asked Americans whether or not they approved of President Truman's decision to send US military aid to South Korea. At that time, 78 percent approved. By February 1951, only 48 percent of Americans thought it was right for President Truman to have sent American forces to fight in Korea.[79] Campbell and Cain also found the Korean War failed to elicit the sustained period of support evidenced in World War I and, to a slightly lesser extent, World War II. Between October 1950 and January 1951, overt support for the conflict dropped from 65 percent to an average of 31 percent.[80]

Americans also felt they had sacrificed enough for the war. In July 1950, 44 percent of people answered that Americans had not been asked to make enough sacrifices in support of the war. Between July 1950 and February 1951, this survey was administered seven times. The average response was that 38 percent felt they had not been asked to sacrifice enough. In March 1951, this figure dropped dramatically, with only 20 percent of respondents feeling they had not been asked to sacrifice enough.[81]

In addition to reduced support for the war, Truman's approval ratings plummeted. Greatly affecting his ratings was the firing of General Douglass MacArthur in April. In June 1951, 58 percent of Americans believed that in the disagreements between Truman and MacArthur about how to carry on in Korea, MacArthur was right, whereas only 27 percent felt Truman was right.[82] In the spring of 1951, around the time the Revenue Act of 1951 was being considered in Congress, the public's general approval for the president hit an all-time low at just above 20 percent.

In addition to decreasing public support for the war effort and President Truman, the belief that the country was in a world war was gone and with it the notion that it was necessary to economically mobilize for World War III. After 1950, there were no more Gallup Poll questions asking the public if they believed the country was in World War III. Even the American Federation of Labor Advisory Committee, writing to the CEA, was aware of the decreased fear, "Since the stalemate following the initial truce negotiations in Korea and the easing of the sense of imminent danger of war, the relaxed attitude toward defense needs has carried over into the expectation that defense expenditures are likely to be sharply curtailed."[83]

Starting in March 1951, both the White House and the Department of Defense had taken notice of shifting public opinion regarding the war and that this shift was affecting the ability to spend and fund the conflict. In a cabinet meeting in late March, Robert Lovett, deputy secretary of defense, stated, "The Defense Department has 3 enemies—(1) Risk of visual aggression . . . (2) Inflation. That has cost us 2 billion out of every 10 billion since June . . . (3) Relaxation. This has been shown itself by reversal of attitude of Congress. In December Congress was talking full war mobilization. It was in an attitude of gluttony. Now the attitude is to minimize the need for vital projects."[84]

At the same time, the CEA and Treasury were trying to figure out what this change meant for the president's war finance policy. In a memo to John Snyder, the secretary of the treasury, the CEA stated that the public was no longer threatened by events in the Korean Peninsula. Consequently, there was less congressional interest to pass the tax bill. "A number of factors account for the lack of Congressional interest in tax legislation," the CEA noted. "The relaxation of public concern over the international situation is one important reason. Recent developments in Korea and in other troublesome areas have not been particularly alarming."[85] A month later, in their quarterly report, the CEA went on to make the connection between the fact that the public no longer believed themselves to be in the next world war, the stalemate in Korea, and the ability to raise taxes: "The Reluctance of the [Ways and Means] Committee to take immediate action probably reflected in considerable part the heavy mail reaction from constituents. Objection was raised to further increases of taxes until prices had stabilized. There was also widespread feeling that expenditures could and should be greatly cut and no further tax increase should be made until this had taken place."[86]

How the war was unfolding affected public attitudes, which in turn shaped the ability of the Truman administration to fund the war effort. Once the public believed that it was not engaged in World War III, it no longer felt that the nation needed to mobilize to such a large extent. Consequently, Americans no longer felt that extensive defense expenditures needed to be maintained. This belief extended to fiscal policy—because expenditures should be reduced, taxes should not be increased, at least not by the amount Truman was asking for. In addition to the removal of an existential threat, the public was dissatisfied with the events of the war. As casualties mounted and little territory was being won, support for the war, as well as for the president, plummeted. The decreased support made raising taxes even more politically costly. Truman, with low approval ratings, had little capital to sway either the public or Congress.

## The Revenue Act of 1951

On February 2, 1951, Truman asked Congress to enact revenue legislation to yield at least $10 billion annually. Truman recommended an immediate increase in personal income taxes to bring in $4 billion in additional revenue. In addition, he recommended an increase in corporate income taxes to yield an additional $3 billion and selective excise taxes to yield $3 billion dollars. Last, he asked Congress to continue the program started in the previous year to close loopholes in the present tax laws.[87]

The removal of the inflation rationale coupled with low support for the war effort gave the administration little leverage to raise taxes. The passage of the Revenue Act of 1950 took only forty-five days. The passage of the Revenue Act of 1951 took nine months. Over the nine months the bill was in Congress, it became a shell of its former self. Aside from reduced revenue, the bill was weakened with a number of special provisions and exemptions. It is important to note that opposition to the bill was not restricted to conservatives. A group of liberal senators offered the most persistent and serious opposition that had ever been launched against a Finance Committee revenue bill.[88] The final bill raised individual income tax liabilities 11 percent for those with incomes under two thousand dollars a year and 11.75 percent for those over that level, with a termination date of December 31, 1951. Corporate rates were raised to 30 percent on income under twenty-five thousand dollars and 52 percent on income over that level. The bill raised about $5.4 billion in revenue.[89]

## Epilogue

The years 1952 and 1953 were uneventful for war finance. In March 1952, faced with a 65 percent disapproval rating, President Truman announced that he would not seek reelection. In April, truce talks in Korea were still deadlocked, principally over the issue of the exchange of prisoners. In November, Republican Dwight D. Eisenhower overwhelmingly defeated Democrat Adlai Stevenson. In addition, the Republican Party also took control of Congress. Although President Eisenhower did not raise taxes, he did not want to lower them either. Like Truman, Eisenhower was committed to fighting inflation and maintaining a balanced budget. However, his party felt differently. The Excess Profits Tax Law was set to expire on December 31, 1953. To Eisenhower's disapproval, Republicans passed legislation that moved forward the termination date to June 30, 1953.[90] The war ended in on July 27, 1953, with the signing of an armistice.

The financing of the Korean War demonstrates how the fear of inflation and the public's support for the war affects how a conflict is financed. When the fear of inflation and public support for the war is high, direct resource extraction, specifically taxation, dominates a state's war finance strategy. When the fear of inflation decreases along with support for the war, it is no longer feasible to pay for the war by taxation. The following chapter demonstrates how a state's war finance strategy is affected when these variables are reversed.

3

# JOHNSON AND THE VIETNAM WAR

The US financing of the Vietnam War effort, primarily by indirect resource extraction, has been connected to inflation, high interest rates, a balance of payments problem, a world financial crisis, and the end of the dollar-gold peg.[1] Similar to President Truman, President Johnson could have paid for a larger percentage of the war with taxes, potentially avoiding these negative consequences. However, Johnson chose to rely on domestic debt for the early years of the war. It was not until January 1967 that Johnson announced he would ask Congress to raise taxes. A year and a half later, in June 1968, a 10 percent surcharge on corporate and income taxes was implemented.

The dominant narrative of Vietnam War finance is the classic of guns versus butter. Johnson avoided asking Congress for a tax increase because he was afraid Congress would cut his Great Society welfare program.[2] Johnson's counterpart, Truman, drastically cut his Fair Deal program to help pay for the Korean War and avoid inflation. Why did Truman relinquish his welfare program and raise taxes to pay for the Korean War outright, whereas Johnson did not? Why did Johnson not raise taxes earlier to fight inflation? Why did it take more than a year to get a tax increase passed through Congress?

I argue that differing inflation fears and public support for the war explain the variation in outcome. Johnson did not want to relinquish his Great Society, for unlike Truman, Johnson did not fear inflation. He believed that the US economy could absorb a large increase in government spending without raising taxes to pay for it. Consequently, Johnson believed he could fund both programs simultaneously, without economic detriment.

By 1967, when prices started to rise, the Johnson administration was unable to increase taxes. While inflation fears where high within the administration, members of Congress and the public were not similarly concerned. The difficulty of implementing a tax increase in 1967 was compounded by low public support for the war effort. Whereas during the Korean War, Truman acted to raise taxes at the onset of the war, when public support was at its peak, the Johnson administration did not request a tax increase until two years into the Vietnam War, when support for the war was beginning to falter. Declining support for the Vietnam War increased the political cost of a tax increase for both the Johnson administration and Congress, delaying passage of the surcharge.

## Background

The Vietnam War was costly. Of the more than 2.5 million personnel deployed to Vietnam by the United States, 153,303 came home wounded, while in-theater deaths totaled over 58,000.[3] Between 1965 and 1975, the Vietnam War cost Americans $111 billion dollars.[4] This cost reflects not only the US war effort but also the funding of its allies. Beginning in 1964, the United States endeavored to involve the military forces of other countries in order to create an allied effort against the communists in Vietnam. This program, titled More Flags, cost an additional $2.1 billion. Under More Flags, the United States funded the involvement of South Korea, the Philippines, and Thailand.[5] In addition, the United States funded a large percentage of the Government of South Vietnam's (GVN) war effort. Military assistance to the GVN between 1966 and 1975 totaled $14.5 billion.[6]

Around the time the United States began to send large numbers of troops into Vietnam, in March 1965, President Johnson was moving forward with his Great Society welfare plan. The budgetary cost of this War on Poverty program during the Johnson Years (1965–1969) amounted to $239 billion, almost three times what Johnson spent on the war.[7] Total expenditures for the Great Society at the peak of the program's cost were 6.72 percent of GDP in 1969. One of the early components of Great Society was a tax cut. On June 21, 1965, three months after sending troops into Vietnam, President Johnson signed H.R. 8371 into law, an excise tax reduction with an estimated cost of $1.3 billion annually.[8] The Vietnam War was the first war in US history in which the government was simultaneously financing a war and welfare program. The result of this concurrent financing was a $37.4 billion deficit created between 1965 and 1969.[9]

To understand the political and economic events that shaped Vietnam War finance, I focus primarily on President Johnson and his administration. The Council of Economic Advisors—Chairman Gardner Ackley (1964–1968), Chairman

Arthur Okun (1968–1969), Otto Eckstein, and James Dusenberry—were in constant contact with President Johnson. As Ackley recalled, "LBJ encouraged us to keep sending him a maximum amount of information on economic questions. We often sent three or four [memos] a day, certainly fifteen a week, on the average, maybe twelve, at the minimum."[10] Other notable agencies and figures include the Treasury Department and its secretary, Henry Fowler, and the Bureau of the Budget (BoB) and its director, Charles Schultze. Together, the CEA, the Treasury, and the BoB made up the Troika, which was responsible for macroeconomic policy.[11] The Troika informally expanded in 1966 to include William Martin, the chairman of the Federal Reserve Board. The four-member group became known as the Quadriad.

Conversations on Vietnam War finance also included Special Assistant to the President Joseph Califano and Secretary of Defense Robert S. McNamara. Joe Califano, while he did not advise on policy, was the intermediary between the CEA and the president.[12] Defense Secretary Robert McNamara did more than just advise the president on defense matters and the budget for Vietnam; in conjunction with the CEA, he advised Johnson on war finance policy. McNamara's advice was included in the majority of memos from the CEA to President Johnson. Moreover, Johnson would explicitly ask McNamara for economic advice.[13]

While I stress the executive, in order to understand the financing of the Vietnam War, it is also necessary to examine the role of Congress, and in particular the House Ways and Means Committee, chaired by Wilbur Mills (D-Arkansas), and the Senate Finance Committee, chaired by Russell Long (D-Louisiana). Last, integral to my analysis of Vietnam War finance is the role of the public and the relationship between public opinion and finance policy.[14] I complement polling data with data compiled by presidential aide Fred Panzer, the White House "poll person" during the Johnson administration.

## Vietnam War Finance Phase I: March 1965 to Fall 1966

### Fear of Recession, Not Inflation

When Johnson sent troops into Vietnam the dominant concern was combating a recession, not protecting the economy from a costly and inflationary war. A memo to Johnson from his CEA dated May 5, 1965, reflected the recession fear: "For the next two or three years, we should see the following as our dominant economic problem: Sustaining the growth of total demand and forestalling recession, by appropriate fiscal policies."[15] Stable prices throughout 1965 reinforced the belief that inflation was not on the horizon and confirmed that no new taxes would be needed to finance the war. In November 1965, the CEA believed that prices might even decrease the following year: "Our best expectation is that the rise of consumer prices and wholesale prices in the next 12 months will be no greater than in the past 12 months, and could be smaller."[16]

Whereas the fear of inflation for the Truman administration had its origins with previous war inflation experiences, the Johnson administration believed the Vietnam War would be different. Even before Johnson sent troops into Vietnam, the CEA rejected any similarity to the Korean War. In August 1964, Ackley wrote to President Johnson, "There is no likelihood that an over-all excess demand inflation will develop like that following the World War II or accompanying the Korean conflict."[17] After the war began, this belief persisted. In October 1965, Ackley reiterated that the CEA did not expect inflation similar to that experienced during the Korean War, "but we do not expect a repeat of the 3 percent-a-year crawling inflation of 1956 and 1957, much less the trotting inflations of the Korean War or 1945–48."[18]

The Korean War was different for two reasons. First, the American economy of the 1960s had the capacity to absorb a defense increase.[19] Second, the American consumer was different. The 1950 consumer had World War II inflation in mind when the Korean War started. The 1950s consumer, fearing a repeat of World War II supply shortages, hoarded when the Korean War started, driving up demand. The 1960s consumer was different and did not recall the price increase of the previous war. Thus he did not hoard and prices remained stable.

> The analogy with Korea simply does not hold water. We started the Korean War with defense purchases running at a $12 billion rate; we doubled them in 9 months and tripled them in 15. Our defense capability is incomparably greater today. Even so, the real reason for the surge in prices in late 1950 and early 1951 was not the pressure of defense orders or outlays. . . . Fresh memories of wartime rationing and shortages drove households in a hoarding binge. The consumer [in 1965] has been living in a world of plentiful supplies and well-stocked shelves for a dozen years now. He is not about to panic.[20]

Five months into the war, the Johnson administration still believed that a repetition of Korea was unlikely.[21] In August 1965, CEA chairman Ackley argued that "on prices, the only really serious hazard is possible fear of war scarcities. But a repetition of the Korean scare psychology seems unlikely."[22]

With fears of recession rather than inflation, the prescription to forestall an economic slowdown was a fiscal stimulus. The CEA, in conjunction with various economists, argued for increasing government spending,

> We will almost surely see a slower rate of growth over the next four quarters, with gradually rising unemployment. . . . All agreed that they

> would like to see more fiscal stimulus in early 1966 . . . they urged a strongly expansionary budget for fiscal 1967. . . . They would like to see a $7 or $8 billion of combined stimulus, from increases in Administrative budget expenditures, income tax reductions, or possibly some new form of grants to State and local governments.[23]

Accordingly, to raise taxes to fund the war effort outright would result in a harmful economic contraction. In a memo to Johnson on July 30, 1965, the CEA explained that both guns and butter were possible:

> Our economy has lots of room to absorb a defense step-up. There is still a $15–$20 billion margin of idle industrial capacity and excessive unemployment. Our productive capacity is growing by $25–30 billion a year, making room for both more butter and, if needed, more guns. . . . In the first half of 1966, the impact on output and employment will be more significant. But it means extra *insurance against slowdown or recession* during that period—*not a threat of overheating.*[24]

President Johnson articulated this same sentiment to the public. In his 1966 budget message, he argued that the United States was a "rich nation" that could "afford to make progress at home while meeting obligations abroad." He explained, that it was for "this reason, [he had] not halted progress in the new and vital Great Society programs in order to finance the costs of our efforts in Southeast Asia."[25] Thus the fear of a recession and the desire to stimulate the economy led the administration to believe that the American economy was able to absorb an increase in defense spending while also pursuing an expansive welfare program.

Prices, however, briefly rose in response to increased war expenditures in the spring of 1966, resulting in a push to increase taxes to fund the war effort. In May, Bureau of the Budget (BoB) Director Charles Schultze argued to President Johnson for a tax increase to avoid inflation: "In short, under almost every conceivable circumstance—except a Vietnam settlement between July and November—a decision to raise taxes at least for the remainder of the year and early 1967 is clearly warranted. And even under that circumstance, the risks of serious inflation, in my view, far outweigh the dangers of having a tax increase extend a few months past the date of a possible Vietnam settlement."[26]

Exactly when and to what extent to increase taxes was up for debate among Johnson's advisors. CEA Chairman Garner Ackley and BoB Director Schultze preferred a tax increase immediately. While Treasury Secretary Fowler and Johnson's advisor Joe Califano felt an immediate tax increase should be considered, they were not strongly committed to one.[27] Defense Secretary McNamara preferred to wait until he knew more about the course of the war.[28]

One reason for delaying the tax increase in the spring of 1966 was the belief by some within the administration that the price rise culprit, the war, would end soon.[29] In February 1966, Schultze wrote to President Johnson, "The military expenditure estimate . . . assumes that the shooting stops on June 30, 1967."[30] Once the war ended, prices would stabilize. Thus an anti-inflationary fiscal policy, such as a tax increase, would no longer be warranted. That said, if Vietnam were to continue, then it was agreed that the war would result in inflation. In April 1966, Fowler, Schultze, and Ackley all agreed that if the projected decline in defense expenditures in January 1967 did not take place a tax increase would be necessary to halt inflation,

> Given the January fiscal program, both tax rates and expenditures, we would expect intensifying price pressures for the rest of the year. . . . However, the January budget program projects a decline in defense expenditures in the first half of 1967. On that assumption we would expect only a moderate pace of advance in overall demand early next year. . . . However, the 1967 Budget program was planned on the assumption that Vietnam hostilities would be over by the end of the 1967 fiscal year. To deal with the possibility (or probability) that we will have to continue military operations in Vietnam after that date, we have considered the economic implications of raising FY1967 defense outlays $4 billion above the January estimates. This would make a major difference in prospects for the first half of 1967, implying a clearly inflationary economy in the absence of restraining fiscal measures.[31]

By the fall of 1966, before any decision had been made, prices stabilized and the fear of recession reemerged. As prices stabilized, the impetus to increase taxes to fund the war effort was delayed.[32] In October, Treasury Secretary Fowler wrote to President Johnson, boasting of American price stability while fighting a war: "Our record of price stability in the face of the impact of active hostilities and persistently enlarging defense needs is the envy of nations throughout the world."[33] By December 1966, it was again believed by the administration that the economy would slide into a recession.[34] Joe Califano advised President Johnson, "The economy is more likely to need a stimulant in the next several months than a sedative."[35] Thus the Vietnam buildup was once again almost welcomed to improve the economic outlook.[36]

## Public Support for the War

While the Johnson administration saw no need to resort to direct resource extraction to combat inflation, it also preferred an indirect resource extraction strategy. The administration preferred to avoid public interaction with the war. Once taxes were raised, the public would become more aware of the course of the war, including unpopular casualties. Thus Johnson deliberately chose to avoid public scrutiny by attempting to shield the costs of the war through a war finance policy that did not raise taxes. Secretary of State Dean Rusk explained this logic at a staff conference on October 5, 1967.

> The Administration made a deliberate decision not to create a war psychology in the United States. There have been no war bond campaigns, etc. The decision was made because it is too dangerous for this country really to get worked up. Maybe this was a mistake; maybe it would have been better to take steps to build up a sense of a nation at war. The course we have taken has meant expecting a great deal of our men in Vietnam, against the background of a home front going about business as usual.[37]

It has been suggested by scholars that the lesson Johnson took from the Korean War was a fear of casualties and public opinion versus a fear of inflation. Historian Paul Hammond argues the economic costs of the war were never a serious issue. Instead, "it was the human costs—the casualties suffered by American military personnel in Korea—that ultimately sapped American support for the war. . . . The pessimistic lesson was that the American public would not sustain its initial support of a foreign war.[38]

There is evidence for Hammond's claim. In a July 21, 1965, National Security Council meeting, Johnson's undersecretary of state, George Ball, directly compared public opinion in Korea and Vietnam. He argued that mounting casualties would produce increasing pressures on the president to escalate the war beyond prudent levels and cause a serious fall-off in public support: "In a long war, I said the President would lose the support of the country. I showed him a chart I had prepared showing the correlation between Korean casualties and public opinion."[39] Thus Johnson did not want to "loose the flood of debate on Vietnam for which a tax increase proposal would provide the tempting occasion."[40]

## Indirect Resource Extraction

At the onset of the war, the administration was optimistic that inflation would not appear. As Ackley wrote to Johnson in 1965 on the economic aspects of Vietnam, "Nobody can seriously expect that the kind of program you outlined is going to overheat the economy, strain industrial capacity, or generate a consumer buying boom."[41] With no fear of inflation, there was no need to raise taxes to fund the war effort, and both guns and butter were possible. Compounding this inflation optimism was a desire to avoid raising taxes to shield the public from the war effort. Thus the war was financed by general public debt.

## Phase II: January 1967–June 1968

In January 1967, President Johnson announced in his State of the Union that he would request a surcharge on corporate and individual income taxes to combat rising prices due to the Vietnam War effort.[42] Johnson did not make a formal request for a tax increase until August. Eighteen months later, in June 1968, the Revenue and Expenditure Act of 1968 was signed into law. The bill was delayed due to differing fears of inflation and public opinion vis-à-vis the war effort. While the fear of inflation was high within the Johnson administration, there was an internal disagreement about how quickly prices would rise and, therefore, the structure of tax increase and when it should be requested. In addition, Congress held a different view of America's economic health. Throughout 1967 and early 1968, the House Ways and Means Committee was unconvinced severe inflation was taking place. Furthermore, Chairman Wilbur Mills believed the cause of inflation was not demand driven but caused by collective bargaining and government spending. Thus a tax increase to finance the war would not stop inflation, only a cut in government expenditures would.

Three events in 1968 increased the fear of inflation in Congress enough to break the stalemate. First, the Tet Offensive in Vietnam demonstrated to the administration as well as to Congress that the war was far from over. Military expenditures were only going to expand, placing even more pressure on the budget and an already overheating economy. Second, inflation was rising to levels last seen during the Korean War. Third, an already weakened dollar was put to the test with an international speculative gold run. The only long-term fix to the dollar crisis was to control inflation. As a result of these events, Johnson was eventually able to get his fiscal policy passed.

### Phase II: Fear of Inflation and Direct Resource Extraction

As previously discussed, the administration budgeted the war to end by June 30, 1967. The war, however, only escalated. On January 24, 1967, Schultze wrote to President Johnson asking for an additional $12.3 billion in supplemental appropriations for FY1967 to support expanding military operations in Southeast Asia.[43] The unanticipated escalation placed further pressure on the budget and, therefore, rising prices.[44]

The realization that the war would continue prompted the administration to request a tax increase. On the morning of December 8, 1966, various advisors, including McNamara, Fowler, Ackley, Schultze, and Clifford, concluded a tax increase would be necessary to reduce the budget deficit: "The most generally discussed increase was a 5 percent surcharge on corporate and individual income taxes, which would raise roughly $4.5 to $5 billion annually."[45] Yet, the advisors were divided about when to raise taxes.[46] Six months later, on June 17, 1967, all agreed that the tax proposal should not be sent to Congress until after the recess. They recommended that they "begin intensive discussion among ourselves as soon as McNamara returned from Vietnam and have some feel for the cost of whatever decisions are made subsequent to his trip"[47]

By July, Johnson's advisors agreed on a tax program. They advised that Johnson should immediately ask Congress for a tax program larger than what he suggested in January. Instead of a 6 percent surcharge, they recommended that Johnson request a 10 percent surcharge on both individual and corporate taxes.[48] On August 14, 1967, Treasury Secretary Fowler described the president's tax program before the House Ways and Means Committee. He directly connected the tax increase to rising Vietnam costs and, consequently, rising inflation:

> That decision was reached by the President because of the hard and inescapable facts. These are that the special Vietnam costs are being incurred at a rate in excess of $22 billion per year; that without the temporary surcharge the budget deficit in the current fiscal year would increase to unacceptable levels; and that we are witnessing a return of long-term interest rates to levels near their peaks of late last summer . . . government borrowing will increase the pressure on the money market and contribute to high interest rates . . . the surcharge is a measure of insurance against the risk that without the temporary tax increases the levels of growth will give rise to unacceptable inflationary pressures.[49]

## Fearing Inflation, Just Not Enough

Throughout 1967, Johnson found himself in a similar situation to President Truman in 1951. While Johnson and his administration feared inflation, Congress did not. Within a month of Johnson's announcement of a tax increase, it was clear that support in Congress would be hard to get. In February, the Congressional Joint Economic Committee (JEC) concluded hearings on Johnson's economic report. The crux of the report was that there was no support for the tax proposal unless the economy started to overheat. Gardner Ackley reported the results of the hearings to Johnson: "The jury is still out on the key issues of taxes and wage policy. . . . Only a couple of the outside witnesses before the JEC and none of the Committee members actually supported the tax proposal. A fair number, however, withheld their judgment, admitting that the bullish economic developments might swing them in favor of tax action by May or June."[50]

Wavering prices throughout 1967 reinforced Congressional skepticism, making it harder for the Johnson administration to sell the surtax to Congress. By May 1967, the administration was at best able to convince Americans that a recession was no longer imminent. A memo from Ackley to Johnson illustrates the effect wavering prices had on the tax increase:

> Our economic statistics have wiggled around in recent months without establishing a clear pattern. . . . Last month's indications of a big rebound in consumer buying have now gone up in smoke. Autos have picked up significantly, but other consumer markets still look soggy according to the latest reports. . . . On the other hand, there has been bullish news in some areas. The outlook is now sufficiently bright to kill the talk of recession, to produce general agreement among the experts that the economy will be moving ahead rapidly by the end of the year. . . . Taking account of these favorable factors on the horizon, nearly all economic forecasters are reaching the objective technical verdict that we are building up steam for a new surge. Still, the surge has not started. There is no compelling hard evidence to convince the non-expert that it lays ahead. Thus, we could not make an airtight case today to the Congress that fiscal restraint will be needed.[51]

In July, the JEC completed its midyear hearings on the economy. The Johnson administration was hoping that Congress would be swayed by expert testimony that inflation was pending and a tax increase was necessary. Congress was unresponsive. Ackley provided a snarky description of the hearings, explaining that while "most of what the specialists presented was fully consistent with our forecasts," the "Committee wasn't sharp enough to see it." The hearings concluded with more delay. Ackley explained, "[Senator] Proxmire (we are told) plans to issue a statement soon saying we should wait on any tax increase decisions until economic indicators show unexpected strength, or the administration is ready to predict a sizable increase in defense spending over the Budget."[52]

By fall 1967, the administration thought it obtained what was needed to propel the tax increase forward: rising prices and the support of businesses and academics. Ackley expressed this hope, "The Consumer Price Index rose by 0.4 percent in July, larger than any monthly increase since last August. . . . The only comfort is that it is another timely argument for the tax increase."[53] In October, a group of academics drafted a statement in favor of Johnson's fiscal policy: "The economic case for a tax increase . . . is based on the fact that rapidly rising federal expenditures will be injected into an economy in which total expenditures are moving steadily upward and that the interplay of these increases threatens renewed inflation."[54] By September, the National Association of Business Economists (NABE) joined the academics, sending a statement of support to Ways and Means signed by 455 business leaders.[55] In October, Ackley reported that 90 percent of economists favored a tax hike and 75 percent expected that the surcharge would be enacted effective January 1.[56]

Yet the Johnson administration was still unable to convince Congress to increase taxes. While evidence was mounting for an anti-inflationary policy, what that policy would be was up for debate. Chairman Mills believed that the cause of inflation was not demand-pull but cost-push. The current rise in prices was not caused by high consumer demand but businesses passing along higher costs of negotiated wage settlements to consumers through higher prices. Mills believed that the remedy to cost-push inflation was not a tax increase but a decrease in government spending. Thus, while the Johnson administration was advocating for a tax increase, Mills was advocating for a decrease in government spending.[57] The difference in proposed policy created a stalemate between Mills and Congress and the Johnson administration.

## Phase II: Public Support for the War

In addition to the lack of fear about inflation in Congress, by 1967, public support for the war had plummeted. By mid-1966, support had dropped to levels more familiar to the later stages of the Korean War.[58] Aside from a couple of interludes in late 1966 and early 1967, the loss of support was never regained.[59] National Security Council member Chester Cooper, whose tasks included dealing with groups in opposition to the war, also placed the decrease in public support for the war in the years 1966–1967: "The war wasn't really popular in 1964, it just wasn't unpopular. By 1965 the marches and teach-in began . . . there was plenty of opposition to the war without the casualties. But the casualties were the kind of thing that was oppressive. . . . It was getting so that by 1966 and 1967 one could meet people whose sons or husbands had died or had been seriously wounded in Vietnam."[60]

Johnson was aware of declining public support. Every week Johnson received a memo that summarized weekly mail received. Throughout 1967 and 1968, the first line of that summary pertained to US policy in Vietnam.[61] A White House summary of all mail received in 1967 on the subject of US policy regarding Vietnam found that there were 10,644 classified as pro and 47,267 classified as con.[62] During the last week of March 1968, at the height of the surcharge debate, there were 550 letters classified as prowar and five times as many letters (2,958) classified as against the war.[63]

This decline in public support contributed to an overall war finance policy characterized by a low percentage of the war paid for by taxation. First, the public did not want to pay for a failing policy. Between March 1965 and July 1967, there were four surveys asking the public if they would be in favor of a tax increase to pay for the war in Vietnam.[64] As shown in figure 3.1, in October 1966, only 19 percent of people polled responded that they would favor an income tax increase to help pay for the war in Vietnam.[65]

Congress was aware of the public sentiment against the war and the relationship between the war and the tax increase. Consequently, members were reluctant to support the tax bill. On January 13, 1967, three days after Johnson delivered his State of the Union address announcing the surcharge, Fowler met with various Democrats in Congress to survey their support for the surcharge. Representative Frank Karsten (D-MO) responded that lack of public support would inhibit his ability to support a tax increase. Fowler summed up Karsten's response for Johnson, "No sympathy in Missouri for the Vietnam War. It is impossible to convince the people out there of either the need or the existence of the war. The party 'is in a helluva fix in Missouri unless Vietnam is settled.' He would much prefer a corporate tax increase only and thinks it would be rough sledding in any event for the tax bill."[66]

In August 1967, when Johnson officially requested the surcharge, he requested that his staff secretly survey Democratic members of Congress to find out the

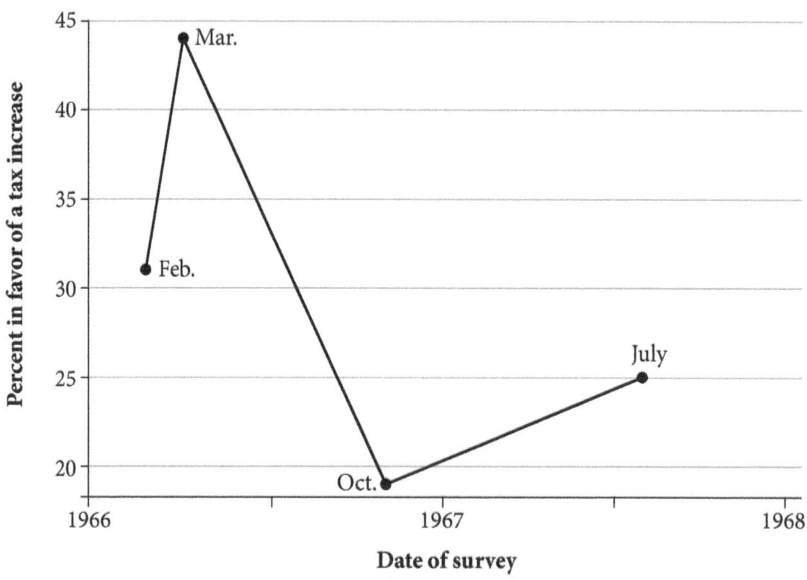


**FIGURE 3.1** Percentage of Americans in favor of a tax increase, 1966–1968

current state of opinion for the war and tax increase. In all, 169 interviews were conducted during August and September (137 representatives and 32 senators), and 104 were categorized as negative with respect to the war.[67] Typical of the responses of the survey were Senator John Pastore (D-RI) and Representative Julia Butler Hanson (D-WA), both influential and respected members who supported the administration on the war. Pastore commented that, "Our problem is Vietnam—boxes coming back, casualties going up—back home not a good word from anyone for us and this attitude is reflected in the Senate."[68] Congresswoman Hansen stated that the public "wants the war over quickly, not because it wants to win but because it wants out. People would rather pull out without victory if this would avoid new taxes. They think Vietnam is not worth the tax increase."[69]

## Phase II: Fear of Inflation Revisited

Congress reopened the tax surcharge debate in January 1968. The fear of inflation was still low among members of Congress and the standoff between Johnson and Mills over the extent of budget cuts remained. In March, the JEC released its 1968 Economic Report. On the issue of the tax increase, the majority report "decided against making a recommendation on a tax increase at this time." The report "acknowledged the current economic strength and inflationary pressures" but remained unconvinced that "a 'boom' will materialize or that a tax increase will head off price increases 'at least for the year ahead.'"[70] Three events in the spring of 1968 turned the fiscal policy tide.

First, throughout the spring, prices rose at historic rates. The increases from December 1967 to March 1968 were the largest the US economy had experienced in more than a decade. There was a 1.1 percent increase in the consumer price index, higher than any quarterly increase in ten years; an overall wholesale price rise of 1.3 percent, exceeding any quarterly increase since mid-1965; and a 1.1 percent rise in wholesale industrial commodities, which topped any quarter since late 1956.[71] New CEA chairman Arthur Okun reported to Johnson that "the 4% rate of price increase we are now experiencing is the most rapid in 17 years. This Nation has never been willing to tolerate that much inflation for very long."[72] In May 1968, the CEA forecast that the rate of inflation would be more costly than a tax increase: "An extra 2% rate of price increase costs the average American who is defenseless against inflation twice as much as the penny-on-a-dollar surcharge. For the poor who are exempted from the surcharge, the cost of inflation is even relatively greater: Inflation is indeed the cruelest tax and—unlike the surcharge—it is not temporary." The memo concluded with grim words from Okun, "The financial mess that would follow failure of the surcharge could jeopardize our 87-month record prosperity. It could bring on a recession and a slump.

Even a mild recession would cost $30 or $40 billion of production and 1½ million jobs."[73]

With rising prices, Congress acknowledged that demand-pull inflation was evident. In April, Okun wrote a letter to Mills urging him to accept the tax increase, citing new demand-pull inflation: "Particularly worrisome is the increasing evidence that, in the early months of this year, consumers have been spending more freely. This development is adding further to the demand-pull pressures that emerged in the second half of 1967 and exacerbated our cost-push inflationary problems."[74] Adding support to the administration's cause was a May report by the Bureau of Labor Statistics on price and wage developments during the first quarter. Okun described the report to Johnson: "It is unpleasant reading about growing inflationary tendencies on all fronts. Troublesome cost-push forces have been compounded by a surge of demand throughout the economy. The need for prompt fiscal restraint to cool off demand is the clear lesson conveyed by the hard facts."[75] When Mills decided to accept the surcharge in June, he acknowledged that the shift from cost-push to demand-pull inflation was the primary cause.[76]

Perhaps more important, the rise in prices was seen as a contributing factor to a global economic crisis.[77] In March 1968, there was a speculative run on gold that *Time* magazine called the "largest gold run in history."[78] This economic crisis raised the fear of inflation to high enough levels to break the stalemate. Johnson, in retrospect, agreed that the crisis provided an important impetus, but he emphasized its impact on his opposition: "The international crisis had done what we could not do: arouse the American public and many congressional leaders to the need for decisive action." Mills did indeed subsequently report that the "severe run on the dollar in the international market during the early months of 1968" and the "drastic outflow of gold" were "important to . . . [the Ways and Means Committee] in reaching a decision to agree to the surtax proposal."[79]

Third, adding to the fear of inflation was the escalation of the Vietnam War. On January 30, 1968, the Communist forces of Vietnam launched an offensive campaign against the GVN, the United States, and their allies. In response, Johnson sent eleven thousand additional marines and airborne troops. On March 31, 1968, he announced to the nation that responding to the Tet Offensive would cost Americans $2.5 billion for FY1968 and $2.6 billion for FY1969.[80] With this announcement he furthered his case for the need to combat inflation with a tax increase,

> These projected increases in expenditures for our national security will bring into sharper focus the Nation's need for immediate action: action to protect the prosperity of the American people and to protect the strength and the stability of our American dollar. On many occasions

> I have pointed out that, without a tax bill or decreased expenditures, next year's deficit would again be around $20 billion. I have emphasized the need to set strict priorities in our spending. I have stressed that failure to act and to act promptly and decisively would raise very strong doubts throughout the world about America's willingness to keep its financial house in order. Yet Congress has not acted. And tonight we face the sharpest financial threat in the postwar era—a threat to the dollar's role as the keystone of international trade and finance in the world.[81]

Rising prices driven by consumer demand, a global financial crisis tied to a weak dollar, and the realization that the war was far from over created such a high fear of inflation that it broke the deadlock. Johnson agreed to further reductions in spending and Mills agreed to the surcharge.

## The Revenue and Expenditure Control Act of 1968

On June 28, 1968, Johnson signed H.R. 15414, the surcharge, into law. In addition to a 10 percent surcharge on individual and corporate taxes, the bill sped up corporate tax payments and raised excise taxes on automobiles and telephones. The bill also mandated that federal expenditures be reduced by $6 billion in FY1969, exempting cost related to the Vietnam War, interest on the debt, veterans services, and social security. Moreover, the legislation required that requests for future spending increases be reduced by $10 billion. The bill promised to increase federal revenues by $15.5 billion in 1969, with about $11.6 billion coming from the surcharge.[82]

## Alternative Means to Combat Inflation—Monetary Policy

Why did Johnson decide to pursue a tax increase when he could have chosen to let the Federal Reserve fight inflation through monetary policy? As with the Truman administration, the Johnson administration viewed fiscal policy as the most effective means to control inflation. It was the preference of both the Johnson administration and the Federal Reserve to increase taxes to pay for the war. Thus by 1967 the Fed and the Johnson administration were working together in order to force Congress to pass the surcharge. However, when inflation became severe and passage of the surcharge seemed unlikely, the Fed acted autonomously.

The Johnson administration, as well as various members of Congress, was adverse to the high interest rates that accompanied a tight monetary policy. Johnson believed high interest rates placed additional pressure on homebuilding, threatened the solvency of savings and loans associations, and penalized small businessmen, farmers, and middle-class homebuyers.[83] Thus, in making the case for a tax increase, Ackley told Johnson that if he did not raise taxes the Fed would tighten money, placing the administration's economic values at risk,

> If we do not restrain demand by a tax increase, the Fed will inevitably be forced to tighten money a great deal more: putting further pressure on homebuilding; threatening the solvency of many savings and loans associations; penalizing small businessmen, farmers, and moderate-income homebuyers. A tax increase would allow the Fed to keep monetary policy about where it is, or even loosen up a little.[84]

In an October report to President Johnson, Treasury Secretary Fowler also pointed out the connection between increased interest rates and its effect on residential housing: "This situation . . . reflects the adaptation of monetary and fiscal policies which have dampened inflationary forces and minimized the inevitable adjustments that characterize a free market economy operation under heavy and shifting power. One of these adjustments—in residential construction—has been too drastic."[85]

Various congressmen were also adverse to high interest rates. Congressman Al Ullman (D-OR) of the House Ways and Means Committee echoed the concerns Ackley identified above. On July 7, 1966, he wrote to President Johnson, "High interest rates will not do the job. They are inflationary in themselves. They have not succeeded in slowing investment in plant capacity, nor—with the single exception of housing—have they slowed the rising level of personal debt. They have instead contributed significantly to higher costs that are certain to be reflected in the consumer price index."[86] Chairman Wilbur Mills also condemned tight money. Mills told Ackley that he was going to meet with members of the Fed in an attempt to prevent them from further increasing interest rates.[87]

The Fed preferred a rise in taxes rather than a hike in interest rates to combat inflation. The primary reason the Fed wanted a tax increase was to control rising prices that were contributing to a balance of payments problem. Federal Reserve associate economist Robert Solomon made the case before the September 1967, Federal Open Market Committee Meeting (FOMC).

> Our price level is now on an upward tilt and that will certainly not help our competitive position. One not very startling conclusion from all this is that the domestic case for the tax increase is strongly reinforced by balance of payments considerations. . . . On the basis of this review, the road to balance of payments improvement appears to have three elements: recovery in Europe; avoidance of inflation here; and a tightening of the Commerce Department program on direct investment.[88]

The Fed's urgency for a tax increase was compounded with the 1967 Sterling Crisis. In November, when rumors circulated that the British pound would be devalued, sterling came under heavy pressure, and on November 18 British prime minister Harold Wilson announced that the pound would indeed be devalued.[89] The Fed feared that if interest rates were raised further, there would be a rush to purchase more dollars, placing further pressure on the pound.[90] However, if the surcharge was passed, prices would stabilize without having to resort to higher interest rates.

In addition to the balance of payments problem, the Fed preferred to raise taxes to avoid high interest rates that were negatively affecting the banking sector.[91] In the September 1967 FOMC Committee Meeting, Federal Reserve board member William Sherrill expressed his hope that the tax would be passed as high interest rates would result in serious disintermediation, or withdrawal of funds from banks so these could be invested in federal bonds. He stated, that "even a small increase in short-term interest rates at present could result in a serious problem of disintermediation, and in his judgment the potential gains from firming somewhat were not sufficient to warrant running that risk."[92]

Given the Johnson administration's and the Fed's preferences for low interest rates, they began to work together to coordinate economic policy. Johnson's advisors believed that if they coordinated economic policy with the Fed, it would be easier to get a tax bill through Congress. Specifically, they hoped to reassure Congress that once the surcharge was passed, the Fed would simultaneously stimulate the economy. In August, Ackley advocated to get the Fed on record as promising to ease monetary policy if Johnson increased taxes.[93] Thus in late 1966 the Troika—the CEA, Treasury, and BoB—was expanded to include the Fed and became the Quadriad. In addition, there were regular lunches between the CEA and the Fed as well as staff members from both agencies attending meetings.[94] The result of this coordination was the "policy mix model" in which Johnson would raise taxes and the Fed would ease monetary policy.[95]

In the fall of 1967, with prices rising at an alarming rate, the Fed purposely held down rates in order to persuade Congress that a tax increase was urgent.[96] The administration and members of the Fed believed that if the Fed tightened monetary policy then Congress would see no need for a tax increase. Almost every board member agreed that raising rates would interfere with passage of the surcharge. Chairman Martin summed up the tone of the meeting,

> With fiscal policy strongly stimulative pending action on the President's tax program, the simple logic of the economic situation implied the desirability of changing monetary policy, as it probably had as much as two months ago. But the overriding need at this point was to get

> some restraint from fiscal policy through a tax increase, and in his judgment that would be less likely if Congress came to believe that adequate restraint was being exercised by monetary policy.[97]

Thus, while monetary policy should have been tightened, the administration and the Fed preferred to wait in hopes of getting the surtax through Congress.

On October 3, 1967, Congress shelved the surcharge, and in December Congress adjourned. The Fed interpreted these actions as a sign that the surcharge was not going to get passed. More important, even if it did pass in early 1968, it would be too late. Chairman Martin compared the current inflation to a horse running loose and monetary policy, while it could not return the horse to the barn, could at best keep it from running too fast.[98] Vice Chairman Alfred Hayes had the same concerns. He believed that the prospects for a tax increase in early 1968 were at best dubious and further inflationary pressure was imminent. Thus monetary policy had to be tightened in order to protect both the US economy and the long-term stability of the dollar.[99]

Given a worsening economy in early 1968, the Fed engaged a tight monetary policy without much debate.[100] The Tet Offensive in January meant increasing defense expenditures that would only add further pressure to already increasing prices.[101] With no passage of the tax bill in sight, the Fed continued to believe that it had to fight inflation alone. Once the surtax was passed in June, the board eased monetary policy, lowering the discount rate in August 1968.

Comparing the financing of the Korean and Vietnam wars demonstrates the importance of leadership preferences and the effect of public opinion in facilitating opportunities and constraining leadership behavior. Both Truman and Johnson preferred to avoid economic ruin. Neither leader wanted the US economy or its citizens to be subject to high inflation. Truman, however, feared inflation immediately. Mindful of inflation after World War II, he wanted to avoid the mistakes he believed were made by his predecessor. He believed that Roosevelt did not raise taxes high enough and borrowed too much, thus, creating inflation. In order to protect the US economy, Truman not only raised taxes immediately but also announced he would pay for the entire war with taxes. What would have been a politically costly endeavor was facilitated by public support for the war and, therefore, Truman's policy. Thus, when Truman submitted his tax proposal to Congress, it was approved immediately.

President Johnson, on the other hand, was not afraid of high inflation, believing that the economic conditions that created Korean War inflation were not present during the Vietnam War in the mid- to late 1960s. When inflation did arise a year and a half into the war, Johnson attempted to raise taxes to curb it. Whereas Truman was aided by public opinion, Johnson was constrained. By 1967, support for the war had ebbed. Consequently, when Johnson asked Congress for a tax increase he was unable to get it. A comment made by Johnson's advisor McGeorge Bundy to the president in March 1968 impeccably summed up the difficulty of getting a war surtax passed in Congress, "I now understand, as I did not when I got here, that the really tough problem you have is the interlock between the bad turn in the war, the critical need for a tax increase, and the crisis of public confidence at home. If I understand the immediate needs correctly, the most important of all may be the tax increase, simply because without it both the dollar and the economy could come apart—and with them everything else."[102]

# 4

# BRITAIN AND CURRENCY RESERVES DURING WORLD WAR II AND THE CRIMEAN WAR

The British government's domestic financing of World War II was cost effective. The state raised taxes to keep inflation down, borrowed cheaply at a set rate of 3 percent, and borrowed progressively with a bond campaign that reached the entire population.[1] Nonetheless, the state had to incorporate external extraction into its war finance strategy. The British engaged in a loan from the United States, Lend-Lease, in which it was subject to costly demands from the US government.[2] In contrast, during the Crimean War, the British were able to finance the entire war domestically, via a combination of taxation and domestic debt. Why did Britain resort to costly external war finance during World War II and not in the Crimean War?[3]

I argue that this variation is explained by the source of war inputs and a state's ability to cope with low currency reserves. When a state needs to procure inputs for the war effort from outside its borders and does not have the currency to pay for those goods, it will be forced to borrow from abroad to meet its war finance needs. In contrast, external extraction is not necessary if the state does not need to purchase goods from abroad or it has the currency to pay for them.

During World War II, to match German war production, the British had to supplement their own military supplies with those purchased from the United States. To procure these goods, the British needed dollars. Yet dollars, like material inputs for the war, were in short supply. The British had an adverse trade balance with the United States and there was general decline in dollar-earning exports from the Sterling Area. Despite efforts to decrease nonessential war imports and promote dollar exports, the British ran out of currency. Consequently, to continue the war, the British had to engage in a costly loan from the United States.

During the Crimean War, the British were able to produce a majority of goods for the war within its territory. There were two exceptions, meat and fodder purchased in Turkey and mercenaries hired from Italy, Switzerland, and Germany. Given Britain's trade balance with these various countries, London as the world's financial center, and the status of the pound, the British were billed in sterling and not the countries' respective currencies. Consequently, there was no need for the British to incorporate external war finance into its war finance strategy.

## British External War Finance during World War II

British external war finance can be understood in four phases. Phase I, September 1939 to May 1940, coincided with the Phony War in which there were no major military operations. Before the war escalated, the British knew they were going to need dollars to purchase supplies from the United States. The United States agreed to sell goods to Britain, but only under the strict conditions of "Cash-and-Carry." Under this agreement, Britain had to pay for all purchases outright with dollars and was responsible for transporting the goods back to Britain. The British agreed, believing that they could supply the dollars themselves through an elaborate mechanism of import and export controls.

Phase II of British external war finance lasted from June to December 1940, from the evacuation of British forces at Dunkirk to the American announcement of the plan to lease war supplies to the British. Losses of supply at Dunkirk required the British to compensate with even larger purchases of goods from the United States. Larger purchases meant more dollars. The British warned the United States that it was going to be dollar bankrupt by Christmas 1940. Unfortunately, American policymakers' hands were tied by the Johnson Act and isolationist public opinion. In order to compensate for these limitations, in December 1940, President Roosevelt announced the United States was going to "give" supplies to the British and the method of repayment to be sorted out once the war ended.

Phase III began after the press conference announcing the Lend-Lease Act through 1942. To pass this "gift" through Congress, the British had to prove to a skeptic American public that they were really out of dollars. In addition Lend-Lease only applied to orders placed after implementation, compounding the dollar problem as the British did not have enough liquid assets to complete existing orders let alone place new badly needed ones. Thus the British had to strip itself of nonliquid assets, sell its US investments, borrow gold from the Belgium government in exile, and ship gold from South Africa.

Phase IV began in January 1943 and lasted to the end of the war. By 1943, British holdings of dollars were increasing. When Lend-Lease was negotiated, the British and United States agreed that a safe minimum of dollar reserves was $600 million; by 1943, the British held $1 billion. Once the British reached $1 billion, American policymakers felt that the Lend-Lease program was no longer necessary. The British felt differently. They now had to convince the United States to continue the program. The British argued that they still faced a balance of payments problem. Not only was the dollar increase temporary due to American soldiers in Britain, but also the British were responsible for the empire. Thus they had dollar commitments to countries other than the United States.

To understand the political and economic events that shaped British external war finance, I focus on members of the Roosevelt and Churchill administrations tasked with negotiating the loan. These men reported the situation in Britain as they saw it, negotiated with their counterparts across the Atlantic, and reported back to their superiors, ultimately President Roosevelt and Prime Minister Churchill. I use their correspondence, cataloged by *Foreign Relations of the United States*, to understand how British war finance strategy evolved throughout the war.

Key figures in the Roosevelt administration include Secretary of State Cordell Hull, Assistant Secretary of State Dean Acheson, and Chief of the Division of European Affairs Jay Pierrepont Moffat. American ambassador to Britain Joseph Kennedy consistently reported about the state of British financial affairs in the early years of the war and gave his opinion to the mood in London. Secretary of the Treasury Henry Morgenthau Jr. had multiple conversations with President Roosevelt regarding the feasibility of passing the Lend-Lease bill through Congress. Edward Stettinius Jr. played a large role in the later years of the war as both administrator of the Lend-Lease program and undersecretary of state. As administrator of Lend-Lease, Stettinius Jr. made multiple trips to Britain to observe the effects of the war and evaluate the program's need.

Each of these men had counterparts in the Churchill administration. British ambassador to the United States, Philip Kerr, Marques of Lothian, constantly conversed with Secretary of State Hull. British chancellor of the exchequer Sir Kingsley Wood and the British Treasury made pleas to their American counterparts. John Maynard Keynes, advisor to the Treasury and lead negotiator during the Bretton Woods conference, greatly influenced the British delegation. In addition, to understand the effect of the war on British production I look to volumes commissioned by Her Majesty's Stationary Office (HMSO), the official printer and publisher of all acts of parliament since 1889, and reports of the

Interdepartmental Committee to President Roosevelt on Policy Decisions Relating to Dollar Position of Lend-Lease Countries.

## Phase I: September 1939–May 1940

Britain not only had to supply itself with goods to fight the war but also to support the war effort of the empire, including India, Egypt, Iraq, Jordan, and Syria. In the first fifteen months of the war, the United Kingdom supplied 90.7 percent of the empire's munitions for the first year of the war, 81.8 percent the second, and a total of 69.5 percent of munitions throughout the course of the war.[4] While this figure is impressive, taken in a comparative prospective, British war production was no match for Germany. Germany outproduced Britain in almost every aspect of war supply until 1941.[5] In order to supplement British production to support the war effort, the British had to purchase goods from the United States.

To pay for these goods the British needed dollars, a currency already in short supply.[6] In 1939, Britain's export industries were languishing and a net deficit on the international balance of payments had announced that the nation, even in advance of war, was already beginning the process of overseas disinvestment.[7] According to a State Department memo in 1938, UK exports to the United States were as low as they had been four years earlier. Moreover, the British chancellor of the exchequer forecast that the Sterling Area would have a negative balance of payments of £117 million sterling, or $470 million, with the United States from September 1939 to August 1940.[8]

Exacerbating the balance of payment problem was short-term balances, dollar commitments, and the Neutrality Act of 1934. The British ambassador to the United States reported that short-term obligations in 1939 were not available to purchase supplies in the United States. Aside from being low in amount, they were needed to maintain banking relationships.[9] In addition, the Neutrality Act, which forbade private loans to belligerents, intensified British dollar commitments. The ambassador noted, "The passage of the Neutrality Act has caused the withdrawal by the United States of an unknown but substantial amount of short-term credit formerly available to the United Kingdom . . . the London exchange market was over-sold on United States dollars when the war broke out to the extent of $107 million, and this had to be covered shortly after by the sale of gold."[10]

The British government, aware of its dollar woes and knowing dollars were crucial to the war's outcome, was worried. Less than a month into the war, in October 1939, the British explained to the Americans that they had to protect their dollar holdings. The American ambassador to Britain, Joseph Kennedy, described the British fervor to US secretary of state Cordell Hull: "I have just spent an hour with [British chancellor of the exchequer Sir John] Simon and [British Board of Trade president Oliver] Stanly and their two topside men. . . . Every time you mention getting any money out of the country, they talk about the length of the war and that they must protect themselves by not sending American dollars."[11]

With the inability to borrow dollars from the United States, the British had to procure the currency themselves. They began an internal campaign to promote the flow of dollars into the country and keep any they had from flowing out. On September 1, 1939, the House of Commons passed the Import and Exports Customs Powers (Defense) Act, which was a series of import controls and export promotion.[12] According to the British Board of Trade the object of the order was to limit "the imports of luxuries and of goods of which there are sufficient home supplies in order to conserve exchange for the additional purchases of other products required in war time."[13] Ambassador Kennedy explained the act to Secretary of State Hull,

> The British government is desirous of maintaining such exports as are possible in order to acquire foreign exchange but certain exports have been put under license in order to (1) conserve essential products needed for prosecuting the war and (2) preventing certain essential supplies reaching the enemy. Stanly told me that the import list will of necessity be drastic in order to conserve available resources of foreign exchange.[14]

In addition to import reduction, the British sought to promote exports to the United States. The government encouraged exports of jute, rubber, tin, whisky, and furs because they were recognized as dollar earners.[15] Moreover, the government forced exporters to bill clients at the official sterling-dollar exchange rate, which was higher than the free rate that was currently being used. Finally, the British government also enforced "dollar invoices," versus the often-used sterling invoices. The goal was to bring dollars from the bulk of certain exports with as little administrative interference as possible.[16]

Fear of dwindling dollar reserves also affected how the British purchased war inputs from the United States. The British government believed itself to be too sparsely supplied with dollars to justify any considerable expenditure on American finished munitions and was determined to limit its purchases as stringently as possible to indispensable materials and tools for use by British workers in British factories.[17] The case of the British Air Ministry provides an example. While Britain stressed unmanufactured goods, the chief exception was aircraft production. The Air Ministry intended to purchase everything the Americans could produce, even investing in US production capacity, spending £100 million to £150 million in the first year.[18] The shortage of dollars, however, forced the Air Ministry to drastically revise its program: £2 million for machine tools and £3 million for materials. Its second priority was airframes and engines, a value of £15 million–£17 million.[19]

Even before the supply disaster at Dunkirk the British system of import and export control was proving itself to be inadequate. First, as the British required more expensive furnished munitions, the amount of imports needed from the United States was underestimated. In July 1939, it was projected that the minimum expenditure for the army from the United States during the first year of the war was going to be £8.1 million for first-priority requirements, £10–15 million if second-priority requirements were included, and if there were no financial restrictions, £50 million. Once raw materials were included, total imports for the war from the United States were expected to be about £75 million.[20] By 1940 these figures were drastically revised upward. In January 1940 the figure for total imports was revised to £197 million.[21] A month later, this amount was again upwardly revised as the British Ministry of Defense decided to increase purchases of airplanes from the United States.[22]

Second, in order to fight the war Britain had to focus all of its manufacturing on the war effort, forcing it to abolish its export drive. In July 1940, the British Embassy sent the State Department a memo explaining their need to decrease exports,

> The natural tendency of all democracies engaged in rearmament is to believe that it is possible to expand the production of guns and to enjoy a full supply of butter at the same time. Her Majesty's Government has found by bitter experience that this is not true and that full production cannot be secured solely by expansion and development of munitions and auxiliary industries, other industries being left unaffected. The establishment of requisite priority for labor, materials, machines tools, etc., necessarily involves the early curtailment of production for domestic civil consumption.[23]

As a result of increased purchases for the war and dwindling exports, shown in table 4.1, British holdings of gold and dollar reserves fell rapidly. British ambassador Lothian wrote to Secretary of State Hull that the effect of increased plane orders "brings the exhaustion of our resources measurably nearer, and shows how the scale of war requirements is capable of rising."[24] On March 1, the British reported that at the current rate of purchases, within two years the UK would have given the United States all of its dollar assets.[25] On March 15, 1940, the eve of the Battle of Dunkirk, British prime minister Churchill told President Roosevelt that "we shall go on paying dollars for as long as we can, but I should like

**TABLE 4.1** Monthly drain on dollars and gold reserves held by the British, January to June 1940 (millions of dollars)

| | 1939 | 1940 | | | | | |
|---|---|---|---|---|---|---|---|
| | 31 DECEMBER | 31 JANUARY | 29 FEBRUARY | 31 MARCH | 30 APRIL | 30 MAY | 29 JUNE |
| UK holdings of gold and dollars | 2,100 | 2,002 | 1,954 | 1,883 | 1,772 | 1,694 | 1,572 |
| Change on the month | | –98 | –48 | –71 | –111 | –78 | –122 |
| Add sale of securities | | –16 | –26 | –30 | –30 | –18 | –7 |
| Total drain in the month | | –114 | –74 | –101 | –141 | –96 | –129 |

*Source:* Adapted from H.D. Hall, *North American Supply* (London, Her Majesty's Stationery Office, 1955), 250, table 7.

to feel reasonably sure that when we can pay no more you will give us the stuff all the same."[26]

## Phase II: June 1940–December 1940

On May 10, 1940, the Churchill government took power in Britain. That same day the Phony War ended as the Germans launched their offensive in the west, invading France and the Low Countries. On May 20, the British government commenced Operation Dynamo, evacuating the British Expeditionary Forces (BEF) from Dunkirk. On May 27, the Belgian army capitulated and three days later the French First Army surrendered. By June 4, the last ship drew away from Dunkirk and 337,000 Allied soldiers had been saved from capture.[27]

The Battle of France and the evacuation at Dunkirk significantly affected British war finance. At Dunkirk the British left recently produced equipment that had been delivered and incorporated in the field. Churchill wrote,

> We had lost the whole equipment of the Army to which all the first fruits of our factories had hitherto been given: 7,000 tons of ammunition, 90,000 rifles, 2,300 guns, 120,000 vehicles, 8,000 Bren guns, 400 anti-tank rifles . . .We had very little field artillery, even for the Regular Army. Nearly all the new 25-pounders had been lost in France. There remained about five hundred 18-pounders, 4.5 inch and 6-inch howitzers. There were only 103 cruiser, 132 infantry, and 252 light tanks. Fifty of the infantry tanks were at home in a battalion of the Royal Tank

> Regiment, and the remainders were in training schools. Never has a great nation been so naked before her foes.[28]

The loss of supply at Dunkirk did not go unnoticed by the Americans. On June 12, 1940, Ambassador Kennedy wrote to Secretary of State Hull describing the effect of supply on the British ability to fight.

> The condition of Britain's preparedness equals [*sic*] her ability to fight the kind of war Hitler wages still appears to be appallingly weak. I am of the opinion that outside of some air defense the real defense of England will be with courage and not with arms. . . . The point of all this is the fact that the preparedness for carrying on a war here is pitiful, this in spite of the fact that production and war effort are now for the first time going ahead in excellent fashion.[29]

Churchill had every reason to be worried; except for tanks, the Germans were outpacing British production of all principal army weapons and the British war industry was still in its formative years.[30] In addition to having to compete with German production, the British war effort was expanding beyond continental Europe. The British needed arms to defend the British Isles against direct attack by Germany and the Suez Canal against direct attack by Italy. In the light of Japanese infiltration into French Indo-China, Great Britain, Australia, and New Zealand were also in need of arms for the defense of Singapore and the Southwest Pacific.[31] Moreover, the Dunkirk evacuation changed Britain's war strategy. Before Dunkirk, the British were satisfied behind the Maginot Line—the main French fortifications—in the belief that rearmament and economic warfare were continually sapping Germany's ability to fight.[32] Now British survival depended on the efforts of the next weeks and days.

In order to compensate for the loss of supply and the widening of the war, Britain increased purchases from the United States.[33] Five days after the last British ship left the continent, the British and French spent $43 million on American arms surplus.[34] On July 5, 1940, the British government wrote to the Americans asking for destroyers, powerboats, airplanes, guns, rifles, and ammunition.[35] By November 1, 1940, British orders to the United States totaled $3.2 billion, and the British still owed $1.98 billion to complete them. Yet this increase in material was not enough. On December 20, 1940, British Prime Minister Churchill wrote to President Roosevelt requesting an immediate order of two thousand more aircraft a month.[36]

British takeover of French contracts further increased American orders. The French had thousands of contracts for planes, machine tools, raw materials, trucks, powder, explosives, and guns. Many of the contracts covered supplies the British needed to fight the war. Others were for special French equipment, unhelpful for the British war effort. With no time to sort through the contracts, the British took responsibility for all of them. Outstanding French commitments to the United States totaled over $500 million.[37]

These purchases furthered the drain on British dollar reserves. It was clear that British dollar requirements for the next year far exceeded what the British held. The chancellor of the exchequer warned the British government on August 22 that new expenditures looming in the United States would run the deficit up to $3.2 billion by June 1941—an amount far beyond the resources of the Treasury. The chancellor then reported that the "mere continuance of such losses . . . would run us out of gold by the end of December."[38]

The British were no longer able to finance the war on their own. They needed to turn to external war finance. On July 5, in the same memo asking the Americans for more supplies after Dunkirk, the British warned American policymakers that their ability to continue paying for goods was coming to an end.

> So long as gold and other foreign assets at their disposal permit, Her Majesty's Government will of course continue to pay cash for essential armaments, raw materials and food stuffs. They feel however that they should in all frankness inform the United States Government that it will be utterly impossible for them to continue to do this for any indefinite period in view of the scale on which they will need to obtain such resources from the United States. Their immediate anxiety arises from the necessity of entering into long term contracts.[39]

They hoped, however, when they ran out, the US government would continue to deliver the goods anyway. Unfortunately for the British, American policymakers had to wait until after the November presidential election to aid the British. When the British sent Sir Frederick Phillips to the United States after Dunkirk to negotiate future purchases, he received "no commitments or promises of any kind of credits, nor would this be possible before the election."[40]

That aid ultimately came in the form of the Lend-Lease Act. The origins of Lend-Lease lie in the US Treasury Department.[41] According to the administrator of the Lend-Lease program Edward Stettinius Jr., "Treasury lawyers found an old statute of 1892, the Secretary of War 'when in his discretion it will be for the public good,' could lease Army property 'not required for public use,' for a period of not longer than five years."[42] President Roosevelt embraced the concept and attempted to sell it to the American public in his December 17, 1940, press conference. He stated that a simple person would assume the only way to aid the British would repeal the Neutrality and Johnson Acts. However, there was another way to aid an ally and that was a gift.

> It is possible . . . for the United States to take over British orders, and, because they are essentially the same kind of munitions that we use ourselves, turn them into American orders. We have enough money to do it. And thereupon, as to such portion of them as the military events of the future determine to be right and proper for us to allow to go to the other side, either lease or sell the materials, subject to mortgage, to the people on the other side. . . . Now, what I am trying to do is to eliminate the dollar sign. That is something brand new in the thoughts of practically everybody in this room, I think—get rid of the silly, foolish old dollar sign.[43]

## Phase III: January 1941–December 1942

On January 10, 1941, H.R. 1776 was introduced on the floor of the House of Representatives "to promote the defense of the United States and for other purposes." The act gave President Roosevelt wide-ranging discretion. He could extend aid to any country he saw fit, "to manufacture in arsenals, factories, and shipyards under their jurisdiction, or otherwise procure, to the extent to which funds are made available therefore, or contracts are authorized from time to time by the Congress, or both, any defense article for the government of any country whose defense the President deems vital to the United States." Moreover, payment in return for this "gift" was also subject to the president. The only two limitations was the limit of goods that could be dispensed, $1.3 billion, and the time frame, set to expire on June 30, 1943.[44]

The introduction of the Lend-Lease Act to Congress only semirelieved British war finance anxieties. The Roosevelt administration now had to get the bill through Congress. American response to Lend-Lease and the British was mixed. While many Americans wanted the British to defeat the Germans, they were reluctant to aid them beyond selling supplies for cash. When Lend-Lease was proposed in December 1940, only 36 percent of Americans were in favor of the British receiving credit form the United States to purchase war materials.[45]

There were a number of reasons for American skepticism, ranging from British inability to pay back a loan to strong isolationist beliefs.[46] While these reasons were important for the overall passage of the Lend-Lease Act, only one had real implications for the British government. Americans were leery of the British proclaimed financial position. One of the most persistent complaints heard at the congressional hearings on the Lend-Lease Bill was that the legislation was unnecessary because Britain was nowhere near being as financially strapped as the state made out to be.[47] They did not believe the British were actually out of dollars.[48]

American policymakers believed the British needed to prove how broke they were to sway public opinion. In response, Treasury Secretary Henry Morgenthau began a campaign to ensure and demonstrate the British were dollar bankrupt. He exerted pressure on London to liquidate British-owned direct investments located in America, ship South African gold to the United States, and force French gold held in Canada turned over the United States.[49] Moreover, he suggested that the British should provide a further 2 billion in cash before arms began to be supplied under Lend-Lease. Finally, he asked for statements of British financial reserves and commitments.

Morgenthau's requests were resented in Britain. Prime Minister Churchill once again wrote President Roosevelt, not only reminding the president of Britain's financial position but also suggesting that forcing British to sell its assets was morally wrong.

> The more rapid and abundant the flow of munitions and ships which you are able to send us, the sooner will our dollar credits be exhausted. They are already very heavily drawn upon by payments we have made to date. Indeed as you know orders already placed or under negotiations, including expenditures settled or pending for creating munitions factories in the United States, many times exceed the total exchange resources remaining at the disposal of Great Britain. The moment approaches when we shall no longer be able to pay cash for shipping and other supplies. While we will do our upmost and shrink from no proper sacrifice to make payments across the exchange, I believe that you will agree that it would be wrong in principle and mutually disadvantageous in effect if, at the height of this struggle, Great Britain were to be divested of all saleable assets so that after victory was won with our blood, civilization saved and time gained for the United States to be fully armed against all eventualities, we should stand stripped to the bone.[50]

Moreover, while the British did have nonliquid gold and dollar assets, they preferred not to liquidate them. They wanted to keep the South African gold to maintain confidence in sterling and for other needs outside of purchases in the United States. In addition, some gold was needed to sustain the Greeks and Turks, who required some dollars for essential war supplies. Furthermore, Belgian and French gold was at best a slow and uncertain option.[51] Finally, the British believed that it was a threat to their interest to show the world, including Germany, just how broke they were.

In desperate need of dollars, the British hands were tied. Arthur Purvis, director general of the British Purchasing Commission, wrote to President Roosevelt,

> (a) Between 23rd December and the end of February the British Purchasing Commission would have to pay out $400 million on existing, and essential, continuation orders; (b) It needed to spend $250 on new orders; (c) the remaining cash reserves on the 28th December were $385 million. (Of this only some $295 was available; the rest was locked up in various ways); (d) Newly accruing resources from the sale of securities in the period could not amount to $100 million; (e) These reserves were the last balance of the Exchange Control and had to cover much else besides the purchase of arms in the USA.[52]

Thus the British began to liquidate their assets. In January 1941 the United States diverted a ship, the USS Louisville, to Simonstown, South Africa where it took on £42 million of gold, arriving safely in New York on January 26.[53] In addition, the British arranged the sale of American Viscose Corporation. A deal was negotiated, a minimum price was paid by a New York banking syndicate and the Treasury received 90 percent of any price paid by investors when public marketing took place.[54] Finally, the British received $300 million in gold from the exiled Belgian government.[55]

The dollars procured were not enough to meet present contracts. On January 21, Purvis sent Morgenthau a list of orders that were deemed imperative to be placed in this interim period. The value of the order (cost of product and capital assistance) was $1.25 billion, $884 million for US-type equipment and $375 million for British-type.[56] In order to meet this cost, the Reconstruction Finance Corporation would loan the money to the British and finance plant production. A $425 million loan was extended against collateral in the form of British securities in the United States, valued at some $500 million.[57]

The ratification of Lend-Lease could not come fast enough. On March 11, 1941, the House of Representatives accepted the bill by a vote of 317 to 71. President Roosevelt signed the act into law that afternoon. Within three hours after signing the bill, the president issued a directive putting the Lend-Lease program in motion. The directive declared the defense of Great Britain vital to the defense of the United States.[58] From mid-March 1941, the US government paid for new contracts for munitions and defense. However, the UK had to continue to pay cash for existing pre–Lend Lease orders until those contracts ran out. The British government still had to preserve all the dollars it could find.[59]

## Phase IV: January 1943–August 1945

The final phase of British external war finance began on January 1, 1943. That month a report by the Interdepartmental Committee to President Roosevelt on

Policy Decisions Relating to Dollar Position of Lend-Lease Countries found that British dollar reserves were nearing $1 billion.[60] When Lend-Lease was signed, it was agreed that the British dollar holdings be above a desired minimum of $600 million but below $1 billion.[61] Yet, throughout 1943, gold and dollar holdings of the British government continued to rise. In January 1944, Hull reported to Roosevelt that the "British Government's liquid dollar exchange assets have continued to rise and are now over $1.7 billion, or $1,350 million more than at the time the Lend-Lease Bill was presented in Congress."[62]

With such high reserves, US policymakers began to question the continuation of aid. The British once again had to defend their gold and dollar reserve levels. First, they argued that the rise in dollar reserves was temporary, due to an increase in spending by American troops abroad.[63] Moreover, because the British agreed to give raw materials to the United States under the policy of Reverse Lend-Lease, they were no longer exporting these materials for sale. Thus they were not receiving dollars for them, further lowering their currency reserves. The chancellor of the exchequer explained to newly appointed Undersecretary of State Edward Stettinius Jr., that "as a result of the recent reductions in Lend-Lease and the increases in Reverse Lend-Lease, however, it is estimated that the net increase in British gold and dollar balances will only be $300,000,000."[64]

Second, they argued that they were in an equally or more perilous dollar position than they had been in 1941. Between 1939 and 1942, the British financial problems were caused by a shortage of dollars for the purchase of imports from the United States. Now, the current financial position was due to greater dollar and gold liabilities of the Sterling Area. The British chancellor of the exchequer explained this situation to Secretary of State Morgenthau in a letter sent on September 3, 1943.

> In the North American Continent our financial problem has been largely solved by the generosity of the United States Government and of the Dominion of Canada. In many other parts of the world however, we have to provide the finance for the war. We can only do this in the main by borrowing local currencies against a credit in sterling to the respective countries, and thus we are incurring unfunded indebtedness on a vast scale. We could not continue this policy indefinitely without having some proportion of liquid assets out of which the more pressing part of the liquid indebtedness could be met if called for from time to time. But our liabilities, which are liabilities of the United Kingdom alone, are several times as great as our reserves, and the disproportion between our reserves and liabilities is also reflected in their growth.[65]

The British then explained that they were responsible for meeting the local cash expenditures for the area of hostilities from Tunis to Burma. "At the present time the United Kingdom's local cash expenditure in Egypt, the Middle East and India, over and above the supplies shipped across the seas, is amounting to some $2½ billion annually, the greater part of which has been borrowed from the countries concerned."[66]

In addition to increased liabilities, the British were in an even worse currency position. The gold and dollar balances were not just that of the United Kingdom but also the pooled reserves of the Sterling Area. Wood informed Morgenthau, "As you know, the members of the Sterling Area turn over to us their surplus dollar earning in exchange for sterling credit. But this carries with it an implied obligation on our part to turn back, so far as we can, the sterling into dollars when other parts of the Sterling Area need them."[67] Thus given the fact that some of their dollars did not technically belong to the British government, their reserves were inadequate once overseas liabilities were taken into account.[68]

By November, the American policymakers agreed they should not restrict British and dollar resources to a rigid ceiling. Assistant Secretary of State Dean Acheson confirmed that the British argument was valid.

> The British contend that the increase in their gold and dollar balances does not reflect an improvement of their financial position. On the contrary, their net overseas position is deteriorating at a rate of about $2.5 billion a year. Some growth of their liquid reserves is, they argue, indispensable to the delicate system by which they finance the war on credit through a large part of the world. To allow such growth could not legitimately be criticized. The British argument appears to be valid.[69]

Thus, US policymakers agreed with British assessments and Lend-Lease continued until the end of the war.

## Epilogue

Lend-Lease aid came to an abrupt stop once the war ended. By mid-1944, businessmen and foreign traders were lobbying vigorously for the return of trade to normal commercial channels. Conservatives, concerned by the vast expenditures of the war and the mounting national debt, insisted that American participation in reconstruction be on a strictly business basis. Democratic and Republican congressmen agreed that Lend-Lease was exclusively an instrument of war and must not be extended afterward, a position the administration never challenged.[70]

Anti–Lend-Lease sentiment continued throughout 1945. In August, the Truman administration began preparations to liquidate Lend-Lease. On August 13, the army terminated shipments of munitions to the United Kingdom. That same day, without consulting the British, Truman ordered the termination of all Lend-Lease on V-J Day, "in order that the best faith may be observed toward Congress and the administration protect itself against any charge of misuse of Congressional authorization."[71]

By the time the war was over, Britain had paid cash for $4.4 billion in goods and received $27 billion in Lend-Lease aid from the United States.[72] John Maynard Keynes described the financial state of Britain's dollar and gold reserves in August 1945, as "without exaggerating and without implying that we should not recover from it, a financial Dunkirk."[73]

## Crimean War Finance

Why did the British resort to costly external war finance during World War II and not in the Crimean War? As demonstrated in the World War II case, a state will resort to external war finance when it needs to procure inputs for the war effort from outside its borders and does not have the currency to pay for those goods. In contrast to World War II, during the Crimean War the British were able to produce a majority of goods for the war within its territory. There were two exceptions to British production—meat and fodder purchased from the Ottomans and mercenaries hired primarily from Italy but also from Switzerland and Germany. Britain's trade balance with these states coupled with London's status as a financial center meant the British were billed in sterling and not the countries' respective currencies. Consequently, there was no need for the British to pay in another currency and resort to an external war finance loan.

In this section, I present a brief description of the Crimean War, its cost, and the state of British finance in the mid-nineteenth century. Then I discuss the procurement of inputs for the war effort and how goods procured abroad were financed.

### Background

The Crimean War was a two-and-a-half-year conflict in which England and France joined forces with the Ottoman Empire against Russia. While the catalyst for the dispute was possession and control of Christian holy sites in Ottoman territory, the aim of the Anglo-French alliance was to check Russia's power.[74] The first open act of hostility took place on March 18, 1853, when Napoleon III sent a squadron from Toulon to an island off the coast of Greece. Britain followed suit on June 2, 1853, by sending ships to the entrance of the Dardanelles. After failed diplomatic negotiations, the Ottomans declared war in October 1853. In the same month, the British deployed their fleet to the Turkish Straits and Black Sea to protect Turkey. Britain and France officially declared war on March 22, 1854. The war continued until the Treaty of Paris was signed in March 1856.

The Crimean War, while shorter in duration and less intense than World War II, was costly.[75] The war cost the British government around £70 million.[76] At the height of the war in 1855, military expenditures were 56.8 percent of total government expenditures.[77] The war was paid for through a combination of taxation and general domestic debt.[78]

At the time of the Crimean War, Britain dominated the world both industrially and financially. World demand for British goods skyrocketed during the 1850s. The value of British exports in 1848 was £53 million. In nine years, this figure more than doubled, to £122 million in 1857.[79] At the same time British exports were increasing, Britain profited from an 1848 gold discovery in California and an 1851 discovery in Australia. Thus gold was flowing into the country at a rapid rate and Britain became the center for the world distribution of much of this new gold.[80]

The implications of this financial dominance were twofold. First, most countries at this time were trading with or in Britain. That meant that these countries were using pounds to complete these transactions. Because the volume of transactions was so high throughout much of the nineteenth century, the pound sterling was the prevailing reserve currency.[81] Second, because the pound was the prominent reserve currency, states were willing to accept pounds for transactions instead of their native currency.[82]

## Inputs for the War Effort

The majority of inputs for the war were secured on the Isle of Britain. The Crimean War was the first major war the British fought in which the innovations of the industrial age were fully incorporated in the army and navy. Until the late 1850s, guns were smoothbore muzzle-loading canons. The Enfield rifle, an improved version of the Minié rifle, had been introduced in the British army in 1853.[83] In addition to arms, the new ironclad, steam-propelled "floating batteries" with revolving gun turrets put the Industrial Revolution on the high seas.[84]

Regarding other inputs for the war effort, there is scant data on what was used and where it was procured. However, it can be inferred from data describing the period that the basic needs of the army in terms of iron, coal, textiles, and food were procured in Britain. With regard to cotton, the years immediately preceding and during the Crimean War were historically prosperous. Beginning in 1851 and 1852, there was new investment and additions to old factories, while existing capacity continued to be fully employed. One government reporter expressed awe at the cotton textile industry in 1853: "At no period during the last seventeen years that I have been officially acquainted with the manufacturing districts of Lancashire have I known such general prosperity."[85] The British were even supplying cotton to their Turkish ally during the war. About half of the increase in cotton exports in 1855 went to Turkey. The Sultan's government received a loan of £5 million from Britain to aid in purchasing goods in Britain for their war effort. As a result, Turkey's cotton imports from Britain rose dramatically.[86]

Iron and coal follow the same pattern as cotton, with periods of heavy investment and rising output arriving immediately before war broke out. The expansion of iron production in Britain began in 1851, and dependence on coal in the iron-making process gave British coal producers a new market that enabled them to achieve an extensive enlargement of their production. Moreover, the proximity of British coalfields to the newly developed iron ore deposits provided iron producers with adequate fuel supplies to exploit the advantages of their abundant ore supply.[87] Thus, with abundant supply and production at home, there was no need for Britain to look elsewhere for primary war inputs.

One area where inputs for the war were not secured in Britain was in the area of fresh meat and fodder. However, the reason for procuring inputs abroad was not due to insufficient British production but shipping. Animals and hay were shipped to Balaklava, a port city on the southern part of the Crimean peninsula, and redistributed throughout Crimea for the war. When the war began, Britain was shipping meat and fodder from the British Isle to Crimea. However, in the late fall and winter of 1854, the British began to encounter serious shipping constraints. The first disaster was a storm on November 14, 1854, when four-fifths of the pressed hay on board was lost. This supply disaster was followed by harsh winter weather that rendered sailing vessels useless.[88] Therefore, in order to feed the troops and animals, the British purchased these goods from the Ottoman Empire.

The British also had to hire mercenaries from abroad.[89] Relative to the other belligerents, the British army system was the weakest in regards to manpower.[90] Until 1847, men enlisted for life, or twenty-one years. There were two problems with this policy: soldiers in the ranks were worn out by age and there was no reserve of discharged soldiers in civilian life to fill out the regiments in the event of a major conflict.[91] Making matters worse, there was no compulsory service in Britain and volunteers were not forthcoming due to high civilian wages and general antiwar sentiment.[92] Thus when the Crimean War began, the British army was much smaller than that of its French ally. In the summer of 1854, the British army of the east numbered 21,500 men; the French army was about triple the size.[93] Moreover, most of the army's 153,000 men were scattered throughout the colonies and hence unavailable for war against Russia. Casualties from disease further weakened the numerical strength of the army. In December 1854, British secretary of war Sidney Herbert estimated British strength at 20,000. By the end of January effective strength had fallen to 13,000 due to rigors of winter.[94] Unfortunately for the British, there was no trained reserve to be called up to compensate for such high losses.[95]

Unable to secure more manpower in Britain, the British had to look outside its borders. In December 1854, the Aberdeen government tabled a foreign enlistment bill that allowed the British government to hire foreign mercenaries. The British government found success in Germany, Switzerland, and the Kingdom of Sardinia. About ten thousand men were recruited from Prussia and other German states, three thousand men from the Kingdom of Sardinia (particularly from Novara, Suza, and Chivasso), and eleven officers and three thousand men from Switzerland. The cost for mercenaries totaled £1.11 million.[96] Eventually Sardinia would send fifteen thousand men from Sardinia at no cost to the British.[97]

## Purchasing War Inputs

How did Britain pay for these goods? When a state purchases a good from abroad, it typically must sell its currency and buy the currency of the exporting state in order to finalize the purchase. However, because the pound was the dominant reserve currency at this time, the British government was able to pay for war inputs with its own currency. Food and fodder was billed in pounds instead of Ottoman lira.[98] Thus the British did not need to call on its Turkish currency reserves or engage in an external loan with the Ottomans to pay for these supplies.

The payment of mercenaries was also in pounds. Recruits were paid a bounty of £10. Of this sum £6 was payable on enlistment and the rest was withheld until disbandment in order to cover the cost of possible damage to barracks and equipment.[99] In addition to troops, the British also had to hire and pay a recruitment committee to find and enlist men. Each committee member would be paid £1 per day and £5 per each person they persuaded to enlist.[100] Finally, the British began to recruit officers. The pay for each of officer enlisted was negotiated individually; all were paid in pounds.

Unlike German and Swiss mercenaries, the Kingdom of Sardinia had ulterior motives to fight on behalf of the Anglo-French alliance. At the time of the Crimean War, Austria controlled the Lombardy region of northern Italy. The Sardinians hoped that fighting in the Crimean War would increase their leverage vis-à-vis the Austrians with the end goal of gaining independence in order to unify Italy. Sir James Hudson, head of the British legation at Turin, was instructed to take on ten thousand Sardinian regulars into British pay. Hudson approached Sardinian foreign minister Dabormida and was assured Sardinia would send fifteen thousand soldiers to be an independent force under Sardinian command.

The Sardinian government, however, did not want the British to pay for its troops. It was believed that accepting financial help from Britain would place Sardinia in the embarrassing position of supplying what were virtually mercenaries instead of an equal ally.[101] Thus the costs of the troops were to be borne by the Sardinians. Unable to pay for the troops outright, they negotiated a loan from Britain. On January 26, 1855, Sardinia signed a military convention with Britain and France. According to its terms, Sardinia was to furnish 15,000 men "under the command of a Sardinian general" and France and Britain were to "guarantee the integrity" of Sardinia during the war. A supplementary convention between Sardinia and Britain was signed on the same day, under which Britain was to lend Sardinia £1 million, half of which was to be paid at once, and the other half six months later; the interest on the loan was to be 4 percent and Britain was to pay for all the transport needed by Sardinia.[102]

In all, during the Crimean War, Britain was able to avoid the costs of external war finance as a result of high domestic war production and ability to procure currency due to the sterling's status as an international currency

When fighting World War II, the British did their best to protect their domestic economy, financing the war through various taxes, debts with low interest rates, and a bond campaign. This domestic war finance policy was economically prudent as it kept inflation and interest rates low. Yet, needing to procure imports from abroad to fight the Germans and lacking the currency to pay for them, the British had to engage in costly external war finance. After the war, the British found themselves stripped of their dollar assets and badly needed gold and dollar reserves. Moreover, they were straddled with an enormous amount of dollar debt, $30 billion dollars that would take more than fifty years to pay back; the last payment was made on December 29, 2006.[103]

In addition to economic costs, external war finance cost Britain its autonomy.[104] Britain had to sell its dollars assets at lower than market prices against its will and the state was subject to financial audits. The United States even sent a Lend-Lease program administrator to ensure that the British were not profiting from Lend-Lease aid.[105] The extent to which the United States violated British autonomy is evidenced in Stettinius Jr.'s recounting of scrap metal when in Britain in April 1944.

> Several things about the British and steel picture disturbed me. In Bristol, I had seen the steel frameworks of many blitzed buildings still standing. And in London, near the American Embassy, I saw day after day the

> huge steel girders of some large buildings which had been wrecked in the air raids many months before . . . It seemed to me that the British were not making the most of their scrap collections, and I pointed this out at Ashorne Hill. I told them we could not continue to supply them under Lend-Lease at the present rate unless they were collecting all the scrap iron and steel they possible could at home.[106]

By accepting aid from the United States, the British subjected themselves to both the economic and political costs of external war finance.

During the Crimean War, to confront the Russian army, the British government was able to procure all its imports for the war from within its borders, except for fresh meat, fodder, and manpower. Poor weather conditions affected British ability to ship food to its men and hay for its animals in the Crimean War in a timely manner. As a result, the British government had to secure these goods from the Ottomans. In addition, given the inability to conscript and recruit volunteers, the British government had to import troops from abroad, hiring mercenaries from Switzerland, Germany, and Sardinia. The dominance of the pound as the reserve currency allowed the British to pay for these inputs in pounds, effectively avoiding the need to turn to external war finance. There was no need to engage in external extraction, allowing them to avoid a reliance on other states or creditors and, thus, a potentially exploitive costly relationship.

5

# TAXATION AND CURRENCY RESERVES DURING THE RUSSO-JAPANESE WAR

The Russo-Japanese War, rooted in the imperialist desires of Russia and Japan to expand in the Pacific, was an eighteen-month conflict fought between 1904 and 1905. Two territories were of particular interest, Manchuria and Korea. In the years leading up to the war, Russia was in the process of completing the Trans-Siberian railway connecting St. Petersburg to the Pacific. The quickest route was through Manchuria to Port Arthur. Like the Russians, the Japanese had interests in the region. After the Sino-Japanese War of 1894–1895, China ceded the Liaodong Peninsula (southeast Manchuria) to Japan. In early 1904, after years of negotiations over its rival ambitions, Tokyo broke off talks with Russia and withdrew its minister from St. Petersburg. On February 8, 1904, the Japanese declared war and attacked the Russian fleet at Port Arthur.[1]

The Russo-Japanese War was a success for Japan. Not only did Japan gain control over Manchuria and Korea, it financed the war in a less costly manner than Russia. Japan financed its war effort through higher levels of taxation and foreign debt at lower interest rates than Russia. Japan's war finance success relative to Russia is puzzling. First, in the years leading up to the war both the Russian and Japanese governments reformed their fiscal system in order to expand their extractive capacity. Yet, despite similar efforts, the Japanese government was able to pay for a larger percentage of the war via taxation than Russia. This feat is even more impressive given that the war with Russia was the first war fought by Japan to include taxation into its war finance strategy.[2] Second, the financing of the Russo-Japanese War was Japan's debut into international credit markets whereas

Russia was a seasoned veteran. Given that the Japanese government had little experience raising tax revenues, how was it able to incorporate direct resource extraction into its war finance strategy whereas Russia was not? Moreover, with no international credit history, how was Japan able to secure relatively cheaper credit abroad?

The previous chapter addressed under what conditions belligerents are constrained by their capacity to cope with inputs from abroad and low currency reserves and, therefore, are forced to resort to external war finance. This chapter continues to explore external war finance while also emphasizing the capacity to extract revenue. By comparing Japanese and Russian war finance policies I demonstrate that when a state has low bureaucratic capacity, direct resource extraction will comprise a low percentage of its war finance strategy. Low extractive capacity does not result in capitulation. Given that the state continues the war, we should expect to see a war finance strategy that reflects higher levels of indirect and external resource extraction.

I argue that in the decades preceding the war with Russia, the Japanese government enhanced their extractive capacity with the introduction of the yen and created an effective revenue administration. These institutions allowed the Japanese government to change tax rates when necessary, implement new taxes, and collect and process revenue. Russia, on the other hand, lacked these institutions. Russia's economy was only partially monetized and the state's administrative capacity to collect tax revenue was marred with inefficiencies. Thus, if Russia wanted to continue with the war effort, it would have to turn to other sources of revenue.

For different reasons, both states engaged in external war finance. While the Japanese exercised their capacity to raise taxes, similar to the British during World War II, they needed inputs for the war effort from abroad, specifically ships and steel, but did not have the currency to pay for them. In the years leading up to the Russo-Japanese War, the Japanese had a consistent balance of payments deficit. Thus, the Japanese government engaged in external war finance by floating debt in the United States and London. Japanese creditworthiness was contingent on its capacity to service the debt, which was bolstered by a gold indemnity received from China before the war, the aid of an American investment bank, and success in military battles against Russia. Russia, on the other hand, unable to increase tax revenue, turned to domestic debt. However, domestic debt soon proved a difficult way to finance, as the state was committed to the gold standard and needed to maintain a strict reserve ratio; thus the state had no other choice but to seek loans abroad. Russia's creditworthiness declined as it experienced military losses and as it appeared it would no longer be able to repay its debt due to worsening economic conditions and domestic disturbances.

## Japan and Russia in the Prewar Era

In the years leading up to the war, Japan and Russia shared many similarities. Beginning in the 1860s, both countries began a period of political centralization and economic modernization. The transformation period in Japan began with the Meiji Restoration in 1868, which was followed by the abolition of feudal divisions in 1871, and the Meiji Constitution in 1890. In Russia, this period began in 1861 with the emancipation of the serfs. The "Great Reforms" continued through the latter half of the 1800s and lasted until 1917.[3]

Both countries reorganized their societies. The Japanese government dissolved the local village as the center for political activity and economic revenue and replaced it with administrative townships loyal to the central government. Similarly, the Russian government formed new local assemblies, zemstvos, which strengthened the role of the gentry in local self-government and emphasized the class principle within that government.[4] In addition to new administrative centers, this period was one of bureaucratic reform. Both governments were attempting to create a value system that stressed the predominance of common interests over individual interests, the belief that central government should play a leading role in development, and sacrifice to the national interest as defined by authoritative political figures.[5]

In addition, both states experienced a transition from an agrarian and rural to an industrial and urban way of life.[6] In addition to the timing of their transformation, their per capita levels of growth mirrored each other. Between 1889 and 1902 Japan's average annual growth rate was 2.8 percent where as Russia, between 1860 and 1900, was 2.5 percent.[7] The two countries also had similar average annual growth rates of industrial output—Japan at 5.5 percent in 1887 and Russia at 6.7 percent in 1900.[8]

These reforms caused both Japan and Russia to experience a rapid rise in the potential tax revenue that could be extracted. Both states vastly increased their tax bases and placed their populaces within the direct purview of public policy.[9] The potential to extract revenue increased as the ability of the states to reach their citizens expanded with the advent of modern technology and its application to communications through railroads and postal, telegraph, and telephone systems.[10] Given these similarities of political centralization, bureaucratic reform, growth patterns, and expanding tax base, why was the Japanese government able to raise taxes to finance the war and the Russia government was not? Moreover, why was Russia's war finance policy so much more politically and economically costly than Japan's?

## Japanese War Finance

The war with Russia cost Japan around ¥1.98 billion.[11] It was eight times more costly than the previous war, the First Sino-Japanese War, fought a decade earlier.[12] A fifth of the male working population was mobilized for some form of war service, a million men were sent to the front, and casualties mounted over 100,000.[13] The war was paid through a combination of taxation and foreign loans with a minimal reliance on domestic debt.[14]

### Tax Capacity

Before the Meiji Restoration, Japan was ruled by the feudal regime of the Tokugawa clan.[15] Under this system of government there was neither a central currency nor a central administrative tax bureaucracy. During this period, gold, silver, and copper coins of different weights and fineness were in circulation as well as an assortment of notes. Moreover, the source of note issue was not the central government but local towns and villages. At the time of the Meiji Restoration there were 1,694 different issues of paper money in circulation, with their relative values frequently changing.[16]

The primary form of revenue in Tokugawa Japan was a land tax that was payable in rice by farmers and levied on the basis of crop-sharing arrangements. This form of revenue was highly unstable, fluctuating with the vagaries of the weather.[17] Other taxes were also inefficient as citizens were subject to a large number of miscellaneous taxes that scarcely repaid the cost of collection.[18] Moreover, taxes were levied on the villages as a whole, rather than on individual plots, and then allocated by a consultative process within the village.[19] Thus the central government did not interact with citizens directly.

Japan had to consolidate the currencies in circulation before any administrative reforms could be successfully implemented. The yen was introduced in 1871 and the central government became the sole issuer of currency. For the next thirty years, the Japanese government removed all previous forms of coins and notes from circulation.[20] By the time of the Russo-Japanese War, almost all locally issued paper money and bank notes had been taken out of circulation making the yen the dominant currency.[21]

In addition to the dominance of the yen, the Japanese government reformed and created a variety of institutions that allowed it to raise more taxes during the Russo-Japanese War than it would otherwise had been able to. These improvements included reforming the land tax, consolidating miscellaneous taxes, transferring revenue extraction from local villages to the central government, transferring loyalty from villages to the central government, hiring competent bureaucrats, and establishing a Ministry of Finance and national bank.

Tax reform began in 1873 with the land tax. Instead of paying the tax in rice, the tax was now to be paid in currency. Moreover, the land tax was now based on the land instead of the harvest, making it more stable as harvests varied from year to year.[22] In addition, the government created a more efficient tax structure by removing miscellaneous taxes and implementing nationwide taxes on specific goods. In 1875, the whole system was drastically transformed, and in the course of the next five years, the number of taxes was reduced from nearly 1,600 to 74.[23]

In addition to removing various inefficient miscellaneous taxes, the Japanese government diversified its tax portfolio. This diversification increased the sources of potential revenue. Between 1885 and 1895, the primary taxes collected were on land and liquor. After 1895, the government implemented and increased taxes on income, liquor, tobacco, sugar, textiles, and beverages, as well as custom duties.[24] Initially, the land tax alone made up about four-fifths of the total tax revenue. In 1876, total tax revenue was ¥57.8 million, of which ¥50 million came from the land tax. By 1883, total tax revenue was ¥69.2 million, of which only ¥39 million came from the land tax.[25]

The government also created a tax bureaucracy to collect and process revenue. First, the government assumed responsibility for local administration. Before the Meiji Restoration, local lords received and kept local taxes. Now these revenues were due to the central exchequer.[26] Second, beginning in 1888, the government transferred loyalties from the village to administrative towns. By the time of the Russo-Japanese War, more than seventy-six thousand Tokugawa hamlets had been reduced to some twelve thousand administrative towns and villages.[27] Third, the government created a competent bureaucracy. The government replaced leaders from old regimes with civil servants who were university educated, passed the required civil service exam, and were assured tenure.[28] Finally, in March 1882, the government established a central bank to deposit collected revenue.[29]

In the period immediately before the Russo-Japanese War, Japanese tax capacity was reinforced and broadened. In order to pay the domestic debt from the Sino-Japanese War (1894–1895), the government instituted a national business tax and a registration tax for the first time. In addition, the land tax was increased, as were taxes on alcoholic beverages and sugar. As a result of these measures, the total tax revenue in the ten years following the Sino-Japanese War, ¥124 million, was roughly double that of the ten years preceding the war, ¥65 million.[30] By 1902, Japan's ratio of national and local tax revenue to national income was increasing faster than its western counterparts, 15.0 percent in Japan, 10.7 percent in Britain, and 6.5 percent in the United States.[31]

By the time of the Russo-Japanese War, Japan had emerged with a uniform currency system, a central bank, a system of note-issuing commercial banks, a government-owned bank to finance foreign trade, a postal saving system, a few small private savings banks, and a Deposit Bureau in the Ministry of Finance.[32] These institutions allowed Japan to raise more taxes than it ever had before.

## Taxation and the Russo-Japanese War

The Japanese government raised taxes twice during the war. One month into the war, in March 1904, the Diet approved a myriad of tax increases and new taxes. This first scheme of war taxation increased the following taxes: land, income, business, sake, soy, sugar excise, mining, registration, bourse, shooting licenses, as well as various import duties. In addition, the government imposed consumption taxes on woolen textiles and kerosene; increased the amount of stamps to be affixed to documents; and put into operation the tobacco manufacture monopoly. The government raised taxes again a year later. This second scheme of increased taxation further increased various taxes and import duties. It also implemented a traveling tax, stamp duties on checks, a placer tax, imposed a consumption tax on textiles other than woolens, and established a succession tax.[33]

There was some increase in the land tax, but the sharpest rise was in various excise taxes on such consumer commodities as textiles, kerosene, sugar, and salt. Indirect taxes rose 300 percent in five years: from ¥96 million in 1903 to ¥152 million in 1905 and to ¥231 million in 1908.[34] The government also reduced spending and responsibilities for public works and education as financial responsibilities for these services were increasingly delegated to local government, causing local taxes to grow, bringing their total to over 40 percent of the national tax revenue after the turn of the century.[35]

## Inputs for the War Effort

While the Japanese were successful in raising tax revenue to pay for their domestic war costs, they needed foreign currency in order to purchase goods for the war from abroad. Before the Russo-Japanese War, the Japanese were purchasing warships overseas.[36] In the 1870s, the Japanese navy purchased a few small cruisers and torpedo boats, and three British corvettes costing $1 million each.[37] In the 1880s, a Japanese commission visited England and ordered a pair of sleek protected cruisers of 4,150 tons, mounting a 12.6-inch turret gun, costing $1.7 million each. Two more protected cruisers were ordered from France, costing $2.2 million apiece. By the late 1890s, a 14,850-ton battleship cost about $5 million and the Imperial navy bought four of them and six first class cruisers of 9,800 tons, mainly from Britain.[38]

Shipyards had been forbidden to build oceangoing ships in Tokugawa times, the period before the Meiji Restoration. After the war with China, the Japanese government began a crash program to produce more warships internally. By the early 1880s, the Japanese government managed to build a 1,000-ton wooden side-wheel steamer and a royal yacht. Not until 1894, after six years of construction, did the yard at Yokosuka complete a 4,217-ton lightly armored cruiser with French ordnance. Guns, engines, and armor of the naval revolution lay far beyond Japan's infant industries.[39] While the current Japanese government was expanding its production capacity, this expansion was still not enough to effectively fight the Russians. Thus they had little choice but to purchase ships from abroad.

The onset of the war with Russia not only increased demand for warships built abroad but also increased demand for raw materials. Though the total tonnage of foreign-made warships exceeded that produced domestically, Japanese capacity to build and equip larger warships continued to improve following the Sino-Japanese War.[40] This rise in internal production increased the demand, supplied by imports, for iron and steel.[41]

In 1888, a group of private individuals established Nihon Steel. The mill was legally charged with "meeting the needs of the military as its primary objective" and planned to produce 60,000 tons of steel.[42] Yet in 1904 the mill's capacity failed to exceed 40,000 tons. At the same time, the nation's total demand neared 310,000 tons of steel due not just to naval expansion but the buildup of the army and the rapidly expanding railroad network and other industries.[43] Thus the Japanese did not only need to purchase warships from abroad but steel as well.

Before the Sino-Japanese War, Japan was able to purchase warships from abroad as a result of a balance of payments surplus. However, after the Sino-Japanese War, an excess of imports over exports characterized Japan's foreign trade every year until long after the Russo-Japanese War.[44] To make matters worse, Japan's primary export, silk, had suffered due to a world recession, with prices falling 30 percent in 1903.[45] The annual average of foreign trade between Japan, including its colonies, and abroad between 1899 and 1903 yielded an import surplus of ¥26 million. Between 1904 and 1908, the annual average surplus of imports over exports increased to ¥105 million.[46] This adverse trade balance created a dearth of foreign exchange. As shown in table 5.1, Japan's foreign exchange balance was negative beginning in 1903 and worsened throughout the war.

**TABLE 5.1** Japanese foreign exchange balance, 1901–1906

| YEAR | FOREIGN EXCHANGE BALANCE (¥ MILL.) |
|---|---|
| 1901 | 16 |
| 1902 | 26 |
| 1903 | -6 |
| 1904 | -131 |
| 1905 | -326 |
| 1906 | -24 |

*Source:* Adapted from R.W. Goldsmith, *The Financial Development of Japan, 1868–1977* (New Haven, CT: Yale University Press, 1983), 38.

Consequently, Japan did not have the currency to import the goods needed to effectively fight the war. In order to compensate for this lack of foreign exchange, Japan went to London to float a loan.

## External War Finance

Japan was a novice on the foreign currency market when the war began. When Japan opened itself to world trade in 1859, it had no credit standing or national currency.[47] Moreover, it had little experience in floating loans. Except for two relatively small foreign loans in the 1870s (to finance Japan's first seventeen miles of railroad and nominally to pay off feudal pension rights), the government adopted the policy of opposing the inflow of foreign direct investment or portfolio capital.[48]

In the years immediately prior to the Russo-Japanese War, Japan increased its creditworthiness. The state built credit through a $185 million gold indemnity received from China in 1897.[49] Initially, the indemnity was to be paid in silver. Since China had to finance the indemnity by borrowing in Europe, the Japanese were successful in negotiating for it to be paid in pounds held in London, readily convertible into gold.[50] Thus the funds remained in London and were used to purchase armaments.[51] The Japanese knew that pounds held abroad would not be enough to finance their military buildup. Thus they began to stabilize their currency. Using the indemnity as a basis, in 1897, Japan adopted the gold standard and pegged the yen at 0.75 grams of gold, equivalent to £2.57, or $0.49, a value it maintained for thirty-five years.[52]

Stabilizing Japanese currency aided in floating debt, but stabilization alone was not enough. Few Western observers thought Japan could beat the world's largest army and a fleet with more battleships. Moreover, British prime minister Arthur Balfour was hesitant to extend credit to Japan, worried about offending Russia, an ally of England's other ally, France.[53] To combat these problems,

Japan dispatched Korekiyo Takahashi, vice governor of the Bank of Japan, to raise money overseas. In April 1904, Takahashi persuaded a London banking group to agree in principle to float a bond issue of £10 million, secured with Japanese customs receipts as collateral. The bankers, however, were only prepared to underwrite an initial tranche of £5 million, despite Japan's need for more.[54]

Fortunately for the Japanese war effort, while in London, Takahashi met Jacob H. Schiff, head of New York Banking house of Kuhn, Loeb & Company.[55] Schiff, who disliked Russian treatment of its Jewish population, offered to aid the Japanese in floating its loan.[56] Schiff, on behalf of Kuhn, Loeb & Co., agreed to underwrite the remaining £5 million in New York through a syndicate headed by the firm. The expertise of Kuhn, Loeb & Co. allowed Japan to act like a seasoned debtor. Although they underwrote only 44 percent of the foreign bonds, the company set the pace and conditions for every issue.[57]

Japan's credit was also aided by its military successes.[58] No longer was the country seen as a weak adversary who would be overtaken by the larger Russian army. On May 1, Japan achieved a decisive victory against Russia on the Yalu River. On May 10, £10 million in 6 percent bonds were issued in London and New York. The issue was a huge success and immediately oversubscribed.[59] Each loan proved more successful than the last. The first two loans had interest rates at 6 percent, but by 1905, after numerous Japanese battlefield successes, it was perceived by many in Europe and the United States that Japan was going to win the war. In March and July, the interest rate was lowered to 4.5 percent. Moreover, Russia's allies, France and Germany, were also subscribing to the loan.[60] On April 1, 1905, *The Economist* wrote, "The striking success which has attended the issue of the new Japanese loan, both here and in the United States, ought to present itself to the Tsar and his advisers as a potent argument in favor of peace. . . . Japan's credit has improved with successive victories, while that of Russia has declined with her corresponding defeats."[61]

## Epilogue

Japanese financing of the Russo-Japanese War was impressive. As a result of increased tax capacity, with the introduction of the yen, and a new effective and efficient national tax structure, the Japanese were able to finance a portion of the war with taxes. It was the first war fought by Japan to incorporate taxation into a war finance strategy. More important, the Japanese government did not have to resort to other costly means of war finance.

In order to fight the war effectively, the Japanese also needed to engage in foreign war finance. Regardless of how much tax revenue the Japanese gathered to pay for the war effort, they needed foreign currency to buy war supplies from abroad. The small country that had only once before floated a foreign loan was able to secure vast amounts of credit at a low interest rate. In the words of Edward S. Miller, "What ensued was an international financial coup. Meiji Japan, a minor league borrower that had raised only $60 million abroad since its origins thirty years earlier, tapped into global lending markets by issuing bonds with a face of $408 million that netted it, after discounts and charges, $343 million.[62]

## Russian War Finance

The war was as costly, if not more so, for the Russians. The total expenditure caused by the Russo-Japanese War amounted to 3 billion rubles.[63] For the years 1904 and 1905, war expenditure consumed 40 percent of the total revenue.[64] Russia attempted to raise taxes and curtail expenditures to pay for the war, raising the urban property tax, excise taxes on beer, yeast, matches, and fuel oils, as well as increasing stamp and death duties. The government also increased the sale price of vodka (a state-owned monopoly), customs duties on certain imports, and railway charges for the transports of passengers and goods. This tax effort, however, was only able to pay for about 5 percent of the war.[65] Russia, unlike Japan, was unable to incorporate taxation effectively into its war finance strategy.

The government then attempted to finance the war by domestic debt. However, at the time of the Russo-Japanese War, the Russian government was committed to maintaining the gold standard, introduced only seven years earlier in 1897. As a result, the government required that all notes issued be backed by gold. This strict reserve ratio meant there was a limit to how many paper notes could be in circulation. After the first few months of the war, the government realized that it would violate this ratio if it continued to fund the war domestically.

In order to continue financing the war, the government had to either print or float its debt abroad. Choosing the less costly option, the Russian government turned to foreign markets. Russia called on its French ally to extend its credit. Unlike Japan, the Russians found that as the war unfolded, credit became more costly as interest rates rose. Repeated Russian military defeats, combined with deteriorating finances due to the war and domestic social unrest, made Russian debt a risky investment. In addition, Russia did not fully participate with the demands of the French government and its banking houses. Therefore, in order to continue securing credit, the Russian government had to pay higher interest rates, increasing the cost of the war.[66]

## Tax Capacity

Russia lacked the capacity to pay for the war by taxation. Low monetization, a regressive tax structure, and an inefficient bureaucracy characterized its tax capacity.[67] At the time of the Russo-Japanese War, while there was widespread use of the ruble and no other competing currencies in use, there was still a significant portion of society that was not using currency to pay for its goods. Russia's large peasant population was often paid in kind as the bulk of the peasants' income was consumed within the households without reaching the market.[68] Consequently, the Russian government did not have access to this income to extract in the form of tax revenue.

Russian capacity to finance the war via tax revenue was also strained by the structure of the tax system. In the decades before the war, Russia's primary source of tax revenue was not from direct taxes but from more inefficient indirect taxes.[69] In 1903, the year before war outbreak, only 6.6 percent of total revenue collected was from direct taxes.[70] Of the indirect taxes collected, the excise taxes on items of mass consumption, such as alcoholic beverages, sugar, tobacco, matches, and petroleum, were the most significant.[71]

The problem with this emphasis on indirect taxation was twofold. First, its regressive nature meant that the tax burden was heaviest on the low-income strata of the population.[72] Not only did this segment of the population engage in fewer commercial transactions because of its poverty level, a large portion of these taxes was also waged on those peasants that were paid in kind. Thus there were fewer points at which the government could extract revenue relative to a direct income tax that targeted the entire population. Moreover, attempting to extract more taxes from an already impoverished class of people limited government revenue. This scenario was exacerbated as the economic strength of the agricultural population was undermined in the year before the war. The harvests of 1903 were poor and in nineteen provinces, the harvest was considered very poor when compared with those of past years.[73] Second, the landed nobility was not taxed.[74] By not seeking revenue from wealthier citizens, the Russian government further limited the amount of tax revenue that could be collected.

Finally, Russia was constrained by its administrative capacity to extract revenue. Like Japan, in the decades before the Russo-Japanese War, Russia was reforming its tax structure.[75] In an attempt to ease the tax burden of the peasantry, Alexander III increased direct taxes. This new direct tax system targeted urban and business income by increasing rates on urban property taxes (1883), introducing death duties and gift taxes (1882), imposing a levy on interest bearing depositions and securities (1885), implementing business income taxes (1885), and an impost (1893) on revenue from urban house and apartment ownership.[76]

In 1898, business tax reform also introduced several new taxes on corporations and banks: a 0.15 percent tax on nominal capital, surcharge on excess profits, and personal income taxes on corporation directors.[77] While it appeared that Russia was increasing its tax capacity, and the government did increase the amount of taxes collected, the administrative capacity to extract revenue remained low, inhibiting the state's ability to collect the amount of revenues needed to fund a costly war.[78]

The ability to collect business taxes illustrates the lack of capacity. In 1885, the Russian government imposed a 3 percent tax on corporate profits. In 1893, this 3 percent flat tax was raised to 5 percent. In addition, the Russian Ministry of Finance, for each year beginning in 1885 and thereafter, decreed a certain sum of revenue to be collected from businesses.[79] Provincial tax offices were allocated their share and they in turn divided this up into smaller sums to be collected by each district. Each district was then assigned portions to business taxpayers.

There were many problems with collecting this tax, including but not limited to auditing, tax evasion, and enforcement. The first problem with collecting tax revenue was auditing businesses. Each business was assigned a tax officer to estimate how much profit the business produced. To estimate profits, the tax offices categorized each enterprise according to its "external signs," information readily available from looking at the kind of business license it held.[80] They also consulted with experts to estimate the average profitability one could normally expect for each type of trade and industry in a given area. Armed with percentages of normal profitability for each category of trade industry, tax offices then set about calculating the profits of each enterprise.[81] Lacking the required knowledge, state agents could never be sure if their assessments of a locality were too high or too low, and they tended to allow arrears to grow unchecked.[82]

Exacerbating the inaccuracy of the estimated profits, until 1898, no precise guidelines existed in the law codes describing what actually constituted corporate net profits. On the advice of the State Council, the definition of net profits was left for interpretation by administrative instructions.[83] In addition to creating problems for the tax officers, businesses exploited this vagueness. Corporations paying the tax sent in accounts designed to obfuscate by being either "unusually brief" or "excessively complete." It was common for corporations to create purely fictitious balance sheets for public consumption in order to hide real profits and reduce taxes.[84]

In addition to auditing difficulties, there was massive tax evasion. The structure of the tax system was such that businesses needed to self-report. Knowing from experience that the Finance Ministry often assigned levies which were beyond business taxpaying ability and that it was pointless to pay what the tax collector asked as more would be asked for later, businesses engaged in tax evasion.[85]

A Finance Ministry report commented that it believed everyone, "everywhere," "equally" tried to avoid the income taxes.[86]

Finally, capacity was limited by the inability to enforce the tax. In order to collect these new direct taxes, the government reformed its bureaucracy. In order to estimate what sum each individual taxpayer should pay, two new institutions were created in 1885: inspectors and district tax officers. Five hundred tax inspectors were dispersed to preside over the tax offices that were composed of both finance officials and merchants or industrialists.[87] The inspectors were given unprecedented powers to assess and collect revenue. Inspectors and tax offices had to estimate profits of privately owned enterprises without recourse to trade books. In an understatement, the Department of Trade and Manufacturing explained the difficulties of the first year:

> Tax inspectors, only just appointed in 1885, were not able to collect sufficiently complete data; therefore the new tax offices, lacking the necessary information, could not always execute their duties with complete success. Moreover, it is necessary to keep in mind that the law of 15 January 1885 by no means required a precise definition of turnover and profits of enterprises, possible only with the obligatory presentation of their trade books by taxpayers, but only required [enough] information [so that] turnover and profits could be hypothetically determined by the tax offices.[88]

Five hundred inspectors were just too few for the enormous task of verifying information in a suspicious and often hostile environment.

Russian tax capacity inhibited the government's ability to include taxation into its war finance strategy. The government's ability to extract revenue was marred by its low level of monetization, its regressive tax structure, and a weak bureaucracy unable to audit society and collect and process revenue. In order to finance the war, Russia would have to resort to other forms of revenue.

## Domestic Debt

Once the Russian government realized that it was unable to finance the war via taxation, it began to raise domestic debt. However, this method of war finance was short lived. At the time of the Russo-Japanese War, the Russian government was zealously committed to maintaining the gold standard. In the latter half of the nineteenth century, Russia's economy was characterized by an unstable and inconvertible paper currency. This currency instability harmed Russia's ability to seek credit abroad, affected foreign trade, and therefore cut into customs duties, a primary source of revenue.[89] The Russian government realized that if it were to maintain and expand its international status, it would have to reform its currency. Thus the primary goal of Russian economic policy was to achieve a state of convertibility of its currency by adhering to the gold standard. In order to fulfill this goal in the period before the war, the government built up its gold reserve and, in 1897, officially adopted the gold standard.[90]

After a series of failed attempts at maintaining convertibility in the past, this time was going to be different.[91] Thus the Russian government set very conservative and strict provisions to maintain it. The required gold reserve was to cover 50 percent of the first 600 million rubles of the new State Bank notes and 100 percent for any amount of paper notes above this level.[92] This convertibility ratio meant that the Russian government could only issue as many paper notes as it had gold. If the Russian government wanted to continue paying for the Russo-Japanese War effort via domestic debt, it had to violate this ratio.[93] On March 17, 1904, new minister of finance, Vladimir Kokovtsov, in his report to the Committee of Finance, insisted that the gold standard be maintained at all costs and then proposed to contract foreign loans in order to strengthen Russia's gold reserves and pay for the war.[94] Once again, if Russia was going to continue fighting the war, it would have to seek money elsewhere.

## External War Finance

As Kokovtsov's report suggested, the Russian government decided to search for funds abroad. Russian comptroller Sergei Witte summarized Russia's predicament in the spring of 1905 in a letter to General A.N. Kuropatkin, the Russian chief of staff, stating that Russia would have to seek funds abroad, specifically France, if it were to continue with the war: "We must count on the fact that further [foreign] financial operations are ahead of us whether or not they can be completed on terms favorable to us."[95]

The Russian government immediately looked to its French ally for financial aid.[96] On May 2, Russian finance minister Kokovtsov met with the French ambassador, Maurice Bompard, to discuss the condition of the loan. The sum of 800 million francs was authorized under the condition that only 400 million be made available immediately. In case of an unfavorable market, the operation would be halted.[97] The Russian government was against splitting the loan. Kokovtsov and Witte attempted to strengthen their bargaining position, threatening that they would float their loan in Germany instead.[98] The French government, unwilling to change the terms, agreed to a high interest rate of 6.5 percent, as well as preference for French companies in foreign purchases.[99] On May 12, 1904, the loan agreement was signed. The loan was a success and the entire 800 million francs (300 million rubles) were issued.[100]

The Russian government needed to float another loan and the next round of negotiations with France began in October 1904. The May loan had been enormously profitable for those who had taken part and now Crédit Lyonnais sent its representatives to St. Petersburg.[101] Once again, this loan, which now included German banks, was successful.[102] The loan was sold at 4.5 percent and was so profitable for the German bankers that the Deutsche Bank's board met in the last days of March to discuss a larger loan to Russia through a different consortium of bankers. But the loan of 1905 turned out to be the last major Russian operation on the Berlin exchange.[103]

In the spring of 1905, with the Battle of Mukden, Russia's financial fortunes took a sharp turn. In March the Japanese forced the Russian Manchurian Army to retreat. The Russians lost about eighty-five thousand men and the army disbanded as a fighting unit.[104] The loss at Mukden was followed by the loss of thirty-two vessels in the Tsushima Straits in May. It was becoming evident that Russia would not win the war. The French foreign minister Théophile Delcassé told the Japanese minister in Paris that a continuation of the war after the battle at Mukden appeared to him utterly useless.[105] On March 13, French bankers wired their delegates in St. Petersburg instructing them to break off negotiations on a 600 million franc loan. This cancellation of credit was a disaster that rivaled the defeat at Mukden, for it would be very difficult for Russia to go on with the war without the continued infusion of French money. Russian Ambassador A.I. Nelidov was convinced that Russia should make peace at once, and he urged his government to avail itself of the services of Delcassé in approaching Japan.[106]

Even before the Russian losses at Mukden and Tsushima, France's willingness to extend credit was waning due to deteriorating domestic conditions in Russia. In January 1905, Russian officials massacred a group of demonstrators marching in St. Petersburg.[107] Russia's bloody suppression outraged the Russian population, leading to hundreds of thousands of workers striking and protesting throughout the country. The massacre quickly received international attention. A wave of protests reverberated throughout the world, and mass demonstrations took place in major cities around the globe. Nowhere were the demonstrations more outspoken than in France.[108] Consequently, the French government and its citizens no longer desired to extend their credit.[109]

The combination of military losses and political upheaval in Russia also caused French financiers to doubt the ability of Russia to repay its debt.

> In January 1905, A.L. Guernaut, head of the department in the French Ministry of Finance dealing with foreign loans, told French Finance Minister Maurice Rouvier, that Russia might not be able to pay the interest on the debt contracted in France. He advised that France's

> policy of 'indefinite' lending to Russia be stopped and that the Russian government be informed that its appeals for French credit had reached their limit.[110]

When the French financiers refused to sign the loan, Delcassé explained to the French ambassador to Russia that French finance minister Rouvier had been studying the internal situation in Russia and the military reverses and was of the opinion that "henceforth great prudence must be shown in the matter of loans to Russia."[111]

The Russian government was in a precarious position. Its French ally was no longer going to extend its credit. Moreover, the German market was incapable of absorbing any more Russian bonds as only part of the 500 million marks granted to Russia had been subscribed.[112] On April 8, Russia told the French government that unless they received a foreign loan, Russia could continue the war no longer than twelve months without abandoning the gold standard.[113]

In order to continue funding the war effort, the Russian government reverted back to domestic debt and short term loans floated in London. On March 24, 1905, the finance committee discussed a 5 percent domestic bond issue for 200 million rubles. Kokovtsov stated that the rates were lower than the previous foreign loans, but last-minute demands by the Russian banks raised commissions further. The high rate made clear the government's dire situation, and the finance committee accepted the loan for lack of other options.[114] The domestic loan was not enough, and Kokovtsov had to return to the German bank of Mendelssohn and Company. Germany could only extend short-term loans. The finance committee authorized Mendelssohn to raise up to 200 million rubles, but in the end only 150 million could be placed at the rate of 7.28 percent.[115]

The Russian government, unable to float any more badly needed external debt, began peace negotiations. On September 5, 1905, the Treaty of Portsmouth was signed, formally ending the war.

Japanese and Russian financing of the Russo-Japanese War highlights the effect of tax capacity on war finance. Japan was extremely successful at financing its war effort. After successfully reforming its tax system and its bureaucratic capacity to extract revenue in the years prior to the war, Japan, for the first time, was able to finance a portion of the war with taxes. Japan, however, needed currency other than yen to effectively fight the Russians. Similar to Britain during World War II, Japan needed to import goods to fight the war. Because a series of balance of payments deficits left Japan with a shortage of reserve currency, the country had to engage in foreign war finance. Under the guidance of a US investment bank and aided by a series of battlefield successes, Japan was able to finance the war via external extraction at a low cost.

Weak bureaucratic capacity to extract revenue limited Russia's war finance strategy. Unable to pay for the war by taxation, Russia turned to other forms of war finance. Initially the Russian government floated domestic debt. However, by maintaining the gold standard, the Russian government was unable to raise enough domestic debt to finance a costly war. If Russia wanted to continue fighting, the government could either print or turn to foreign war finance. In the spring of 1904, the Russian government asked its French ally for credit and France complied. For the first year of the war, Russia had access to cheap credit as French and German investors evinced a high demand from Russian debt. However, the financing of the war became extremely costly in the spring of 1905 as investors no longer perceived Russia to be able to win the war or pay back its debt.

6

# CONFRONTING THE COSTS OF WAR, 1823–2003

The previous empirical chapters provided evidence for my theory of how states pay for war. This chapter seeks to lay the foundation of future war finance studies through a series of descriptive statistics using a novel data set. The data presented seek to commence the debate on the following war finance questions: While the dominant war finance narrative is tax or borrow, how often do taxation and debt alone actually characterize a state's war finance strategy and to what extent? How often do states resort to other means of war finance such as printing and external funding? Have the means of war finance changed over time or remained consistent? Does the cost of war affect a state's war finance strategy? Once these questions are addressed, the data can then be used to explore the effect of war finance on prominent topics in political science. For example, what is the relationship between war finance and military duration and outcome? Does the manner of war finance affect leadership survival? What are the implications of war finance on alliance relationships during wartime?

Until now, there has been no existing work that collected or employed large-N analysis on war finance.[1] Data sets measuring resource potential, the supposed pool of money policymakers could draw on to confront the costs of war, have been used as a proxy. Early works studying war outcome looked at the preponderance of power and, consequently, national capabilities. These studies use indices that account for a state's potential tax revenue and foreign aid.[2] In the same vein there are scholars who look to a state's ability to obtain large amounts of cheap credit.[3]

The counterparts to these resource potential data sets are those measuring military expenditures such as the Correlates of War Project's Composite Index of

National Capabilities or the Stockholm's International Peace Research Institute's Military Expenditures Data Set.[4] While these data sets are important building blocks to understanding a state's potential financial and, consequently, military power, they do not address how states actually pay for war. Through the creation of the war finance data set presented in this chapter, this book bridges this gap between resource potential and actual military expenditures to provide a comprehensive account of how interstate wars have been financed from 1823–2003.

## Confronting the Cost of War Data

The data set encompasses all interstate war principal belligerents in wars over six months long from 1823 to 2003.[5] Principal belligerents are those states considered major decision makers in the war, those whose contributions to the fighting force (i.e., number of troops) are sufficient to make them independent decision makers about the course of the war.[6] Nonprincipal belligerents are excluded in an attempt to isolate states whose war effort places economic stress on their economy. For example, in the Korean War, only the United States, China, North Korea, and South Korea are considered principal belligerents.[7]

The unit of analysis is war finance by participant aggregated over the entirety of a war. As previously discussed, war finance can be an endogenous process, as war finance in year one affects war finance in year two, etc. Unfortunately, war finance information by country-year is not readily available for the majority of observations in the data set. To compensate for data limitations, I use country-war. I use the United States' financing of World War I as an example: instead of taking the percentage of World War I financed by taxation by the United States for each fiscal year (1917, 1918, and 1919—about 30 percent, 25 percent, and 22 percent, respectively), I aggregate over the entire war, of which 26.5 percent was paid for by taxation. It should be noted that while the war ends in November 1918, prior to 1976, the US fiscal year began on 1 July and ended on 30 June. Hence, I include through fiscal year 1919 to capture the entire cost of and financing of the war effort.[8] Of the ninety-four cases in the data set, twenty-five observations take place in the post–World War II era. Geographically, over half of the wars fought involve participants from European states, Russia, and the United States.[9]

The data set captures the primary means by which a state can finance war. I account for how much of the cost of a war is met by taxation as well as domestic borrowing, which encompasses all forms of borrowing, ranging from a bond campaign to general public debt. I also account for printing, including when the state issues nonmonetized debt from its central bank. I also include the extent to which a war is paid for by domestic means. Domestic war finance is a broad variable that encompasses all domestic revenues, including but not limited to taxation, existing coffers, domestic borrowing, and printing money. It is an attempt to capture how much of the war burden was met by the state.

I account for the presence of borrowing (did the state borrow or not and to what extent, and the location of borrowing—if the state borrowed from either the United States or Soviet Union). I also include plunder, which occurs when goods are taken by force from the area of conflict. I then account for various external forms of funding. I account for external extraction (did the state use money or aid from abroad to fund its war effort). External extraction is a broad variable. It includes all forms of aid from outside a country's borders, including plunder, grants, loans, or other means of external extraction.

I triangulate primary and secondary sources to form the majority of observations in the data set.[10] During the interwar years, the League of Nation's statistical publications are an excellent source, particularly for the various Sino-Japanese wars. In the post–World War II era, primary sources include documents collected from the *Foreign Relations of the United States* (FRUS). During the Cold War, US intelligence estimates from various intelligence and defense agencies provide a plethora of information for the various "proxy wars." Specifically, intelligence estimates were helpful to understand funding for the various Southeast Asian wars and Arab-Israeli wars. While primary sources are useful, secondary sources provided the core of information for the data set.[11]

It is important to note some of the data are in the form of numerical estimates of how much of a particular war was financed by a specific mean(s). Most of the data, however, are qualitative in nature. Data availability for the Russian and Turkish war finance effort during the Russo-Turkish War of 1877 provides an example. Data on the Russian war effort are based on an estimate of the actual amount borrowed and printed:

> Since April 12, 1877. . . . The cost of the campaign has been enormous. In November 1877, we concluded three domestic loans for 350,000,000 paper roubles [*sic*] and one foreign loan for 93,750,000 paper roubles or 125,000,000 paper roubles. In addition to this, 285,000,000 roubles were advanced by the Imperial bank, the aggregate sum of the cost amounting to at least 800,000,000 roubles. Beckoning the expensive of the return march at 50,000,00 roubles, we have a grand total of 850,000,000 roubles, which will take 45,000,000 roubles a year in interest and sinking fund. Now as the outlay occasioned by the Imperial debt is given at 108,000,000 roubles a year in the Budget for 1877. It follows that the war has raised our debt nearly one-half. . . . It is estimated in this country that the war has cost in one way and another about L100,000,000.[12]

> Just before the outbreak of the Russo-Turkish war, the notes in circulation amounted to a little over 780,000,000 rubles. During the war there was an additional issue of 417,000,000 rubles.[13]

In contrast, data for Turkey's war effort are qualitative. These sources suggest Turkey attempted to raise taxes, yet the war effort hampered the state's ability to do so. As a result, the army was forced to plunder and the state had to borrow. This data are descriptive in nature:

> They [Turkish Parliament] did, however, accept all the heavy expenditures required for the war, which produced a substantial deficit, and they approved increases in income, property, and animal taxes to compensate. They also approved a compulsory internal loan requiring property owners and civil servants alike to purchase government bonds according to their wealth and means.[14]
>
> A forced loan was voted by the Parliament before its dissolution, and was to have come into operation in August; but owing to the poverty-stricken condition of the people, it was found impracticable to enforce the payment of the double taxes.[15]
>
> If the ordinary taxes could have been possibly collected by the Turks during the campaign, they certainly need not have been embarrassed for lack of the "sinews of war," considered the rather sweeping reductions in their payments. Not only, however, [does] an enemy occupy their most lucrative province, but that enemy, on the 31st July, issued a decree which was to have an important bearing on the payments by those who had hitherto been Turkish tax-payers.[16]
>
> The Turkish army was recruited solely from the Mohammedan population, Christian subjects of the Sultan were not allowed to bear arms, but paid a poll-tax in lieu of military service. It would perhaps be more accurate to say that they were compelled to take out annual licenses to carry their heads, the receipt of the tax bearing the words "The bearer is entitled to keep his head for one year." Exemptions from service were frequent, and easily obtained by the upper classes.[17]
>
> The Army lived almost entirely on the country it occupied.[18]
>
> By 1876 the prosecution of the war had forced the treasury to assume an additional burden of 7.45 billion kurus of debt.[19]

These two examples, Russia and Turkey in the Russo-Turkish War of 1877, demonstrate the complexities of data collection.[20] They also demonstrate, however, information availability. To overcome data limitations, the data set is comprised using a mix of dummy and discrete variables rather than point values. The discrete variables are captured by using an ordinal scale of 0–4: 0 = none of the cost of the war was met by X variable; 1 = under 25 percent of the cost of the war was met by X variable; 2 = between 25–50 percent of the cost of the war was met by X variable; 3 = between 50–75 percent of the cost of war was met by X variable; and 4 = over 75 percent of the cost of the war was met by X variable. Dummy variables are captured through a simple 0 or 1, reflecting whether the method of war finance in question occurred or not.

The following section discusses the data collected. Given that this chapter is the first foray into cross-national war finance data analysis, I provide anecdotal evidence or discussion of unique cases where possible. As the goal of this chapter is to promote future research that incorporates the study of war finance, I highlight examples when the dynamics of the war affect a state's war finance strategy.

## Descriptive Statistics: A Quantitative History of War Finance since 1823

How have wars been financed over the past two hundred years? First, since 1950, printing, plunder, taxation, and domestic debt have comprised a smaller percentage of state's war finance strategies than prior to 1950. In regards to printing, of the thirty cases of printing in the data set, only three have taken place after 1945: the Republic of Korea during the Korean War, the Republic of Vietnam during the Vietnam War, and the United States during the Vietnam War.[21]

Furthermore, there are only two cases in which states relied on printing to finance at least 75 percent of the war: Argentina during the La Plata War and Paraguay during the Lopez War. In both of these cases, the respective belligerents attempted to raise taxes and float debt to secure enough revenues to finance their war efforts. Argentina used a variety of methods to finance the La Plata War. There was a failed attempt to implement a capital tax and land rents were successfully implemented but never made a significant impact in financing the war.[22] As a result of these failed attempts, 200 million pesos were printed to cover the costs of the war.[23]

Similar to Argentina during the La Plata War, when the Lopez War broke out, Paraguayan President Lopez attempted to pay for the war though the selling of yerba mate, loan guarantees (the Paraguayan Congress authorized a loan of 25,000,000 pesos), and by yerba and land revenues. This strategy failed due to the increasingly effective blockade of the Parana River, the decrease in yerba harvesting, and the consumption of yerba by troops.[24] The president attempted to raise

£200,000 sterling on the money markets of Buenos Aires but found no buyers. The republic now had to depend solely on its internal financial reserves, which included property confiscated from the president's political rivals and seized from enemy nationals. Paraguay turned to paper emissions of 2,900,000 pesos in March 1865, more than doubling the amount of paper pesos in circulation. In the same month, Solano Lopez decreed that all government purchases would be paid solely in paper currency, rather than one-third in specie and two-thirds in paper as in the past.

Second, plunder, like printing, was much more prominent in the nineteenth century than the twentieth century.[25] Of the twenty-two cases in which plunder was documented, 81 percent took place prior to 1950. The five cases of plunder in the postwar era are the Peoples Republic of Korea during the Korean War, the Democratic Republic of Vietnam during the Vietnam War and the Vietnamese-Cambodian Border War, Chad during the War over the Aouzou Strip, and Iraq during the Gulf War. When belligerents do resort to plunder, it only comprises a small percent of their war finance strategy. Only two states have financed more than 25 percent of their war by plunder, Germany during the First Schleswig-Holstein War and Chile during the Pacific War.

During the First Schleswig-Holstein War plunder played a large part in financing the war effort. When the town of Rendsburg was captured, the Schleswig Holsteiners also captured stored Danish military funds, which came to about 2.5 million RBD, to cover part of the expenses for the first year of the war.[26] Furthermore, after the move into Jutland, General Wrangel demanded that the local populations supply his army and tasked patrols to collect provisions.[27] During the Pacific War, Chilean military successes resulted both in an increase in the price of foreign bonds on American and European markets and allowed the state to control the disputed territory of Tarapacá, which allowed it to profit from Peruvian owned exports of guano and nitrates.[28]

Third, taxation has consistently comprised a small percentage of a state's war finance strategy and appears to be further decreasing in the postwar era. Half of all belligerents in the data set, forty-eight, enacted new taxes to confront the costs of war. While these states may have set the intention of paying for a significant percentage of the war via taxation, only nine belligerents have financed 25 percent or more of their wars using tax revenues: Turkey during the Russo-Turkish War of 1828–1829; Denmark in the First Schleswig-Holstein War; France during the Franco-Turkish War; Britain during the Crimean War and World War II; the United States during World War I, World War II, and the Korean War; and Russia during World War II. Of these nine cases, four of them are during the World Wars.

While in general taxation plays a small role in war finance strategy, it appears to be declining further. Taxation has not comprised a significant component, 25 percent or more, of a state's war finance strategy in more than sixty years. The last case was the United States during the Korean War. The declining trend is also reflected in the data. Prior to 1950, 63 percent of states included at least some taxation in their war finance strategy, while during the postwar era, only 52 percent have included taxation.

Fourth, of the various war finance means, borrowing is the foremost war finance method. From 1823 to 2003, 88 percent of states have engaged in at least some form of borrowing, either domestic or from abroad to confront the cost of war.[29] In regards to domestic debt, 63 percent of states financed at least some of their war efforts via domestic debt. The majority of belligerents have a moderate reliance, 25 percent–75 percent of their war finance strategy, on domestic debt. Only six belligerents—France during the Crimean and Franco-Prussian War, Japan during the First and Second Sino Japanese War, Austria-Hungary during World War I, and Ethiopia during the Badme Border War—have financed 75 percent or more of their wars by domestic debt.[30] Akin to taxation, domestic debt as a form of war finance is also decreasing in the postwar era. Prior to 1950, 68 percent of states incorporated domestic debt into their strategy, whereas in the postwar era, only 40 percent have.

Fifth, while domestic debt as a percentage of a state's war finance strategy is in decline, foreign borrowing appears to be on the rise. Of the belligerents in the data set, 57 percent engaged in some form of foreign debt. Prior to 1950, 52 percent of belligerents engaged in foreign debt, whereas 72 percent have in the postwar era. Once borrowing from at home and abroad is taken into account, fourteen belligerents financed 75 percent or more of their war via debt. Three of these fourteen cases are in the postwar era—Ethiopia during the Ethiopian-Somalian War and the United States during the wars in Afghanistan and Iraq.

If one takes into account all forms of foreign war finance, the figures are more dramatic. Prior to 1950, 25 percent of states used resources from abroad to cover 25 percent or more of the cost of war. After 1950, 80 percent of states relied on resources from abroad to cover 25 percent or more of the war. Furthermore, three (Ethiopia and Somalia during the Ethiopian-Somalian War and Chad during the War over the Aouzou Strip) of the four cases in which a belligerent relied on foreign finance to cover 75 percent or more of the wars cost occurred in the post–World War II era.[31] Not only are belligerents increasing their reliance on foreign war finance, but also their reliance was specifically on the Soviet Union or United States during the Cold War. After 1950, 68 percent of belligerents received funds from one of the two superpowers.

Finally, to conceive of war finance in the form of tax or borrow misses the broader picture of how wars are financed. Few states finance their wars within this dichotomy. Few belligerents (nineteen) rely heavily (75 percent or more) on just one method of war finance. Even fewer (ten) combine of all four methods—taxation, domestic debt, printing, and external war finance.[32] Most belligerents also incorporate plunder or external extraction into their war finance strategy.

## The Cost of War and War Finance

Economists suggest that as the cost of war rises, states should borrow more and tax less. Tax smoothing theories recommend that states should avoid sharp increases in taxation to meet large exogenous increases in government expenditure (i.e., financing a costly war). A sharp increase in taxation, such that the government achieves a balanced budget, leads to negative externalities on labor supply, consumption, output, and capital. Thus states should borrow to pay for their wars. Accordingly, as the cost of war rises, the percentage of the war paid by taxation should decrease. Unfortunately, data on the cost of war are scant.[33] However, there are reliable data on war cost and financing of wars fought by the United States as well as the primary belligerents in the World Wars.

In regards to US war finance, counter to what we should expect from tax smoothing theories, there is a positive relationship between the cost of war and the percentage of the war financed by taxation. Figure 6.1 presents the relationship between the cost of each interstate war fought by the United States as a percentage of GDP for the most expensive year of the war and the percentage of the war paid for by taxation. Taxation met 50 percent of the costliest war fought by the United States, World War II, whereas tax revenue contributed minimally to the least costly American wars.

The relationship between the cost of World War I for the various belligerents and the percentage of said cost met by taxation suggests no relationship between the two variables. As seen in figure 6.2, taxation met a negligable amount of the cost of war for the costliest belligerent, Germany, as well as the least costly, Austria-Hungrary. Only the United States, France, and Britain were able to incorporate taxation into their war finance strategy.

These two graphs exploring the relationship between war cost and war finance suggest that the relationship between the cost of war and finance is more complex than at first blush. The cost of a war alone does not, as some economists would predict or prescribe, necessarily dictate how much of a war is financed by taxation. However, much more work needs to be done in this area before more conclusions can be drawn.

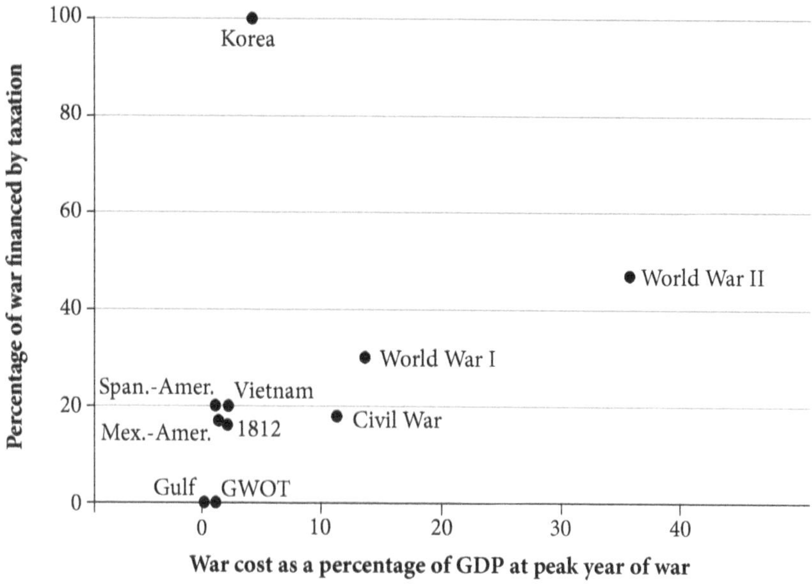


**FIGURE 6.1** The relationship between war cost and percent of war financed by taxation in US war finance

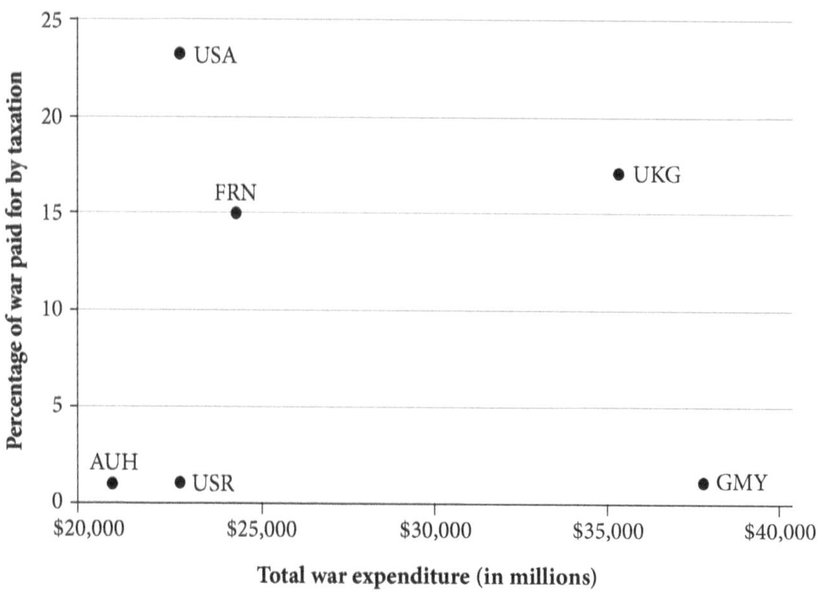


**FIGURE 6.2** Percentage of World War I cost by belligerent met by taxation

## Future Research

This chapter provides the first cross-national descriptive statistics of war finance. As such, it makes large strides toward understanding how states confront the cost of war. This advancement, however, leaves many aspects of war finance unaddressed. In what follows, I suggest how some of the descriptive statistics in addition to data presented in the previous empirical chapters could influence future research.

The data regarding external extraction during the Cold War exemplify the political aspect of war finance. When scholars discuss the role of credit in war finance, they look to sovereign debt yields and floating war debt on financial markets.[34] But war finance is not a purely economic transaction. For example, when the United States was funding the Republic of Vietnam during the Vietnam War, US policymakers were not concerned with the state's credit rating. They were concerned with ensuring that an ally and cobelligerent won the war. Combined with the discussion of how military success affects a state's creditworthiness in the cases of Japan and Russia during the Russo-Japanese War, these findings suggest that the traditional variables that increase a state's creditworthiness, such as regime type, and war finance need to be explored further.[35]

The data also suggest the importance of third parties and alliances.[36] Turning abroad to finance a war may be critical to the war effort, as demonstrated in the case of Britain during World War II. Yet wartime financial alliances are understudied. Under what conditions do states extend wartime financial aid?[37] Why did the United States extend credit to Britain during World War II, before it was a cobelligerent?[38] Would France and Germany have supported Russia's use of their credit markets during the Russo-Japanese War if they were not formal allies? In brief, how do alliances affect war finance?

The extent to which states turn to multiple methods of war finance also suggests that studies regarding the ability of states to mobilize resources for conflict must take an expansive view of resource potential. Even if states are unable to finance the war via taxation or debt, they can turn to printing or external extraction abroad. To pay for one of the longest interstate wars in history, Paraguay during the Paraguayan War incorporated large amounts of printing into its war finance strategy. A state may go bankrupt to pay for a war, but it can continue to pay for it nonetheless.

The data also leave a myriad of research areas to be explored. For example, for this work, the study of war finance begins once war has been initiated. Wars, however, are not fought in a vacuum. States often prepare for war, including financial mobilization, before the war starts. How does prewar mobilization affect war finance? Do states that initiate conflict face different war finance constraints or opportunities than those that do not?

Furthermore, this work focuses solely on long interstate wars. As discussed in chapter 1, short wars have different dynamics than long wars. How is war finance different for these wars? Are leaders constrained by the same set of assumptions? How does the immediacy of the war effort affect the political and economic cost of confronting an enemy? This study also does not take into account civil war finance. Civil wars necessarily divide the domestic population and weaken state capacity. How do these new domestic socioeconomic conditions affect war finance? Do these states increase their reliance on printing and external war finance as my argument would suggest, or do they resort to other means of war finance?

Another avenue of research is the effect of war finance on war outcome.[39] Russian and Japanese experiences in the Russo-Japanese War suggest that war finance contributed to war outcome. The war became so economically costly for the Russians by the fall of 1905 that the Russian government chose to sue for peace. The Japanese throughout 1905, on the other hand, experienced a cascade of foreign credit, reinforcing their war effort. The findings in other chapters do not put forward such a direct connection between war finance and war outcome. Thus, if war finance does affect war outcome, under what conditions does it do so?

In addition to war outcome, how does the manner of war finance affect the dynamic of war? For example, the manner of war finance could signal state capacity and resolve. A state financing a war by taxation may signal that the state has the capacity to raise taxes, and thus, it has access to a renewable source of revenue, implying that the state is capable of fighting a long war and public support for the war is high enough to allow political leaders to raise taxes. On the other hand, if a state is financing a war via printing, one might expect that state either to be constrained by low capacity or low support for the war. Low capacity and low supports suggest a potentially weak war effort. In sum, how do belligerents interpret the war finance strategies of their adversaries?

Moreover, does war finance effect the negotiation of conflict outcome? The manner in which a state confronts the cost of conflict has implications for negotiating settlement.[40] Did the citizens sacrifice to pay for the war? If they did, how did this sacrifice affect the state's war aims? Do the citizens now expect higher results to compensate for their sacrifice? Does the state now have costly debt they need to repay? The answers to these questions are essential for understanding the belligerents' needs and, therefore, mediating conflict resolution.

Another area of research for exploration is the relationship between the location of the war and war finance. When a state is fighting a war that is geographically far away, such as Britain during the Crimean War, it may change war finance. States fighting far away often purchase goods in theater as Britain purchased food and fodder in Turkey and Crimea instead of shipping these goods from the Isle of Britain. These purchases comprised a minuscule percentage of British war purchases, and the British were able to pay for these goods in pounds, as pounds were the dominant reserve currency at the time. However, if these purchases had been much larger, it may have placed stress on the British balance of payments. Thus under what conditions does the location of fighting affect war finance?

How does regime type affect war finance?[41] I argue that works suggesting democracies are better able to borrow and tax ignore crucial elements of state capacity as well as leaders' fears of inflation and support for the war effort. It is possible, however, that regime type affects war finance in more implicit ways than I was able to capture. Given that this is the first systematic study of interstate war finance, this work takes place at a higher level of aggregation with cruder measures of regime type. In regard to democratic regimes, it is possible that parliamentary or presidential regimes finance their wars differently. In regard to authoritarian regimes, it is possible that a military regime will tend to finance wars differently than personalistic dictatorships or single-party regimes. Each type of regime mentioned above interacts with society in a different way, possibly affecting war finance.

Over the past two centuries, how states pay for war has evolved. Plunder, printing, and even domestic debt have declined as the primary means of war finance while external extraction has become more prominent. Taxation has consistently comprised a minimal role in states' war finance strategy. Finally, preliminary analysis suggests the cost of war has either a positive or no effect on the percentage of the war financed by taxation. These findings, coupled with the insights from the empirical chapters, suggest that war finance is a product of both domestic interests and the international political environment. Thus the cross-national study of war finance has implications for understanding how domestic political forces and relative capabilities of great powers affect foreign security policies.

# Conclusion

# LONG WAR FINANCE IN PERSPECTIVE

The most influential ideas regarding war finance focus on the tax-versus-debt dichotomy, regime type, and creditworthiness. These frameworks structure the broader conversations regarding a state's resource potential and, therefore, a state's material capabilities. Thus they underpin the treatment of military power in international relations theory. I argue, however, that these conceptions of war finance do not adequately explain the variation in how states pay for long wars. To do so requires an interactive model that considers the broad array of war finance options at a state's disposal and the relationship between state capacity, domestic interests, the international political environment, and the war effort.

In regard to the array of war finance options, leaders have three broad means to choose from: direct resource extraction, characterized by direct taxation and bond campaigns; indirect resource extraction, characterized by indirect taxes, domestic debt, and printing; and external resource extraction, characterized by procuring resources from outside the state. The combination of means chosen forms a state's war finance strategy.

The war finance strategy that the state ultimately employs is a function of leaders' preferences and state capacity. Leaders are in a constant balancing act, weighing their desire to win the war and stay in power. Because each primary method of war finance—taxation, domestic debt, external funding, and printing—has different economic and political costs, leaders can decide how costly the policy will be. Leaders control these costs by choosing to what extent the war finance strategy is inflationary and the extent to which citizens interact with the policy chosen.

When fear of inflation is high, leaders will attempt to protect the domestic economy through an anti-inflationary war finance policy that emphasizes taxation. President Truman, as discussed in chapter 2, went to great lengths to guard the economy of the United States against rising prices during the Korean War. Influenced by the financing of World War II and confronting postwar inflation while in office, Truman attempted to pay for the entire war outright. The ability to generate this historical war finance anomaly was made feasible by public opinion. The US public, also scarred by the effects of inflation after World War II, was in favor of an anti-inflationary war finance policy. Moreover, public support for the war was high, as many Americans believed that the Korean War was World War III. The shared desire for an anti-inflationary war finance policy and high support for the war lowered the political costs of raising taxes.

The opposite scenario, low inflation fear and low public support, is illustrated in chapter 3 by President Johnson's financing of the Vietnam War. Johnson did not fear inflation during the first two years of the Vietnam War. He believed that the causes of inflation in the previous war were not present in the current US economy. Whereas the US economy in 1950 was destined for inflation, the US economy in 1965, facing a potential recession, was able to absorb the costs of a war without rising prices. This belief caused Johnson to pursue an indirect extraction policy, based not on taxation but on domestic debt. By 1967, rising prices caused a shift in US war finance policy. Now fearing inflation, Johnson attempted to raise taxes to pay for the continuing war effort. Whereas Johnson feared inflation, many Americans and congressional leaders did not. Moreover, by 1967, public support for the war was in sharp decline. Thus the political cost of raising taxes for an ailing policy was high. Consequently, Johnson's war finance tax bill was stalled in Congress for almost a year. The result was a war financed primarily by domestic debt and only minimally by taxation.

Truman's and Johnson's financing of the Korean and Vietnam wars demonstrates that the guns-versus-butter trade-off is not ubiquitous. Policymakers, particularly in developed economies, do not have to choose how to allocate a fixed amount of funds to finance a war, as funds are not fixed. States can borrow domestically, procure funding abroad, or print. Only when the fear of inflation is high does the guns-versus-butter trade-off become relevant. During the first years of the Vietnam War, President Johnson not only believed that both guns and butter were possible, as there was no fear of inflation, but that both guns and butter were necessary to combat a recession. It is only in 1967, when inflation began to negatively affect the economy of the United States, that a trade-off emerged. In contrast to Johnson's war finance policy, President Truman feared inflation from the moment the Korean War began. Thus he engaged directly in the guns-versus-butter trade-off, raising taxes and decreasing spending immediately to protect the domestic economy.

Both chapters also address monetary policy's limited role when combating inflation. During the Korean War, both the Federal Reserve and the Truman administration were preoccupied with managing the volume of World War II debt. Consequently, the traditional means used by the Federal Reserve to combat inflation were ineffective. Hence, emphasis was placed on fiscal policy to combat rising prices. During the Vietnam War, monetary policy was an available tool, yet was not preferred by many members of Congress, the Federal Reserve, or the Johnson administration due to its negative effects on various sectors of the economy, particularly housing. Akin to the Korean War, taxation was the preferred means to combat inflation. The preference of fiscal policy over monetary policy in both cases suggests the efficacy and role of central banks to fight inflation during wartime needs further exploration.

The experiences of President Johnson in the early years of the Vietnam War also suggests that the manner of war finance can either promote or obscure the public's awareness of the war. When a state is fighting a war, only a fraction of its citizens are mobilized as either soldiers or as participants in war-supporting industries. How a war is financed may be the only direct link between all members of society and the war. When a war is paid for by taxation, particularly direct taxes or domestic debt in a form of a bond campaign, society is conscious of the policy for which they are paying. Wars financed via these means allow citizens to evaluate their leader's foreign policy choices and sanction that leader if they disagree. If a leader chooses to finance a war by printing or funding from abroad, that direct connection between citizens and the war is lost. Leaders, consequently, are able to shield their policy choices, lowering the political costs of fighting the war. Controlling this cost is particularly important in longer wars when the rally-around-the-flag effect has faded.

The extent to which leaders can exercise their war finance preferences is conditioned by the state's extractive capacity. When a state is facing low currency reserves yet needs to continue procuring goods from abroad to fight the war, that state has no choice but to engage in external resource extraction. A leader may attempt to promote the flow of currency into the state through increasing exports or decreasing imports, but the dynamics of war suggest this effort is unsustainable. This constraint is evident in chapters 5 and 6 with British financing of World War II and Japanese financing of the Russo-Japanese War. In both of these cases, the respective governments were financing their wars domestically at cheap economic cost through a combination of taxation and domestic debt. Both states, however, were constrained by their need to procure inputs for the war effort from abroad due to low currency reserves. While the Japanese were able to secure cheap credit in the United States and England to finance their war with Russia, the British incurred a costly loan from the United States.

Chapter 5 also discussed the role of extractive capacity and how belligerents cope with low capacity while trying to fight a war. While Japan was able to improve on its tax capacity before the war, Russia was not. Thus Japan was able to incorporate a larger percentage of taxation into its war finance strategy than Russia. Russia, refusing to capitulate, was forced to turn to other means of war finance—domestic debt and external extraction. Russian inability to increase its tax capacity before and during the war implies that the notion that wars make states needs to be qualified. These cases suggests wars increase state capacity to extract tax revenue when leaders are committed to paying for the war via direct resource extraction, the state is sufficiently monetized, and taxes are implemented on citizens and institutions who have the means to pay. However, the pressures of the war effort can obscure a leader's commitment to tax revenue, as the war may force the leader to abandon taxation for other more immediately forthcoming forms of revenue.

How states pay for long wars provides leaders with opportunities to expand or contract the state's economy and shape society's relationship to the war effort. These opportunities, however, are shaped by the state's resource extraction capacity, location of war inputs, and the dynamics of the war.

## The Political Economy of Warfare

As discussed in the Introduction of this book, one cannot understand domestic politics without understanding international forces and vice versa. Thus this study of war finance fits within the expanding body of work that reflects the tenants of neoclassical realism. It complements the domestic interest–international environment interaction embraced by neoclassical realists to explain foreign policy choices and adds to it the dynamics of warfare. This work indicates that the effects of warfare on the ability of the state to mobilize resources from at home and abroad are omnipresent yet undertheorized. More specifically, the characteristics of war—that is, duration or intensity—or how a war unfolds—the timing of battlefield successes—shapes the preferences of political actors as well as state capacity.

Public support for the war is an obvious example of how warfare effects the prosecution of war finance policy. As a war unfolds, battlefield successes and number of casualties shape public support for the war effort, in turn affecting leaders' cost-benefit analysis when deciding what war finance strategy to choose. A more nuanced way to approach public support for war is timing. President Truman, for example, raised taxes as soon as the Korean War began and stated that he intended to pay for the entire war by taxation. He was able to pass these taxes through Congress immediately, as support for the war was high. President Johnson, by contrast, attempted to incorporate taxation into his war finance policy two years after war onset when support for the war was in sharp decline. Thus it took almost a year for Congress to pass his tax bill. How these wars unfolded and their status when Truman and Johnson introduced their war finance strategies to the public were crucial elements of policy implementation for both Truman and Johnson. Their experiences suggest that if a leader wants to finance a war via taxation, it should be done early in the war when support for the war is high.

In addition, the expectation of battlefield success has implications for war finance. If policymakers perceive the war to be short and an easy victory, they will engage in different war finance policies than those who perceive the war effort to be long and arduous. From war onset in Korea, President Truman as well as American citizens believed they were engaging in World War III. As a result, the public horded goods, driving up prices, and Truman prepared a sustainable war economy to finance a long, costly conflict. In addition, wartime creditors respond to expected victory and defeat. During the Russo-Japanese War, Russia initially secured cheap credit, as they were the expected victors, and faced worsening credit as battlefield losses mounted. These findings suggest leaders should consider not just how the war unfolds, but also how to manage the public and other interested parties' expectations of the duration and outcome of the conflict.

The location of the kinetic war effort also affects state capacity. For example, the war can affect extractive capacity, either directly decreasing it through bombing or invasion or indirectly through blockades. States fighting abroad are sheltered from such incursions into their extraction capacity. Hence, wars fought abroad may affect the prosecution of the war effort, and consequently, a state's war finance strategy, differently than wars fought on a state's territory or on an ally's territory.

How the war itself affects the war finance policy suggests that more conceptions of warfare are needed. The expectations of leaders, policymakers, and citizens of how the war will unfold, battlefield outcome and casualty tempo, and conflict locale all have implications for the ability of the state to mobilize resources for war. The cases in this book suggest these variables affect both leadership preferences and state capacity in various ways. Hence as the study of resource mobilization for war continues, future works must take the dynamics of warfare into account.

Regardless of global economic upturns or downturns, financial globalization, or the distribution of power in the international system, states will have to pay for their wars. The variation of war finance options available allows leaders to choose the political and economic costs of war. Leaders can select from various types of taxes and debt, as well as printing, plunder, austerity measures, and external extraction. The preferences of leaders get updated as the war unfolds and leaders confront the state's capacity to extract revenue and ability to purchase inputs for war from abroad.

Wars are painful, tragic events. In addition to casualties, economies can be ruined, leaders and parties can be voted out of office, and state power in the international system may be diminished. These costs of war, however, can be exacerbated or mitigated by how the war is financed. The manner of war finance can protect or destroy the domestic economy, promote or obstruct political transparency, and aid or hinder the war effort.

# Notes

## INTRODUCTION. MAKING MONEY, MAKING WAR

1. E. R. A. Seligman, "The Cost of War and How It Was Met," *American Economic Review* 9 (December 1919): 793. Figures are in 1919 dollars.

2. H. M. Hozier, *The Russo-Turkish War*, vol. 4 (1878; reprint London: Elibron Classics/ William Mackenzie, 2005), 604.

3. "Lack of Funds May End Balkan War," *Wall Street Journal*, July 8, 1913.

4. Seligman, "The Cost of War."

5. Gabriel Ardant, "Financial Policy and Economic Infrastructure of Modern States and Nations," in *The Formation of National State in Western Europe*, ed. Charles Tilly (Princeton, NJ: Princeton University Press, 1975). Select examples of other studies that link war finance and state building are R. F. Bensel, *Yankee Leviathan: The Origins of Central State Authority in America, 1859–1877* (New York: Cambridge University Press, 1990); M.A. Centeno, *Blood and Debt: War and the Nation-State in Latin America* (University Park: Pennsylvania State University Press, 2002); B.M. Downing, *The Military Revolution and Political Change: Origins of Democracy and Autocracy in Early Modern Europe* (Princeton, NJ: Princeton University Press, 1992); T. Ertman, *Birth of the Leviathan: Building States and Regimes in Medieval and Early Modern Europe* (Cambridge: Cambridge University Press, 1997); S. D. Pollack, *War, Revenue, and State Building: Financing the Development of the American State* (Ithaca, NY: Cornell University Press, 2009); K. Scheve and D. Stasavage, "The Conscription of Wealth: Mass Warfare and the Demand for Progressive Taxation," *International Organization* 64 (fall 2010): 529–561; and K. Scheve and D. Stasavage, "Democracy, War, and Wealth: Evidence from Two Centuries of Inheritance Taxation," *American Political Science Review* 106.1 (2012): 81–102.

6. A. C. Lamborn, "Power and the Politics of Extraction," *International Studies Quarterly* 27 (1983): 125–146; and M. Mastanduno, D. Lake, and G.J. Ikenberry, "Toward a Realist Theory of State Action," *International Studies Quarterly* 22 (1989): 457–474.

7. K. Knorr, *The Power of Nations: The Political Economy of International Relations* (New York: Basic Books, 1975); A. F. K. Organski and J. Kugler, *The War Ledger* (Chicago: University of Chicago Press, 1980); J. Kugler and W. Domke, "Comparing the Strength of Nations," *Comparative Political Studies* 19.1 (1986): 39–69.

8. Paul Kennedy, *The Rise and Fall of the Great Powers: Economic Change and Military Conflict from 1500 to 2000* (New York: Random House, 1987); K.A. Rasler and W.R. Thompson, "Global Wars, Public Debts, and the Long Cycle," *World Politics* 25.4 (1983): 489–516; K.A. Rasler and W.R. Thompson, *War and State Making: The Shaping of the Global Powers* (Boston: Unwin Hyman, 1989).

9. K. A. Schultz and B. R. Weingast, "The Democratic Advantage: Institutional Foundations of Financial Power in International Competition," *International Organization* 57 (winter 2003): 3–42. In an unpublished manuscript, Shinju Fujihira also argued that war finance was contingent on regime type. Fujihira asserted that liberal democracies are better able to collect taxes to finance a war because representative institutions characterize them. These institutions enable capital and labor to overcome class disputes and reach a workable compromise between their regressive and progressive positions. S. Fujihira, *Conscripting Money: Total War and Fiscal Revolution in the Twentieth Century* (Ph.D. diss., Princeton University, 2000).

10. David Hume, "Part II, Essay IX," *Essays, Moral, Political, Literary* (1742; reprint Indianapolis: Liberty Fund, 1987); Adam Smith, *An Inquiry into the Nature and Causes of the Wealth of Nations*, 5th ed., vol. 2 (1776; reprint Indianapolis: Liberty Fund, 1981); David Ricardo, "Chapter XVII: Taxes on Other Commodities than Raw Produce," In *The Works of David Ricardo,* ed. J.R. McCulloch (1846; reprint London: John Murray, 1888); David Ricardo, "Essay on the Funding System," in *The Works of David Ricardo*, ed. J.R. McCulloch (1846; reprint London: John Murray, 1888); Alexander Hamilton, "First Report on the Public Credit (Communicated to the House of Representatives, January 14, 1790)," in *The Works of Alexander Hamilton*, vol. 2, ed. H.C. Lodge (New York: Knickerbocker Press, 1904); and Francis Hirst, *The Political Economy of War* (London: J. M. Dent & Sons, 1915).

11. Two twentieth-century examples of such works are A.C. Pigou's *The Economy and Finance of War: Being a Discussion of the Real Costs of the War and the Way in Which They Should be Met* (London: J. M. Dent & Sons, 1916); and John Maynard Keynes's *How to Pay for the War: A Radical Plan for the Chancellor of the Exchequer* (New York: Harcourt, 1940).

12. See R.J. Barro, "On the Determination of Public Debt," *Journal of Political Economy* 87 (1979): 940–971; R.E. Lucas and N. Stokey, "Optimal Fiscal and Monetary Policy in an Economy without Capital," *Journal of Monetary Economics* 12 (1983): 55–93; L.E. Ohanian, "The Macroeconomic Effects of War Finance in the United States: World War II and the Korean War," *American Economic Review* 87.1 (1997): 23–40; L.E. Ohanian, *The Macroeconomic Effects of War Finance in the United States: Taxes, Inflation, and Deficit Finance* (New York: Garland, 1998).

13. Ohanian, *The Macroeconomic Effects of War Finance*, 8.

14. Schultz and Weingast, "The Democratic Advantage."

15. Michael Tomz, *Reputation and International Cooperation: Soverign Debt across Three Centuries* (Princeton, NJ: Princeton University Press, 2007).

16. Charles à Court Repington, *The War in the Far East, 1904–1905* (New York: E. P. Dutton, 1905).

17. There are many studies on the nature of the Japanese regime at the turn of the century. See M. Harries and S. Harries, *Soldiers of the Sun: The Rise and Fall of the Imperial Japanese Army* (New York: Random House, 1994), 37–38; S. Okamoto, *The Japanese Oligarchy and the Russo-Japanese War* (New York: Columbia University Press, 1970); D. Walder, *The Short Victorious War: The Russo-Japanese Conflict* (New York: Harper & Row, 1974), 35.

18. L. Seabrooke, *The Social Sources of Financial Power: Domestic Legitimacy and International Financial Orders* (Ithaca, NY: Cornell University Press, 2006); and S. Steinmo, *Taxation and Democracy: Swedish, British, and American Approaches to Financing the Modern State* (New Haven: Yale University, 1993) discuss the variation of tax rates within liberal regimes.

19. For a discussion of the importance of concept formation see G. Sartori, "Concept Misformation in Comparative Politics," *American Political Science Review* 64.4 (1970): 1035.

20. C. Tilly, ed., *The Formation of National States in Western Europe* (Princeton, NJ: Princeton University Press, 1975); C. Tilly, "War Making and State Making as Organized Crime," in *Bringing the State Back In*, ed. P. Evans, D. Rueschemeyer, and T. Skocpol (Cambridge: Cambridge University Press, 1985); C. Tilly, *Coercion, Capital, and European States, AD 990–1990* (Cambridge: Cambridge University Press, 1990).

21. Thus the study of war finance fits within the tradition of scholars such as Gourevitch's "The Second Image Reversed: The International Sources of Domestic Politics," *International Organization* 32 (1978): 881–912; Mastanduno, Lake, and Ikenberry's, "Towards a Realist Theory of State Action"; Robert D. Putnam's "Diplomacy and Domestic Politics: The Logic of Two Level Games," *International Organization* 42.3 (summer 1988):

427–460; Ira Katznelson and Martin Shefter's *Shaped by War and Trade: International Influences on American Political Development* (Princeton, NJ: Princeton University Press, 2003); and Steven E. Lobell, Norrin M. Ripsman, and Jeffrey W. Taliaferro's *Neoclassical Realism, the State, and Foreign Policy* (Cambridge: Cambridge University Press, 2009).

22. Lobell et al., *Neoclassical Realism.*

23. Stated by General Brehon B. Somerval, Commanding General Army Services Forces, 1942, quoted in K. Detzer, *The Army Reader* (New York: The Bobbs-Merrill, 1943), 266.

24. Pollack, *War, Revenue, and State Building,* 140.

25. R. M. Ketchum, *Saratoga: Turning Points of America's Revolutionary War* (New York: Henry Holt, 1997), 33.

26. Hume, *Essays, Moral, Political, Literary*, 355.

27. O. Anderson, *A Liberal State at War: English Politics and Economics during the Crimean War* (New York: St Martin's Press, 1967), 214.

28. For example, see the works of Scheve and Stasavage, "The Conscription of Wealth" and "Democracy, War, and Wealth."

29. H. E. Krooss, *American Economic Development* (Englewood Cliffs, NJ: Prentice-Hall, 1955), 455.

30. F. R. Fairchild, "German War Finance—A Review," in *War Finance*, vol. 3, ed. L. Neal (1922; reprint Brookfield, VT: Edward Elgar, 1994), 254–255.

31. For an excellent account of war finance policy and the resulting inflation, see G. D. Feldman, *The Great Disorder: Politics, Economics, and Society in the German Inflation 1914–1924* (Oxford: Oxford University Press, 1997).

## CHAPTER 1. HOW STATES PAY FOR WARS

1. The excerpt is from Samuel Johnson's (1749) "The Vanity of Human Wishes" and can also be found as the epitaph to Hirst's 1915 work, *Political Economy of War*, 1.

2. Smith, *An Inquiry into the Nature and Causes of the Wealth of Nations.*

3. Given the difficulty of defining and measuring various war finance concepts, it is not surprising that scholars neglect this important foundational step. Even policymakers avoid the subject. In 1967, Pentagon comptroller Robert N. Anthony, in a testimony regarding the economic effects of Vietnam spending, stated, "As I have discussed with you before, Senator [Stuart] Symington, we do not have a cost accounting system for the Vietnam conflict. I think you and everyone agrees that one does not set up a cost accounting system for a war" ("Economic Effect of Vietnam Spending," *Hearings Before the Joint Committee, Congress of the United States, Ninetieth Congress, First Session, April 24–27, 1967,* vol. 1 [Washington, DC: US Government Printing Office, 1967]). In regards to constructing the cost of US war efforts, Anthony's testimony is not unique. The most recent Congressional Research Service (CRS) report on the costs of the US war efforts in Iraq and Afghanistan report similar difficulties. According to Amy Belasco, the Government Accountability Office (GAO), the Congressional Budget Office (CBO), and CRS have all testified before Congress about the limited transparency in the Department of Defense (DOD) war cost estimating and reporting (see testimony to House Budget Committee, October 24, 2007, July 31, 2007, and testimony to Subcommittee on National Security, Emerging Threats and International Affairs, House Government Reform, July 18, 2006). While the DOD has provided considerably more justification for its war cost requests beginning with the FY2007 Supplemental report, many questions remain difficult to answer—such as the effect of changes in troop levels on costs—and there continue to be unexplained discrepancies in DOD's war cost reports (A. Belasco, *The Cost of Iraq, Afghanistan, and Other Global War on Terror Operations Since 9/11* [Washington, DC: Congressional Research Service, 2011], 42–43).

4. For an early analysis of what may be included in the cost of war, see S.R. Giffen's discussion of the cost of the Franco-Prussian war, *Economic Inquiries and Studies,* vol. 1 (London: George Bell, 1904). For the most recent discussion of what is included in measuring the cost of recent US wars, see Belasco, *The Cost of Iraq*, appendixes C and D. For an expansive conceptualization of the cost of war, see E.L. Bogart's discussion of the cost of World War I or Stiglitz and Bilmes's discussion of the cost of the 2003 Iraq war to the United States: E.L. Bogart, *War Costs and Their Financing* (New York: D. Appleton, 1921), chap. 14; J.E. Stiglitz and L.J. Bilmes, *The Three Trillion Dollar War: The True Cost of the Iraq Conflict* (New York: W. W. Norton, 2008).

5. Seligman, "The Cost of the War," 741.

6. Bogart estimates the net cost of the war effort to be $22.625 billion and advances to allies to be $9.455 billion. Thus the gross cost was slightly more than $32 billion. If we include costs through 30 June 1920, $9.711 billion had been allotted to various allies by the United States. Through June 1920, the United States advanced $4.3 billion to Great Britain, $2.85 billion to France, $1.59 billion to Italy, $187 million to Russia, $341 million to Belgium, $27 million to Serbia, $30 million to Romania, $43 million to Greece, $50 million to Czecho-Slovaks, $10 million to Cuba, and finally, $5 million to Liberia. See E.L. Bogart, *Direct and Indirect Costs of the Great World War* (New York: Oxford University Press, 1920), 231.

7. See Stiglitz and Bilmes, *The Three Trillion Dollar War.*

8. Michael Barnett argued that governments can choose among three broad types of state strategies for war preparation: accommodational, restructural, and international. An accommodational strategy relies on already-existing policy instruments, whereas a restructural strategy occurs when state managers attempt to restructure the present state-society compact in order to increase the total amount of resources available. An international strategy occurs when a state is highly constrained by its domestic context and, consequently, attempts to distribute the costs of war onto foreign actors. The broadness of Barnett's typology does not provide us with the analytical leverage to understand the specifics of war finance, the variation of policy outcomes regarding taxation, borrowing, external extraction, and other less conventional means. Furthermore, Barnett does not offer a framework for how these various strategies interact. For example, a state may be engaged in both an international and accommodational strategy simultaneously. As a result, this work deviates from Barnett's typology in an attempt to more directly understand the dynamics of war finance. See *Confronting the Costs of War: Military Power, State, and Society in Egypt and Israel* (Princeton, NJ: Princeton University Press, 1992).

9. Adapted from the International Labor Organization, Forced Labor Convention from 1930.

10. Forced labor has been present in numerous wars. One prominent example is Russian forced labor during the Russo-Turkish War of 1828. The Russians forced the labor of sixteen thousand peasants who were employed in making hay on the banks of the Danube (F.R. Chesney, *The Russio-Turkish Campaigns of 1828 and 1829* [New York: Redfield, 1854], 76). During the Russo-Turkish War of 1877, the Turkish troops received no regular pay; they were merely lodged and fed by the state (Hozier, *The Russo-Turkish War*, 605).

11. Germany used forced savings plans or involuntary borrowing during World War II (A. Tooze, *The Wages of Destruction: The Making and Breaking of the Nazi Economy* [New York: Viking, 2007]), a method that John Maynard Keynes, in his treatise *How to Pay for the War*, suggested should be a component of Allied war finance. During the Greco-Turkish War of 1919–1922, Greece forced a loan campaign on its population. On April 10, 1922, Greek finance minister Petros Protopapadakis ordered that every piece of paper currency to be cut in two pieces. The side bearing the photograph of Minis-

ter Stavros was used as legal tender for one half of the face value of the note. In other words, 100 drachma notes cut in two became legal tender for 50 drachma and the other 50 drachma became government revenue (M. Mazower, *Greece and the Inter-War Economic Crisis* [Oxford: Oxford University Press, 1991]). Early presence of forced loans can be seen in England under Edward I to finance his campaign in Flanders against the French. "Further, foodstuffs were requisitioned on a massive scale to supply the armies . . . and a large forced loan in wool was ordered in July 1297" (E. Miller, "War, Taxation, and the English Economy in the Late Thirteenth and Early Fourteenth Centuries," in *War and Economic Development: Essays in Memory of David Joslin,* ed. J.M. Winter [Cambridge: Cambridge University Press, 1975], 12).

12. Taxation is a form of government revenue that differs from other forms of finance, including debt; parastatal income, such as revenue from the selling of public land; and user fees, such as revenue from the selling of import licenses, in terms of obligations and administrative requirements. Taxes are "unrequited compulsory payments collected primarily by the central government" (E.S. Lieberman, *Race and Regionalism in the Politics of Taxation in Brazil and South Africa* [Cambridge: Cambridge University Press, 2003], 43). They are levied on a particular base and paid to the government to provide certain public goods or services or to redistribute income or purchasing power within society, but without provision or promise of any specific good or service in return for payment (E.S. Lieberman, "Taxation Data as Indicators of State-Society Relations: Possibilities and Pitfalls in Cross-National Research," *Studies in Comparative International Development* 36.4 [2002]: 91).

13. According to Lieberman, there are "seven major categories of tax revenue—income tax, social security contributions, taxes on payroll and workforce, taxes on property, domestic taxes on goods, taxes on international trade and transactions, and 'other' taxes are generally reported by governments in compliance with IMF guidelines" ("Taxation Data as Indicators of State-Society Relations," 98). For an elaboration of what is considered a direct tax and what is considered an indirect tax and how each reflects the relationship between state and society, see J.S. Mill, *Principles of Political Economy* (1848; reprint London: Longmas, Green, 1909). See Book V, Chapter III, "Of Direct Taxes"; and Book V, Chapter VI, "Comparison between Direct and Indirect Taxation."

14. Buchanan also addresses the various forms of taxes and their visibility (Buchanan, *The Collected Works of James M. Buchanan*, vol. 4 [1967; reprint Indianapolis: Liberty Fund, 1999], 4.10.21–25).

15. Lieberman, "Taxation Data as Indicators of State-Society Relations," 99, 105.

16. Moles and Terry define debt as (a) a sum owed by one party to another; (b) a legally enforceable agreement expressed or implied to pay money to another party (P. Moles and N. Terry, *The Handbook of International Financial Terms* [Oxford: Oxford University Press, 1997], 146). Using Modigilani's definition, I define national debt as consisting of: (a) all claims against the government held by the private sector of the economy whether interest bearing or not (and including therefore bank-held debt and government currency, if any), less (b) any claims held by the government against the private sector (F. Modigliani, "Long-Run Implications of Alternative Fiscal Policies and the Burden of the National Debt," *Economic Journal* 71.284 [1961]: 730–731).

17. As David Ricardo stated, "The people who pay the taxes never so estimate them, and therefore do not manage their private affairs accordingly. We are too apt to think that the war is burdensome only in proportion to what we are at the moment called to pay for it in taxes, without reflecting on the probable duration of such taxes. It would be difficult to convince a man possessed of 20,000*l.*, or any other sum, that a perpetual payment of 50*l.* per annum was equally burdensome with a single tax of 1000*l*" (Ricardo, "Essay on the Funding System," 338). For a review of economic literature repudiating and sup-

porting the Ricardian-Equivalence model, see G.A. Akerlof, "The Missing Motivation in Macroeconomics," *American Economic Review* 91.1 (2007): 4–36.

18. Buchanan, *The Collected Works,* 4.10.16.

19. Ibid., 4.8.16

20. Ibid., 4.8.17.

21. Mastanduno, Lake, and Ikenberry, "Toward a Realist Theory of State Action."

22. Descriptive statistics regarding the variation in how states finance war are discussed in chapter 6.

23. P. Studenski and H.E. Krooss, *Financial History of the United States* (New York: McGraw-Hill, 1952).

24. R.S. Sayers, *Financial Policy, 1939–1945* (London: Her Majesty's Stationery Office, 1956).

25. For a discussion of prewar financing of the various belligerents of the Six Day War, see (about Syria) B. Morozov, "The Outbreak of the June 1967 War in Light of Soviet Documentation," in *The Soviet Union and the June 1967 Six Day War,* ed. Y. Ro'i and B. Morozov (Washington, DC: Woodrow Wilson Center for Scholars, 2008), 44; M. Ma'oz, *Syria and Israel: From War to Peace-Making* (New York: Oxford University Press, 1995), 122; E. Kanovsky, "The Economic Aftermath of the Six Day War: UAR, Jordan, and Syria, Part II," *Middle East Journal* 22.3 (1968): 284; R.F. Pajak, "The Soviet-Syrian Military Aid Relationship," in *The Syrian Arab Republic,* ed. A. Sinai and A. Pollack (New York: American Academic Association for Peace in the Middle East, 1976), 97; A.H. Cordesman, *Jordanian Arms and the Middle East Balance* (Washington, DC: Middle East Institute, 1983), 33; and F.H. Lawson, *Why Syria Goes to War: Thirty Years of Confrontation* (Ithaca, NY: Cornell University Press, 1996), 49; (about Jordan) E. Kanovsky, *The Economic Impact of the Six-Day War: Israel, The Occupied Territories, Egypt, Jordan* (New York: Praeger, 1970); E. Kanovsky, *The Economy of Jordan* (Tel Aviv: University Publishing Projects, 1976), 21; Central Intelligence Agency, Directorate of Intelligence, "Jordan's Armed Forces," *Intelligence Memorandum* (January 17, 1967); Central Intelligence Agency, "The Eastern Arab World," *National Intelligence Estimate* (February 17, 1966), number 36–66; Central Intelligence Agency, "Arms Shipment to Jordan," *Intelligence Memorandum* (January 17, 1967); Central Intelligence Agency, "Probable Soviet Objectives in Rearming Arab States," *Special National Intelligence Estimate* (July 20, 1967), number 11-13-67; and Kanovsky, "The Economic Aftermath of The Six Day War," 288; (about Israel) A. D. Barnett, *China and the Major Powers in East Asia* (Washington, DC: Brookings Institution, 1977); Kanovsky, *The Economic Impact of the Six-Day War*; Y. Gabbay, "Israel's Fiscal Policy, 1948–1982," in *Economic and Policy in Israel: The First Generation,* ed. M. Sanbar (Lanham, MD: University Press of America, 1990), 85–112.; E. Berglas, "Defense and the Economy," in *The Israeli Economy: Maturing Through Crises,* ed. Y. Ben-Porath (Cambridge, MA: Harvard University Press, 1986), 173–191; Y. Plessner, *The Political Economy of Israel from Ideology to Stagnation,* SUNY Series in Israeli Studies (Albany: State University of New York Press, 1994), 179; H.C. Wilkenfeld, *Taxes and the People in Israel* (Cambridge, MA: Harvard University Press, 1973), 112; and P. Rivlin, *The Israeli Economy* (Boulder, CO: Westview Press, 1992), 35); (about Egypt) Kanovsky, *The Economic Impact of the Six-Day War*; J. Waterbury, *The Egypt of Nasser and Sadat: The Political Economy of Two Regimes* (Princeton, NJ: Princeton University Press, 1983), 99; R.L. Tignor, *Capitalism and Nationalism at the End of Empire: State and Business in Decolonizing Egypt, Nigeria, and Kenya, 1945–1963* (Princeton, NJ: Princeton University Press, 1998), 179; and M.N. Barnett, *Confronting the Costs of War,* 99–100.

26. The concept of short- and long-war finance echoes Alex Weisiger's definition of limited and unlimited wars (Weisiger, *The Logic of War: Explanations for Limited and Unlimited Conflicts* [Ithaca, NY: Cornell University Press, 2013], 11).

27. It is also important to note that the quicker means of taxation, indirect taxation, produces less revenue than direct taxation. Indirect tax revenue is contingent on the size and frequency of the transaction. In theory, direct taxes have no limit, as they can be levied against all individuals and businesses within the state.

28. Moreover, even when successful debt is negotiated quickly, transferring specie takes time. Today, states are privileged with technology and transfers can be made instantaneously. However, this was not always the case. For example, in the United States during the Mexican-American War, war expenditures were met by the Independent Treasury Bank in New Orleans. However, two-thirds of government revenue was collected in the northeast and mid-Atlantic. Thus banks had to move the specie to New Orleans. One method was to assume the expense and risk of physically shipping gold and silver coins by express (J.W. Cummings, *Towards Modern Public Finance: The American War with Mexico, 1846–1848* [London: Pickering & Chatto, 2009], 45).

29. Theories of war optimism would suggest that the majority of leaders commence with a short-war finance policy. For select works that discuss optimism, see G. Blainey, *The Causes of War* (New York: Free Press, 1973), chap. 3; and Stephen Van Evera, *Causes of War* (Ithaca, NY: Cornell University Press, 1999), chap. 2.

30. For select works that discuss learning and updating expectations during wartime, see H.E. Goemans, *War and Punishment* (Princeton, NJ: Princeton University Press, 2000), R. Harrison Wagner, "Bargaining and War," *American Journal of Political Science* 44.3 (2000): 469–484; Darren Filson and Suzanne Werner, "A Bargaining Model of War and Peace: Anticipating the Onset, Duration, and Outcome of War," *American Journal of Political Science* 46.4 (2002): 819–838; and R. Powell, "Bargaining and Learning While Fighting," *American Journal of Political Science* 48.2 (2004): 344–361.

31. For statistical and case study selection purposes, I refer to wars over six months long as "long wars," as the average interstate war duration as coded in the Correlates of War Project is only about four months long.

32. See chapters 13 and 14 in Studenski and Krooss, *Financial History of the United States* for a discussion of the change in Civil War finance from 1861 to 1863.

33. See A. Downs, "An Economic Theory of Political Action in a Democracy," *Journal of Political Economy* 65.2 (1957): 138; A. Downs, *An Economic Theory of Democracy* (New York: Harper and Row, 1957), chap. 4; and Mastanduno, Lake, and Ikenberry, "Toward a Realist Theory of State Action," 463.

34. Studenski and Krooss, *Financial History of the United States,* 75. For an excellent discussion of Gallatin's commitment to Jeffersonian ideals, see Raymond Walters's biography, *Albert Gallatin: Jeffersonian Financier and Diplomat* (New York: Macmillan, 1957).

35. Studenski and Krooss, *Financial History of the United States*, 78.

36. A.N. Young, *China's Wartime Finance and Inflation, 1937–1945* (Cambridge, MA: Harvard University Press, 1965).

37. About 70 percent of the war has been paid for with domestic debt and 30 percent with foreign debt. The figure for foreign debt is an estimate of US securities—public debt—owned by foreign and international sources (D. Andrew Austin, "Overview of the Federal Public Debt," *Congressional Research Service*, 2011).

38. E.g., M. Levi, *Of Rule and Revenue* (Berkeley: University of California Press, 1988).

39. Standard taxation is "levied on a particular base and paid to the government to provide certain public goods or services or to redistribute income or purchasing power within society, but without provision or promise of any specific good or service in return for payment" (Lieberman, "Taxation Data as Indicators of State-Society Relations," 91).

40. J.M. Buchanan, *The Collected Works of James M. Buchanan*, vol. 2, *Public Principles of Public Debt: A Defense and Restatement* (Indianapolis: Liberty Fund, 1999).

41. Select influential works include S.S. Gartner and G.M. Segura, "War, Casualties, and Public Opinion," *Journal of Conflict Resolution* 42 (1998): 278–300; S.S. Gartner, G.M. Segura, and M. Wilkening, "All Politics are Local: Local Losses and Individual Attitudes Towards the Vietnam War," *Journal of Conflict Resolution* 41 (1997): 669–694; J.E. Mueller, *War, Presidents, and Public Opinion* (New York: Wiley, 1973).

42. Select literature linking war, war outcome, the cost of war, and leadership survival include B. Bueno de Mesquita and R.M. Siverson, "War and the Survival of Political Leaders: A Comparative Study of Regime Types and Political Accountability," *Americal Political Science Review* 89.4 (1995): 841–855; B. Bueno de Mesquita, A. Smith, R.M. Siverson, and J. Morrow, *The Logic of Political Survival* (Cambridge, MA: MIT Press, 2003); G. Chiozza and H.E. Goemans, "Peace through Insecurity: Tensure and International Conflict," *Journal of Conflict Resolution* 47.4 (2003): 443–467; M. Colaresi, "When Doves Cry: International Rivalry, Unreciprocated Cooperation, and Leadership Turnover," *American Journal of Political Science* 48.3 (2004): 555–570; and Goemans, *War and Punishment*. For a review of economic voting literature, see M.S. Lewis-Beck and M. Stegmaier, "Economic Determinants of Electoral Outcomes," *Annual Review of Political Science* 3 (2000): 182–219.

43. Buchanan, *The Collected Works*, 4.10.15.

44. "The direct costs of government services appear to the citizen as taxes, and the manner in which these are levied may significantly affect his attitudes toward the extension or the contraction of such services" (Buchanan, *The Collected Works*, vol. 4, 5). R.H. Bates ("A Political Scientist Looks at Tax Reform," in *Tax Reform in Developing Countries*, ed. M. Gills [Durham, NC: Duke University Press, 1989]) and J.A. Cheibub ("Political Regimes and the Extractive Capacity of Governments: Taxation in Democracies and Dictatorships," *World Politics* 50 [1998, April]: 353–354) also address the perception by citizens that taxes are associated with government services and politicians are aware of this association and structure policy accordingly to lower political costs.

45. When developing a tax structure, leaders weigh the risk of being removed from office against how much revenue to extract. Levi refers to this as the discount rate (Levi, *Of Rule and Revenue*, 32–33).

46. E.g., R. Chetty, A. Looney, and K. Kroft, "Salience and Taxation, Theory an Evidence," *American Economic Review* 99.4 (2009): 1145–1177; M.A. Ryan, D.M. Finkelstein, and M.A. McDevitt, *Chinese Warfighting: The PLA Experience Since 1949* (Armonk, NY: M.E. Sharpe, 2003)

47. E.g., J. Ashworth and B. Heyndels, "Politicians' Preferences on Local Tax Rates: An Empirical Analysis," *European Journal of Political Economy* 13 (1997), 479–502; S. Landon and L.D. Ryan, "The Political Costs of Taxes and Government Spending," *European Journal of Economics* 30.1 (1997): 85–111.

48. John Stuart Mill articulated this logic, "In England there is a popular feeling . . . in opposition to direct taxation. . . . An Englishman dislikes, not so much the payment, as the act of paying. He dislikes seeing the face of the tax-collector, and being subjected to his peremptory demand. Perhaps, too, the money which he is required to pay directly out of his pocket is the only taxation which he is quite sure that he pays at all. That a tax of one shilling per pound on tea, or of two shillings per bottle on wine, raises the price of each pound of tea and bottle of wine which he consumes, by that and more than that amount, cannot indeed be denied; it is the fact, and is intended to be so, and he himself, at times, is perfectly aware of it; but it makes hardly any impression on his practical feelings and associations, serving to illustrate the distinction between what is merely known to be true and what is felt to be so" (Mill, *Priciples of Political Economy*, bk.V, ch.VI).

49. Buchanan, *The Collected Works*, vol. 4, 4.10.15. In 2005, President Obama's Advisory Panel on Federal Tax Reform "failed to reach consensus on whether to replace part of the existing income tax system with a value-added tax (VAT) in part because of concerns

about how the lower visibility of a VAT would affect the size of government." As the Advisory Panel noted in its report: "'[Some] Panel Members were unwilling to support the [VAT] proposal given the lack of conclusive empirical evidence on the impact of a VAT on the growth of government. Others were more confident that voters could be relied on to understand the amount of tax being paid through a VAT, in part because the proposal studied by the Panel would require the VAT to be separately stated on each sales receipt provided to consumers. These members of the Panel envisioned that voters would appropriately control growth in the size of the federal government through the electoral process (The President's Advisory Panel on Federal Tax Reform 2005, p. 203–204)'" (A. Finkelstein, "EZTax: Tax Salience and Tax Rates," *Quarterly Journal of Economics* 124.3 [2007]: 1).

50. Smith, *An Inquiry into the Nature and Causes of the Wealth of Nations*, chap. 3. Writing almost a century later, David Ricardo echoed Smith's concern, "The burdens of the war are undoubtedly great during its continuance, but at its termination they cease altogether. When the pressure of the war is felt at once, without mitigation, we shall be less disposed wantonly to engage in an expensive contest, and if engaged in it, we shall be sooner disposed to get out of it, unless it be a contest for some great national interest" (Ricardo, "Essay on the Funding System").

51. For example, before the Six Day War in Israel, the Israeli population resisted high taxation. Once the war began, Israeli citizens reversed their stance on taxation. "When the Israeli army began to mobilize at the end of May 1967, reaction among taxpayers was immediate: there was a sharp increase in advance payments by self-employed taxpayers. Some paid their advances in full for the entire year; some made payments in considerable excess of the amounts due, which they asked to be credited against assessments that had not yet been made. A number of taxpayers who had filed objections to pending assessments withdrew their objections, explaining that although they felt their positions were reasonable, they preferred not to press them in the face of the government's obvious need for funds. There were others who refused to accept refund checks" (Wilkenfeld, *Taxes and People in Israel*, 112).

52. The extent of inflation is contingent on three factors: the extent to which the state mobilizes for the war, the amount of goods being purchased combined with scarcity, and the health of the economy, specifically whether the economy has room to grow or is already at full capacity and experiencing rising prices prior to the onset of war.

53. Inflation data from C.M. Reinhart and K.S. Rogoff, *This Time Is Different: Eight Centuries of Financial Folly* (Princeton, NJ: Princeton University Press, 2009). Reinhart and Rogoff have collected annual consumer price indices (CPI) and their relative cost of living indices for seventy countries, some observations dating back as early as 1265.

54. W.M. Pintner, "Inflation in Russia during the Crimean War Period," *American Slavic and East European Review* 18.1 (1959): 82.

55. Two examples of scholarly works that link the German Great Inflation to their financing of World War I are T. Balderson, "War Finance and Inflation in Britain and Germany, 1914–1918," *Economic History Review* 42.2 (1989): 222–244; and Feldman, *The Great Disorder*.

56. M. Feldstein, "The Welfare Cost of Permanent Inflation and Optimal Short Run Economic Policy," *Journal of Political Economy* 87.4 (1979): 749–768; "The Costs and Benefits of Going from Low Inflation to Price Stability," in *Reducing Inflation: Motiviation and Strategy*, ed. C.D. Romer and D.H. Romer (Chicago: Chicago University Press, 1997), 123–156; "Capital Income Taxes and the Benefit of Price Stability," in *The Costs and Benefits of Price Stability*, ed. M. Feldstein (Chicago: University of Chicago Press, 1999), 9–39.

57. M.J. Bailey, "The Welfare Cost of Inflationary Finance," *Journal of Political Economy* 64.2 (1956): 93–110.

58. D.E. Lounge and R.J. Sweeney, "Inflation and Real Growth: Some Empirical Results," *Journal of Money, Credit, and Banking* 13 (1981): 497–501; R.W. Parks, "Inflation and Relative Price Variability," *Journal of Political Economy* 86.1 (1978): 79–95.

59. A. Birati and A. Cukierman, "The Redistributive Effects of Inflation and of the Introduction of a Real Tax System in the U.S. Bond Market," *Journal of Public Economics* 12 (1979): 125–139; E.C. Budd and D.F. Seiders, "The Impact of Inflation on the Distribution of Income and Wealth," *American Economic Review* 61 (1971): 128–138; W.D. Nordhaus, "The Effects of Inflation on the Distribution of Economic Welfare," *Journal of Money, Credit, and Baking* 5 (1973): 465–508; E. Wolff, "The Distributional Effects of the 1969–75 Inflation on Holdings of Household Wealth in the United States," *Review of Income and Wealth* 25 (1979): 195–207.

60. J.M. Keynes, *Essays in Persuasion* (New York: Harcourt, 1932), 77–78.

61. See G.H. Kramer, "Short-Term Fluctuations in U.S. Voting Behavior, 1896–1964," *American Political Science Review* 65.1 (1971): 131–142; S. Peltzman, "How Efficient Is the Voting Market," *Journal of Law and Economics* 33.1 (1990): 27–63.

62. M.J. Gasiorowski, "Economic Crisis and Political Regime Change: An Event History Analysis," *American Political Science Review* 89.1 (1995): 882–987; S.P. Huntington, *Political Order in Changing Societies* (New Haven, CT: Yale University Press, 1968).

63. In the words of John Maynard Keynes, "In peace time . . . the size of the cake depends on the amount of work done. But in wartime the size of the cake is fixed. If we work harder, we can fight better. But we must not consume more" (Keynes, *How to Pay for War*, 4).

64. J.W. Kipp, "M. Kh. Reutern on the Russian State and Economy: A Liberal Bureaucrat during the Crimean Era, 1854–60," *Journal of Modern History* 47.3 (1975): 443–444.

65. E.g., M. Khan and A. Senhadji, "Threshold Effects in the Relationship between Inflation and Growth," *IMF Staff Papers* 48.1 (2001): 1–21; R. Burkdekin, A. Denzau, M. Keil, T. Sitthiyot, and T. Willett, "When Does Inflation Hurt Economic Growth? Different Nonlinearities for Different Economies," *Journal of Macroeconomics* 25 (2004): 519–532; M. Gillman and M. Kejak, "Contrasting Models of the Effect of Inflation on Growth," *Journal of Economic Surveys* 19.1 (2005): 113–136.

66. E.g., Antonia López-Villavicencio and Valérie Mignon, "On the Impact of Inflation on Output Growth: Does the Level of Inflation Matter?" *Journal of Macroeconomics* 33 (2011): 455–464. Barro finds an inverse relation between growth and inflation at high rates of inflation, above 15 percent per year. He found no statistically significant relationship between inflation and growth when inflation rates are below 15 percent per year (Robert J. Barro, "Inflation and Economic Growth," *Annals of Economic Finance* [2013]: 94–95).

67. The oft-discussed example here is the effect of World War II, its corresponding fiscal policies, and US recovery from the Great Depression. The extent to which American recovery from the Great Depression was completed prior to 1942 has been debated. For a review of that debate as well as an argument that World War II fiscal policies were necessary to complete the economic recovery, see J.R. Vernon, "World War II Fiscal Policies and the End of the Great Depression," *Journal of Economic History* 54.4 (1994): 850–868; and Hugh Rockoff, "From Plowshares to Swords: The American Economy in World War II," *NBER Working Paper Series on Historical Factors in Long Run Growth. Historical Paper 77* (Cambridge, MA: NBER, 1995).

68. R. Gilpin, *War and Change in World Politics* (Cambridge: Cambridge University Press, 1981); Knorr, *The Power of Nations*; Kugler and Domke, "Comparing the Strength of Nations"; Mastanduno, Lake, and Ikenberry, "Toward a Realist Theory of State Action"; Organski and Kugler, *The War Ledger*.

69. O.M.W. Sprague, "Loans and Taxes in War Finance," *American Economic Review* 7.1 (1917): 199–213.

70. Bureaucratic capacity is the ability to implement policy effectively (J. D. Huber and N. McCarty, "Bureaucratic Capacity, Delegation, and Political Reform," *American Political Science Review* 98.3 [2004]: 481). Specifically, it is "the ability of the bureaucracy to carry out programs in accordance with a previously specified plan" (D. P. Carpenter, *The Forging of Bureaucratic Autonomy: Reputations, Networks, and Policy Innovation in Executive Agencies, 1862–1928* [Princeton, NJ: Princeton University Press, 2001], 28). Jonathan K. Hanson refers to this process as administrative capacity ("Forging Then Taming Leviathan: State Capacity, Constraints on Rules, and Development," *International Studies Quarterly* 58.2 [2014]: 382).

71. While I emphasize the quantitative aspects of a state's extractive capacity, the size of the bureaucratic machinery (i.e., number of personnel relative to the population), I hesitate to make the claim that capacity is solely reflective of size. I highlight the work of John Brewer and his foundational work, *Sinews of Power: War, Money, and the English State, 1688–1783* (New York: Alfred A. Knopf, 1989) as an example. Brewer discusses the rise of English tax capacity during its various wars. He documents in detail the increase in the number of individuals employed by the state to collect taxes (104–105), yet emphasizes the qualitative component of the tax bureaucracy that led to an increase in tax capacity and, therefore, improved revenue collection. For example, he discusses, the professionalization of tax collection via salaries rather than fees, career ladder of graded appointments, expectation of administrative loyalty, internal monitoring, a system of punishment and awards, and the pace of tax collection operations (69, 72, 91–92). Brewer's work highlights the multitude of components that affect the state's ability to extract tax revenue. Thus I use the notion of complexity to underscore the nonquantitative aspects of a state's bureaucracy that are necessary for revenue collection. While it would be helpful to explore the various subcomponents that comprise a state's extractive capacity, it is beyond the scope of this project.

72. These tasks are similar to the five properties—listability, conduitability, standard clarity, cross-sanctions, and reinforcibility—of tax administrative feasibility identified by Christopher Hood. Listability means easy identifiability of the population to which taxes can apply. Conduitability means the ability to channel taxes through a manageable number of state intermediaries. Standard clarity means capacity to specify and assess tax bases with limited effort and ambiguity. Reinforcibility means taxes can be cross-checked from different administrative vantage points, and cross-sanctions means that evasion of one tax brings extra liability to another (C. Hood, "The Tax State in the Information Age," in *The Nation State in Question*, ed. T.V. Paul, G. J. Ikenberry, and J.A. Hall [Princeton, NJ: Princeton University Press, 2003], 224–225).

73. It should be noted that even if the state has an effective revenue administration, the economy must be developed enough, or sufficiently monetized, in order to draw resources. In an economy where only a small share of goods and services are bought and sold (a relatively nonmonetized society), collectors of revenue are unable to observe or evaluate resources with accuracy. Moreover, the revenue base is much smaller. Thus, as a state's level of monetization increases, its ability to collect more varieties and more efficient forms of revenue increases (Tilly, *Coercion, Capital, and European States*, 85–88).

74. Evan Lieberman points out, "Collection of consumption taxes can be interpreted as evidence of a functioning and competent tax administration, but not to the degree that is generally associated with the collection of income taxes. Taxes on consumption still generally require significant bureaucratic capacity, but not nearly the same amount of information is required as with the taxation of income, and these revenues tend to be easier to collect than taxes on income because they are collected indirectly, incrementally, and generally at the point of purchase" (Lieberman, "Taxation Data as Indicators of State-Soceity Relations," 103).

75. Ibid., 103.

76. For a superb study of the evolution of public credit and supporting institutions, specifically the Bank of England, see P.B.M. Dickson, *The Financial Revolution in England: A Study in the Development of Public Credit, 1688–1756* (London: Macmillan, 1967).

77. James K. Polk, "Third Annual Message, December 7, 1847," in *The American Presidency Project*, ed. Gerhard Peters and John T. Wolley. http://www.presidency.ucsb.edu/ws/?pid=29488.

78. Cummings, *Toward Modern Public Finance,* chap. 5.

79. It was hoped that the Morrill Tariff Act of 1861, which restored duties to the rates in effect before 1857, would produce substantial federal revenue (Studenski and Krooss, *Financial History of the United States,* 139)

80. Ibid., 139.

81. The Revenue Act of 1861.

82. See Bensel, *Yankee Leviathan.*

83. Tilly, ed., *The Formation of National States in Western Europe,* 84.

84. Knorr, *The Power of Nations,* chap. 3.

## CHAPTER 2. TRUMAN AND THE KOREAN WAR

1. For the United States, the lethality of both wars was similar: 54,246 deaths in Korea and 58,153 in Vietnam (M.R. Sarkees and F. Wayman, *Resort to War: 1816–2007* [Washington, DC: CQ Press, 2010], appendix 5).

2. Total defense spending as a percentage of GDP in the peak year of the war during Korea was still more expensive: 13.2 percent compared to 9.5 percent for Vietnam (S. Daggett, *Costs of Major U.S. Wars* [Washington, DC: Congressional Research Service, 2010]; N.A. Tuan, *South Vietnam Trial and Experience: A Challenge for Development* [Athens, OH: Center for International Studies, Ohio University, 1987]).

3. Although the income tax was enacted in 1913, it only applied to high-income individuals for the first thirty years of its existence. To finance World War II, the income tax base was greatly expanded and personal exemptions were reduced. The tax capacity and base created by World War II remained in place for both the Korean and Vietnam wars. Income tax is a fitting example because it is the primary source of government revenue from World War II to the present (J.F. Witte, *The Politics and Development of the Federal Income Tax* [Madison: The University of Wisconsin Press, 1985], 80). During the Korean War, personal exemptions were $600, $1,200, and $600 for single persons, married couples, and dependents respectively. For the first half of the Vietnam War, 1965–1969, these figures were the same. For the latter half of the Vietnam War, these figures were raised slightly (R.A. Wilson, *Personal Exemptions and Individual Income Tax Rates, 1913–2002* [Washington, DC: Internal Revenue Service, 2008], table 1). It should be noted that tax rates were generally lower throughout the Vietnam War than they were during the Korean War. For tax rates before and during the Korean and Vietnam wars, see *IRS Historical Fact Book: A Chronology 1646–1992* (Washington DC: US Department of Treasury, Internal Revenue Service, 1993), appendix 5. For a history of the Internal Revenue Service and its preceding institutions, see *IRS Historical Fact Book: A Chronology 1646–1992.*

4. For a review of the Bretton Woods system and the effect of closed capital controls on macroeconomic policy, see B. Eichengreen, *Globalizing Capital: A History of the International Monetary System* (Princeton, NJ: Princeton University Press, 1996); and E. Helleiner, *States and the Reemergence of Global Finance* (Ithaca, NY: Cornell University Press, 1994).

5. From 1965 to 1972, less than 20 percent of war finance came from increased taxes (T. Riddell, *A Political Economy of the American War in Indo-China: Its Costs and Consequences* [Washington, DC: American University, 1975], 367).

6. C. Blair, *The Forgotten War: American in Korea 1950–1953* (New York: Times Books, 1987); and A.R. Millet, *War in Korea, 1950–1951: They Came from the North* (Lawrence: University Press of Kansas, 2010), provide an excellent review of military events and US involvement.

7. D.M. Condit, "The Test of War, 1950–1953," *History of the Office of the Secretary of Defense*, vol. 2 (Washington, DC: Historical Office, Office of the Secretary of Defense, 1998), 225.

8. A. Leland and M.J. Oboroceanu, *American War and Military Operation Casualties: Lists and Statistics* (Washington, DC: Congressional Research Service, 2010), 10.

9. Blair, *The Forgotten War,* 7; see also Condit, "The Test of War, 1950–1953," 223–224. The army, for example, was below its previously authorized strength of 677,000, numbering only 591,000. Of these only 360,000 were stationed in the United States, with the rest overseas. Moreover, army doctrine was rigidly based on the concept of three-battalion regiments. However, in order to stay within budget, Army chief of staff Joseph Collins was forced to deactivate one in three battalions (Blair, *The Forgotten War,* 28).

10. Blair, *The Forgotten War*, 28.

11. The Korean War is estimated to have cost the United States about $50 billion in 1950 dollars (M. Edelstein, "War and the American Economy in the Twentieth Century," in *The Cambridge Economic History of the United States: The Twentieth Century*, ed. S.L. Engerman and R.E. Gallman [Cambridge: Cambridge University Press, 2000], 348–342), while total defense appropriations from 1951 through 1953 are estimated at $155.579 billion (Condit, "The Test of War 1950–1953").

12. Harry S. Truman, "Special Message to the Congress Reporting on the Situation in Korea, July 19, 1950," *The American Presidency Project,* ed. Gerhard Peters and John T. Woolley. http://www.presidency.ucsb.edu/ws/?pid=13560.

13. Works that discuss South Korean war finance include D. C. Cole and Y.M. Park, *Financial Development in Korea, 1945–1978* (Cambridge, MA: Harvard University Press, 1983); J.W. Lee, "The Impact of the Korean War on the Korean Economy," *International Journal of Korean Studies* 5.1 (2001): 97–118; E.S. Manson et al., *The Economic and Social Modernization of the Republic of Korea* (Cambridge, MA: Harvard University Press, 1980); W.D. Reeve, *The Republic of Korea: A Political and Economic Study* (London: Oxford University Press, 1963).

14. For an excellent review of the costs and reimbursement negotiations with the Commonwealth countries, see J. Grey, *The Commonwealth Armies and the Korean War* (Manchester: Manchester University Press, 1988), chap. 9. For a review of the Korean Operations Pool Account, see A. Farrar-Hockley, *The British Part in the Korean War*, vol. 2 (London: HMSO, 1995), appendix N.

15. S.A. Bank, J.S. Kirk, and J.J. Thorndike, *War and Taxes* (Washington, DC: Urban Institute Press, 2008), 110–111.

16. For a discussion of the veto, see "Memo, Fred Panzer to President Johnson, "The Truman Tax Vetoes," 9/21/1967, EX FI 11, Box 56, WHCF, LBJ Library.

17. The Council of Economic Advisors (CEA), created in 1946 to inform and advise the president when making economic policy decisions, was the hub for financing the Korean War. Not only was the three-man committee tasked with weekly, daily, and monthly reports on the health of the economy, but Truman explicitly turned to them for advice on policy creation. B.M. Gross and J.P. Lewis ("The President's Economic Staff during the Truman Administration," *American Political Science Review* 48.1 [1954]: 114–130) provide an excellent review of the mandate, structure, and role in policy making of the CEA under the Truman administration.

18. In order to understand public opinion for the war effort, I use various sources of polling and survey data: the Gallup Poll, Roper/Fortune Survey, and ORC Public Opinion

Index, using the iPoll databank at the Roper Center. http://www.ropercenter.uconn.edu/data_access/ipoll/ipoll.html#.TihiaM3qo4g.

19. Report, "Economic Indicators December 1951—Prepared for the Joint Committee on the Economic Report by the Council of Economic Advisors," 1952; OF 1565; Truman Papers, Truman Library.

20. Edwin G. Norse to Harry S. Truman, February 4, 1949, WHCF, OF Box 1564, Truman Papers, Truman Library.

21. B.G. Hickman, *The Korean War and United States Economic Activity* (New York: National Bureau of Economic Research, 1955), 17.

22. Ibid., 21.

23. *The Economic and Political Hazards of an Inflationary Defense Economy* (Washington, DC: Joint Committee on the Economic Report, 1951), 5.

24. Gallup Poll Question: "Do you think that prices, in general, will be higher, lower, or about the same six months from now?"

25. Mr. Keith to John Graham, October 13, 1948, Excess Profits Tax folder, Ecker-Racz Papers Box 3, Truman Library.

26. L. Laszlo Ecker-Racz to Harry S. Truman, October 19, 1950, Tax Program folder, Ecker-Racz Papers Box 4, Truman Library.

27. "Unless prompt action is taken to increase taxes, we will be repeating the pattern of World War II financing which resulted in a permanent increase in the public debt. The President has properly said that we must not make this mistake again. It can be avoided only if substantial tax increases are made effective within the next few months . . . to avoid the kind of delay encountered in 1942 when the Revenue Act was not passed until October." John Snyder to Chairman Doughton, "The Dangers in Delaying the 1951 Tax Legislation," February 10, 1951, Papers Box 4, Truman Library.

28. The polling question, "Congress voted recently to increase federal income taxes for all tax payers. To pay the costs of the Korean War and our defense program income taxes will have to be raised even more or the government will have to borrow money and go deeper into debt. Which do you think the Government should do—increase income taxes still more, or borrow more money?" Public sentiment in favor of taxation continued through spring 1941. In February 1951, the preference was still a tax increase; 49 percent of respondents favored taxation whereas only 24 percent favored borrowing. The polling question, "Our government in Washington plans to spend this coming year about $25 billion more than was spent this last year for national defense. How do you, yourself, think this additional money for defense should be raised—mostly by an increase in personal income taxes or mostly by borrowing money to be paid back later?"

29. "Special Message to the Congress Reporting Recommending a 'Pay as We Go' Tax Program," February 2, 1951, Public Papers of the President, Truman Library.

30. *An Economist's Statement on Anti-Inflationary Measures* (Washington, DC: Joint Committee on the Economic Report, 1950), in Report, "General Credit Control, Debt Management and Economic Mobilization," 1951, Keyserling Papers Box 14, Truman Library.

31. For other works that discuss Korea and World War III, see Bank et al., *War and Taxes*, 111, and J.T. Patterson, *Grand Expectations: The United States, 1945–1974* (Oxford: Oxford University Press, 1996), 207.

32. For an excellent graphic representation and analysis of public support for the Korean War, see J.E. Mueller, "Trends in Popular Support for the Wars in Korea and Vietnam," *American Political Science Review* 65.2 (June 1971): 358–375; and J.T. Campbell et al., "Public Opinion and the Outbreak of War," *Journal of Conflict Resolution* 9.3 (1965): 323. Campbell et al. find that public support for the Korean War differed remarkably from public support for World War II. The Korean War "begins with about 65 percent of the population

favoring the already declared 'policy action.' Prior to the actual outbreak of hostilities in Korea on June 25, 1950, and the entrance of the United States two days later, little awareness of pending conflict in Korea is revealed in the polls. Once war was upon us, however, some support was achieved, though not of a magnitude comparable to that occasioned by the world wars" (Campbell et al., "Public Opinion and the Outbreak of War," 323–324).

33. S. Sandler, ed., *The Korean War: An Encyclopedia* (New York: Routledge, 1995), 20.

34. Polling Question: "Some people say the United States should stop fighting and take her troops out of Korea to avoid a third world war. Other people say we should keep our troops even if it does mean a world war. What do you, yourself think—should we take our troops out of Korea, or not?" Twenty-five percent of respondents' felt the United States should withdraw, 66 percent felt the United States should not, and 9 percent had no opinion.

35. The polling question, "Do you think the United States is now actually in World War III—or do you think the present fighting in Korea will stop short of another world war?"

36. *Economic and Political Hazards*, 2.

37. *Inflation and Communism* (Washington, DC: Joint Committee on the Economic Report, 1951), 21.

38. "Special Message to the Congress Reporting on the Situation in Korea," July 19, 1950, Public Papers of the President, Truman Library.

39. Ibid.

40. E. G. Keith, "The Excess Profit Tax Act of 1950," *National Tax Journal* 4.3 (1951): 193.

41. Harry S. Truman to Chairman Robert Doughton, July 25, 1950, Public Papers of the President, Truman Library.

42. As late as June 20, 1950, only a week before the US decision to intervene in the Korean War, Representative Eberharter proposed to include an EPT in the pending revenue bill but was defeated in the Ways and Means Committee (Keith, "The Excess Profit Tax Act of 1950," 193).

43. For the Senate debate on the EPT amendment to postpone the tax, the George-Millikin Amendment, see the Congressional Record of the Senate, 82nd Congress, 1st Session, vol. 96, 14054–14060.

44. Many memos originating from the tax office to Secretary of the Treasury John Snyder emphasized speed. For example: "The need for substantial increases in taxes as quickly as possible to contain inflation is substantially more pressing than the budget results for the current fiscal year are likely to indicate." John Campbell to John Snyder, October 13, 1950, Tax Program folder, Ecker-Racz Papers Box 4, Truman Library.

45. Harry S. Truman to Chairman Robert Doughton, November 14, 1950, Public Papers of the President, Truman Library.

46. Keith, "The Excess Profit Tax Act of 1950," 198.

47. Ibid.; Witte, *The Politics and Development of the Federal Income Tax*, 139.

48. Harry S. Truman to Sec. of Treas., Ch. Of Bd. Of Governors of FRS, Dir. Of Def. Mob, and CEA Chairman, February 26, 1951, Committee on Fiscal and Monetary Policy, 1951 folder, Keyserling Papers, Truman Library. See also Report, "Quarterly Report on the Economic Situation," April 6, 1951, Quarterly and Monetary Reports to the President 1951, folder, Clark Papers, Truman Library.

49. Harry S. Truman: "Annual Message to the Congress on the State of the Union," January 5, 1949. *The American Presidency Project*, ed. Gerhard Peters and John T. Woolley, http://www.presidency.ucsb.edu/ws/?pid=13293.

50. Alonzo L. Hamby, "The Vital Center, the Fair Deal, and the Quest for a Liberal Political Economy," *American Historical Review* 77.3 (1972): 658.

51. "I have sharply reduced expenditures for those programs which can be deferred or eliminated, even though these programs bring clear benefits to the Nation and would

be highly desirable in normal times. . . . Many desirable projects have been retarded or suspended since the beginning of the Korean emergency." Annual Budget Message to the Congress: Fiscal Year 1953, Jan 21, 1952, Public Papers of the President, Truman Library. See also P.L. Hammond, *LBJ and the Presidential Management of Foreign Relations* (Austin: University of Texas Press, 1992), 204. For an in-depth discussion of the relationship between the Fair Deal and the pursuit of Truman's national security agenda as well as the domestic politics surrounding the Fair Deal's demise, see Benjamin O. Fordham, *Building a Cold War Consensus: The Political Economy of U.S. National Security, 1949–1951* (Ann Arbor: The University of Michigan Press, 1998), chap. 5.

52. The Defense Production Act granted President Truman the power to establish priorities and allocations systems; requisition personal property for defense purposes; expand productive capacity and extraction of strategic materials; and invoke wage, price, and credit controls.

53. "Although price and wage controls must go hand-in-hand with higher taxes to achieve an economically and politically defensible anti-inflation program, once assurance of controls has been given and they are announced, the immediate anti-inflationary job of taxes becomes even more critical. At best, it will take several months to make the controls fully effective. Pressure from all sides for price and wage increases will be very great. This will be the make-or-break period for the controls, when they need every possible immediate support from the fiscal side." Walter Heller to L. Laszlo Ecker-Racz, January 21, 1951, 1950 Tax Program I folder, Ecker-Racz Papers Box 4, Truman Library.

54. Council of Economic Advisors to the Treasury Secretary, July 21, 1950, 1950 Tax Program II folder, Ecker-Racz Papers Box 1, Truman Library.

55. A month after the war began, Truman explained to Congress that taxation was the preferred method over controls to fight inflation. "The more prompt and vigorous we are with these general measures, the less need there will be for all of the comprehensive direct controls which involve the consideration of thousands of individual situations and, thus, involve infinitely greater administrative difficulties and much greater interference with individual choice and initiative." Special Message to the Congress: The President's Midyear Economic Report," July 26, 1950, Public Papers of the President, Truman Library.

56. A. Meltzer, *A History of the Federal Reserve*, vol. 1, *1913–1951* (Chicago: University of Chicago Press, 2003), 583. CEA member Roy Blough commented on the dilemma of debt management and inflation on March 12, 1952, before the Subcommittee on General Credit Control on Debt Management: "There would seem to be three general kinds of problems involved in this subject of the relationship between monetary policy and the management of the Federal debt. At the bottom is the economic problem of how to manage the very large Federal debt with the least harmful influence on the economy. . . . Under most economic conditions, a large public debt presents no problem for monetary policy. Under the following circumstances, however, a difficult problem arises in using monetary policy to stabilize the economy while managing the public debt: (1) when there are substantial issues maturing currently that require refunding, or when additional borrowing is necessary because revenues are insufficient to cover expenditures; and (2) when demand for goods and services has pushed employment and production to so high a level that any additions to demand will not result in great production but will give rise to inflationary pressures; and (3) when the combined total of demands for loanable funds by government and private borrows is in excess of supply of loanable funds available from the voluntary savings of individuals and corporations. Conditions of this character have existed during much of the time since the Korean attack in June 1950." "Statement, Roy Blough before the Subcommittee on General Credit Control and Debt Management," March 12, 1952, Keyserling Papers, Box 8, Truman Library.

57. Report, "Report on a Survey of the Problems of Inflation Raised in the President's Memorandum of February 26, 1951," March 2, 1951, Keyserling Papers, Truman Library. See also Harry S. Truman to Secretary of the Treasury, Chairman of the Federal Reserve, Director of Defense Mobilization and Chairman of the Council of Economic Advisors, February 26, 1951, White House Contacts Harry S. Truman folder, Keyserling Papers, Box 8, Truman Library. CEA member Roy Blough: "With about half of the total debt of the Nation in the form of Federal securities, the development of a disorganized market could be a major disruptive force. The action which then might be required by the Federal Reserve to restore financial order might involve larger purchases of Government securities than a flexible support program to maintain stability." "Statement, Roy Blough before the Subcommittee on General Credit Control and Debt Management," March 12, 1952, Keyserling Papers, Box 8, Truman Library.

58. Leon Keyserling and Johnson D. Clark to Joseph C. O'Mahoney, November 20, 1950, White House Contacts—Harry S. Truman, 1947–1953 folder, Keyserling Papers, Box 8, Truman Library.

59. Report, "Report on a Survey of the Problems of Inflation Raised in the President's Memorandum of February 26, 1951," March 2, 1951, Keyserling Papers, Truman Library.

60. Report, "Interim Report for the 4-Member Committee Appointed February 26," April 13, 1951, Committee on Fiscal and Monetary Policy folder, Keyserling Papers, Box 8, Truman Library.

61. Leon Keyserling and Johnson D. Clark to Joseph C. O'Mahoney, November 20, 1950, White House Contacts—Harry S. Truman, 1947–1953 folder, Keyserling Papers, Box 8, Truman Library.

62. "Monetary restriction would be felt by Government credit as well as by private credit, with the possible result of embarrassing the Government in its debt management operations. Taxes, on the other hand, would not have a similar adverse effect on Government credit and would, of course, reduce the amount of borrowing which the Government was obliged to undertake." Council of Economic Advisors to Harry S. Truman, "Report on Monetary Policy and Reserve Requirements," January 25, 1952, Papers of Roy Blough, Box 9, Truman Library.

63. Report, "Interim Report for the 4-Member Committee Appointed February 26," April 13, 1951, Committee on Fiscal and Monetary Policy folder, Keyserling Papers, Box 8, Truman Library.

64. "The period from July 1950 until the present [1951] was characterized by a surplus in the Government budget and very rapid private credit expansion. Some concluded from these facts that inflation in this period obviously was caused by credit expansion, and that the conflict between debt management and credit control was responsible for the failure to prevent inflation. While it is true that the policy of debt management had bearing upon the Federal Reserve System's ability to pursue a more effective anti-inflationary policy, it is by no means certain that Federal Reserve policy could under any circumstances have prevented a substantial inflationary price rise." Report, "Interim Report for the 4-Member Committee Appointed February 26," April 13, 1951, Committee on Fiscal and Monetary Policy folder, Keyserling Papers, Box 8, Truman Library.

65. Council of Economic Advisors to Harry S. Truman, "Report on Monetary Policy and Reserve Requirements," January 25, 1952, Papers of Roy Blough, Box 9, Truman Library.

66. Memorandum, "The Interdepartmental Fiscal Committee Meeting—Met on August 25 from 2:30 to 4:30," 8/30/1950, CEA folder, Blough Papers Box 12, Truman Library.

67. "CEA Quarterly Report on the Economic Situation," April 6, 1951 "CEA Monthly Report on the Economic Situation," March 3, 1951, Quarterly and Monthly Reports to the President 1951–1952 folder, Papers of John D. Clark Box 2, Truman Library.

68. For a table of federal receipts, outlays, and debt during the Korean War, see Edelstein, "War and the American Economy in the Twentieth Century," 369, table 6.6.

69. For a chart of percentage price change since Korean outbreak, January–September 1951, see "CEA Weekly Reports 1951/1952," Papers of Roy Blough, Box 10, Truman Library. For an in-depth discussion for why consumer demand declined, see Hickman, *The Korean War and United States Economic Activity*.

70. Polling Question: "The Government has been asking for further tax increases. Do you think taxes should or should not be increased at this time?" This was not the only polling question that captured the declining support for increased taxes. In February and August 1951, Americans were asked, "In order to pay for the defense, would you approve of the government taxing another five percent of your (your husband's) pay in taxes, on top of what you're paying now?" In February, 41 percent of Americans responded that they would approve another tax increase. By August, this figure declined to 35 percent.

71. "CEA Quarterly Report on the Economic Situation," April 6, 1951, Quarterly and Monthly Reports to the President 1951–1952 folder, Papers of John D. Clark Box 2, Truman Library.

72. CEA to Harry S. Truman, June 5, 1951, White House Contacts—Harry S. Truman 1947–1953 folder, Papers of Leon Keyserling Box 9, Truman Library.

73. "Tax Policy," December 10, 1951, Drafts Proposed by John D. Clark for Council Reports, folder, Papers of John D. Clark Box 1, Truman Library. Emphasis added.

74. "The Presidential Statement on Inflation—Press Conference," June 7, 1951, White House Contacts—Charles. S Murphy folder, Keyserling Papers, Truman Library.

75. "Special Message to Congress—The President's Midyear Economic Report," July 23, 1951, Public Papers of the President, Truman Library.

76. Ibid.

77. Blair, *The Forgotten War*, 716.

78. Ibid., 904.

79. July 1950 polling question: "Do you approve or disapprove of President (Harry) Truman's decision to send U.S. (United States) military aid to South Korea?" February 1951 polling question: "Do you think it was right or was it wrong for President (Truman) to send American forces to fight in Korea?"

80. Campbell et al., "Public Opinion and the Outbreak of War," 324.

81. Polling question: "Do you think the people in this country have been asked to make too many sacrifices, or not enough sacrifices, to support the war in Korea?"

82. Polling question: "In the disagreements between President (Harry) Truman and General (Douglas) MacArthur about how to carry on the war in Korea, who do you think was most nearly right?"

83. "Comments by the Advisory Committee of the American Federation of Labor to the Council of Economic Advisors," June 20, 1952, Council of Economic Advisors folder, Blough Papers Box 11, Truman Library.

84. Robert Lovett in a Cabinet Meeting, March 20, 1951, March 1951 folder, Connelly Papers Box 2, Truman Library.

85. L. Laszlo Ecker-Racz, Memorandum to James Snyder, March 9, 1951, Papers of Ecker-Racz Box 4, Truman Library.

86. The same report stated, "The sense of urgency which was pervasive in the first weeks following the China attack has abated under the influence of better news from Korea without new acts of physical aggression by communist states. The shift in public sentiment is reflected in the Congress, where the administration program for the defense period is now jeopardized by the feeling that it may not be necessary to subject the people to such burdens and restraints. The national leadership is challenged by this shift in public sentiment to make clear that the retarded impact of the defense program upon the

civilian economy which has led to a more complacent view may actually have aggravated the situation in some respects. The economic program can be softened only at the price of real national danger." "Council of Economic Advisors Quarterly Report," April 4, 1951, Quarterly and Monthly Reports to the President 1951–1952 folder, Clark Papers Box 2, Truman Library.

87. "Special Message to the Congress Recommending a 'Pay as We Go' Tax Program," February 2, 1951, Public Papers of the President, Truman Library.

88. Witte, *The Politics and Development of the Federal Income Tax,* 141.

89. Ibid., 142.

90. Ibid., 144–145.

## CHAPTER 3. JOHNSON AND THE VIETNAM WAR

1. For a discussion of the relationship between war finance and inflation, see T. Riddell, "The Vietnam War and Inflation Revisited," in *Lyndon Baines Johnson and the Uses of Power*, ed. B.J. Firestone and R.C. Vogt (New York: Greenwood Press, 1988), 217–232; war finance and the US balance of payments position, see L. Dudley and P. Passell, "The War in Vietnam and the United States Balance of Payments," *Review of Economics and Statistics* 50.4 (1968): 437–442; war finance and pressure on the dollar, see R.W. Stevens, *Vain Hopes, Grim Realities: The Economic Consequences of the Vietnam War* (New York: New Viewpoints, 1976), chaps. 9–10; war finance and world financial crisis, see R.M. Collins, "The Economic Crisis of 1968 and the Waning of the 'American Century,'" *American Historical Review* 101.2 (1996): 396–422; A. Houben, *The Evolution of Monetary Policy Strategies in Europe* (Boston: Kluwer Academic, 2000); and Stevens, *Vain Hopes, Grim Realities.* For the relationship between war finance and high interest rates: Memo, Arthur M. Okun to President Johnson, 5/20/1968, "Costs of Fiscal Inaction," EX BE 5, Box 25, WHCF, LBJ Library; Memo, Gardner Ackley to President Johnson, 10/13/1967, "Notes for Use in Talking with Reporters," EX BE 5, Box 25, WHCF, LBJ Library; Memo, Robert Kinter to President Johnson, 7/26/1966, "Current Banking and Money Market Problems," Confidential File, BE, Box 2, WHCF, LBJ Library.

2. Many scholars discuss Johnson's fear of losing his Great Society welfare program if he were to ask for an increase in taxes to pay for the Vietnam War. See D. Halberstam, *The Best and the Brightest* (New York: Random House, 1972), 606; Riddell, "The Vietnam War and Inflation Revisited," 228–229; Stevens, *Vain Hopes, Grim Realities,* 68.

3. Leland and Oboroceanu, *American War and Military Operation Casualties,* 11.

4. Costs are estimated in current year currency. Daggett, *Costs of Major U.S. Wars, 2.* For a table of military outlays, see Tuan, *South Vietnam Trial and Experience: A Challenge for Development* (Athens, OH: Center for International Studies, Ohio University, 1987).

5. See R. Blackburn, *Mercenaries and Lyndon Johnson's "More Flags": The Hiring of Korean, Filipino, and Thai Soldiers in the Vietnam War* (Jefferson: Mcfarland, 1994); Riddell, *A Political Economy of the American War in Indo-China,* 117, 136–137.

6. Beginning in 1966, military assistance funds for South Vietnam, previously routed through the Military Assistance Program, were transferred to the military services and funded with the Department of Defense Budget. Consequently, military assistance funds since that time are included in DOD estimates of war costs. See U.S. Congress, House of Representatives, Committee on Armed Services, Hearings on Military Posture, 91st Congress, 2nd Session, 1970, 7696; and Riddell, *A Political Economy of the American War in Indo-China,* 9, table 3.

7. A.F. Ott and P. Hughes-Cromwick, "The War on Poverty: Two Decades Later," in *Lyndon Baines Johnson and the Uses of Power*, ed. B.J. Firestone and R.C. Vogt (New York: Greenwood Press, 1988), 53, table 3.1.

8. Memo, Stan Rose to Joe Califano, 5/7/68, EX FI 11, Box 56, WHCF, LBJ Library.

9. For a table of the Johnson budget from 1965–1970 see Memo, Joe Califano to the President, 12/16/68, FI 4, Box 25, WHCF, LBJ Library. According to Edelstein, one consequence of this concurrent financing is the difficulty in isolating the source of a nation's deficit. "During WWI, WWII and Korea, the federal government undertook no other major expenditure or transfer program. Thus, it is possible to treat the movement of federal receipts and expenditures during these earlier war periods as overwhelmingly driven by the financing of national security. However, during the Vietnam War federal expenditures on transfer payments increased as did spending on nonwar goods and services. Thus the financing of the Vietnam War was intertwined with the financing of these other activities, and the task of finding the purely war effects involves a complicated unraveling of various threads" (Edelstein, "War and the American Economy in the Twentieth Century," 376).

10. E.C. Hargrove and M.A. Samuel, *The President and the Council of Economic Advisers: Interviews with CEA Chairman* (Boulder, CO: Westview Press, 1984), 227.

11. Explicitly excluded from the Troika were departments that represented strong constituencies such as Labor, Commerce, Agriculture, etc. See ibid., 7–8).

12. Ackley described Califano's role: "Much of our [CEA] contact with LBJ involved, or occurred through, Joe Califano, who had policy responsibility for domestic economic matters . . . as far as I can recall, all important economic questions funneled through Joe." Ibid., 226–227.

13. Ackley described their relationship: "LBJ was very impressed with Bob McNamara's mental capacities and used to try out ideas of all kinds of economic questions on him. We were always delighted to have him do so because McNamara almost invariably supported our views on what the correct answers were." Ibid., 224.

14. In order to understand public opinion for the war effort, I use various sources of polling and survey data: the Gallup Poll, Roper/Fortune Survey and ORC Public Opinion Index, using the iPoll databank at the Roper Center. http://www.ropercenter.uconn.edu/data_access/ipoll/ipoll.html#.TihiaM3qo4g.

15. Memo, Gardner Ackley to President Lyndon Johnson, 5/5/1965, BE 5 Box 23, "Thinking Ahead on Economic Problems, WHCF, LBJ Library. An alternative but consistent argument explaining why the CEA failed "to convince President Johnson to propose a tax increase in 1966 was that it was so ideologically committed to growth that it was insensitive to the early signals of growing inflation. . . . For the CEA, the real danger was recession, which would lead to unemployment. Its policy instruments were trained and aimed to combat recession, not inflation." J. Sloan, "President Johnson, The Council of Economic Advisors, and the Failure to Raise Taxes in 1966 and 1967," *Presidential Studies Quarterly* 15.1 (1985): 92.

16. Memo, Gardner Ackley to Bill Moyers, Jack Valenti, and Joe Califano, 11/29/1965, "Briefing Materials—The Outlook for Price-Cost Stability," BE 5, Box 23, WHCF, LBJ Library.

17. Report to the President, CEA Staff Memorandum—"The Outlook for Price Stability in 1965," 7/8/1964, BE5-1 Box 28, WHCF, LBJ Library.

18. Report to the President, CEA Staff Memorandum—"The Outlook for Price Stability in 1965—A Second Look," 10/8/1964, BE5-1 Box 28, WHCF, LBJ Library.

19. "The economy can absorb the reasonable foreseeable demands of the Vietnam conflict and essential civilian needs within the framework of a free market economy—without the resort to the harsh economic controls that have characterized past wars." Memo, Henry Fowler to President Johnson, 10/15/1966, "The Current Economic and Financial Situation," BE 5, Box 24, WHCF, LBJ Library.

20. Memo, Gardner Ackley to President Lyndon Johnson, 7/30/1965, "Economic Aspects of Vietnam," BE 5, Box 23, WHCF, LBJ Library.

21. A consistent and additional argument made regarding the Vietnam-Korean analogy and war finance is differences in mobilization. "In 1965, most of the administration's economic and military planners did not see a parallel to Korea because, in their view, the economy could handle an escalation. . . . The force level in 1965 was much greater, so it would seemingly not require drastic measures. . . . Budget director Charles Schultze pointed out that 'one of the accomplishments over the past 4 years has been to build a military force with the capability of moving into a situation like this, giving us time to make the appropriate evaluation.' This probably led many to assume that the war could be handled adequately without going on a war footing." J.W. Helsing, *Johnson's War/Johnson's Great Society: The Guns and Butter Trap* (Westport, CN: Praeger, 2000), 191–193.

22. Memo, Gardner Ackley to President Johnson, 8/25/1965, "The Price Situation and Outlook," BE 5-1 Box 28, WHCF, LBJ Library. Memo, Kermit Gordon to Joe Califano, 1/25/66, "Why Economists Dread Mandatory Price Control," BE 5-1, Box 28, WHCF, LBJ Library.

23. Memo, Gardner Ackley to President Lyndon Johnson, 6/2/1965, BE 5, Box 23, WHCF, LBJ Library.

24. Original emphasis. Memo, Gardner Ackley to President Lyndon Johnson, 7/30/1965, "Economic Aspects of Vietnam," BE 5, Box 23, WHCF, LBJ Library.

25. W.C. Gibbons, *The U.S. Government and the Vietnam War: Executive and Legislative Roles and Relationships*, Part IV, *July 1965–January 1968* (Princeton: Princeton University Press, 1995), 218. For other works that argue the CEA believed that both guns and butter were possible, see D.K. Pickens, "LBJ, the Economic Council of Advisors, and the Burden of New Deal Liberalism," *Lyndon Baines Johnson and the Uses of Power*, ed. B.J. Firestone and R.C. Vogt (New York: Greenwood Press, 1988), 196; and Hammond, *LBJ and the Presidential Management of Foreign Relations* (Austin: University of Texas Press, 1992), 201–209.

26. Memo, Charles Schultze to President Lyndon Johnson, 5/11/1966, "The Effect of a Tax Increase," FI 9, Box 55, WHCF, LBJ Library.

27. "Our best forecasts are bound to be imprecise, but we do not know the direction nor the extent of the error. . . . If demand turned out significantly softer than expected, it would be essential to move very quickly in order to avoid a recession. On the other hand, if demand were stronger than expected, delay in action to moderate it could be costly, but not as damaging as in the opposite case. . . . It seems clear that if we regard a recession as the worst possible outcome, and take seriously the possibility that demand may be weaker than our forecast, we should not ask for a tax increase." Memo, Joseph Barr, Charles Schultze, and Gardner Ackley to President Johnson, 12/14/1966, "A Second Look at the Economic Outlook and Policy for 1967," BE 5, Box 25, WHCF, LBJ Library.

28. Memo, Joe Califano to President Johnson, 5/7/1966, Confidential File, BE (1966), Box 2, WHCF, LBJ Library.

29. For dissenting arguments see A. Downes, "How Smart and Tough Are Democracies? Reassessing Theories of Democratic Victory in War," *International Security* 33.4 (2009): 9–51; and J.M. Schuessler, "Democracy, Deception, and IR Theory," *International Security Studies Forum Roundtable* 5.4 (2012), chap. 3.

30. Memo, Charles Schultze to President Johnson, 2/18/1966, Agency File, Box 7, NSF, LBJ Library. Moreover, in a Memo from Fowler, Schultze, and Ackley to President Johnson, they stated, "The pattern of defense outlays in the fiscal 1967 budget assumes a phasing out of our capabilities for continued hostilities in Vietnam." Memo, Henry Fowler, Charles Schultze, Gardner Ackley to President Johnson, 4/8/1966, "Troika Review of the Economic and Fiscal Outlook," BE 5, Box 2, WHCF, LBJ Library. In a letter from Schultze to President Johnson in January 1967, Schultze stated, "Rather than request an amount not based upon firm requirements, it was decided to request funds based on the assump-

tion that combat operations would terminate on June 30, 1967." Letter from Schultze to President Johnson, 1/24/1967, National Security File, LBJ Library. See also Gibbons, *The U.S. Government and the Vietnam War,* 216–217.

31. Memo, Henry Fowler, Charles Schultze, Gardner Ackley to President Johnson, 4/8/1966, "Troika Review of the Economic and Fiscal Outlook," BE 5, Box 2, WHCF, LBJ Library.

32. "Our recent price performance shows encouraging signs. The index of raw material prices, which moves far in advance of wholesale and consumer prices, has dropped almost fifteen percent since March. Wholesale industrial prices have held steady since July. The rise in wholesale food prices has been reversed in recent weeks. These developments should be favorably reflected in consumer prices in coming months." Memo, Henry Fowler to President Johnson, 10/15/1966, "The Current Economic and Financial Situation," BE 5, Box 24, WHCF, LBJ Library.

33. Memo, Henry Fowler to President Johnson, 10/15/1966, "The Current Economic and Financial Situation," BE 5, Box 24, WHCF, LBJ Library.

34. Joe Califano to President Johnson in December 1966, "It is clear that the models uniformly involve a projected rate of growth below our target. Indeed, projected growth is sufficiently slow that—with bad luck—the economy might stall and head into recession." Memo, Joe Califano to President Johnson, 12/21/1966, "Your FY '68 Tax Decision," FI 11–3, Box 18, WHCF, LBJ Library.

35. Ibid.

36. As an August 7, 1966, article in *Business Week* stated, "In a cold mathematical view, the Vietnam build-up thus far ordered by President Johnson changes the economic outlook for the better." See Helsing, *Johnson's War/Johnson's Great Society*, 195.

37. Gibbons, *The U.S. Government and the Vietnam War*, 906.

38. Hammond, *LBJ and the Presidential Management of Foreign Relations*, 204.

39. M. Lorrell, C. Kelly Jr., and D. Hensler, *Casualties, Public Opinion, and Presidential Policy during the Vietnam War* (Santa Monica: Rand-Project Air Force, 1985), 52–53.

40. W. Heller, *New Dimensions of Political Economy* (Cambridge, MA: Harvard University Press, 1966), 94.

41. Memo, Gardner Ackley to President Lyndon Johnson, 7/30/1965, "Economic Aspects of Vietnam," BE 5, Box 23, WHCF, LBJ Library.

42. "Now we have been greatly concerned because consumer prices rose 4.5 percent over the 18 months since we decided to send troops to Vietnam. . . . I recommend to the Congress a surcharge of 6 percent on both corporate and individual income taxes—to last for 2 years or for so long as the unusual expenditures associated with our efforts in Vietnam continue . . . this surcharge will raise revenues by some $4.5 billion in the first year." *Public Papers of the Presidents of the United States: Lyndon B. Johnson, 1967*, vol. 1, entry 3 (Washington, DC: Government Printing Office, 1968), 2–14.

43. Letter, Charles Schultze to President Johnson, 1/24/1967, NSF, Box 7, Agency File, LBJ Library.

44. Ackley estimated an $11 billion budget deficit for FY1967 and an $18 billion deficit for FY1968. Memo, Gardner Ackley to President Johnson, 1/4/1967, "Briefing Paper on Economic Policy for 1967," Confidential Files, BE (1966), Box 2, WHCF, LBJ Library.

45. Memo, Joe Califano to President Johnson, 12/8/1966, FG 11-3, Box 18, WHCF, LBJ Library.

46. Memo, Joe Califano to President Johnson, 6/12/1967, EX FG 11-3 Box 60, WHCF, LBJ Library.

47. Memo, Joe Califano to President Johnson, 6/17/1967, EX FG 11-3 Box 60, WHCF, LBJ Library.

48. "We recommend the following program: Speed up corporate tax collection; Postpone reduction of excise tax on automobiles and telephone service; 10% corporate tax surcharge and 10% on individual income tax; exempt lowest income brackets; keep civilian expenditures within the January budget and reduce non-Vietnam defense expenditures." Memo, Henry Fowler, William Wirtz, Alexander Trowbridge, Robert McNamara, Charles Schultze, Gardner Ackley, and Joe Califano to President Johnson, 7/22/1967, FI 11, Box 56, WHCF, LBJ Library.

49. Memo, Henry Fowler to President Johnson, 8/14/1967, EX BE5, Box 25, WHCF, LBJ Library.

50. Memo, Gardner Ackley to President Johnson, 2/25/1967, "Reactions to Your Economic Policy Program," BE 5, Box 25, WHCF, LBJ Library.

51. Memo, Gardner Ackley to President Johnson, 5/22/1967, "Economic Situation and Strategy," EX FG 11-3, Box 60, WHCF, LBJ Library.

52. Memo, Gardner Ackley to President Johnson, 7/1/1967, "Joint Economic Committee Hearings," EX FG 11-3, Box 60, WHCF, LBJ Library.

53. Memo, Gardner Ackley to President Johnson, 8/21/1967, "Economic News Notes," EX FG 11-3 Box 60, WHCF, LBJ Library.

54. The economists responsible for drafting and circulating the statement were professors G. L. Bach of Stanford; Walter W. Heller, former CEA chairman, from the University of Minnesota; and Dr. Joseph A. Pechman, director of economic studies at the Brookings Institution. Memo, Gardner Ackley to President Johnson, 8/16/1967, "Economists' Statement on Tax Policy," EX FG 11-3, Box 60, WHCF, LBJ Library.

55. The statement read: "We, the undersigned members of the business community, believe that: (1) congress should enact a temporary uniform tax increase on corporations and individuals for such period as the Vietnam war requires; and (2) the Congress and the administration should control and reduce Federal expenditures. . . . The combined result of the tax increase and expenditure reductions should hold the deficit to manageable proportions. These steps are necessary to prevent a federal deficit so large that it could lead to dangerous inflation, spiraling interest rates, tight money, and a serious weakening in our balance of payments positions." "Statement of Principles," 9/13/1967, EX FG 11-3, Box 60, WHCF, LBJ Library.

56. Memo Gardner Ackley to President Johnson, 10/27/1967, "Meeting with Business Economists," EX BE 5, Box 25, WHCF, LBJ Library.

57. J.E. Zelizer, *Taxing America: Wilbur D. Mills, Congress, and the State, 1945–1975* (Cambridge: Cambridge University Press, 1998), 268; P. M. Simpson, "Lyndon B. Johnson and the 1964–1968 Revenue Acts: Congressional Politics and 'Fiscal Chickens Coming Home to Roost,'" *Lyndon Baines Johnson and the Uses of Power*, ed. B. J. Firestone and R.C. Vogt (New York: Greenwood, 1988).

58. Mueller, *War, Presidents, and Public Opinion*, 53.

59. A Rand report found similar trends: "The single largest decline in public support occurred as it became evident—in the spring of 1966—that the war would be neither low-cost nor brief. Support for the war then stabilized at about 50% for approximately a year. But in the spring of 1967, it fell permanently below 50%. Thereafter, a steady decline set in at roughly a constant rate until support declined to an all-time low of 28 percent in May, 1971." Lorrell et al., *Casualties, Public Opinion, and Presidential Policy During the Vietnam War*, 20.

60. Interview, Chester Cooper, March 10, 1982, quoted in ibid., 79.

61. The mail was classified as "Vietnam–U.S. policy, general" and categorized every letter, card, or telegram received as "pro, con, or comment." See Papers of LBJ, Mail Summaries, LBJ Library.

62. The rest—7,011—were classified as "comment." White House Mail Room, Volume Mail Receipts, Recapitulation for 1967, 1968, Mail Summaries, Box 1, LBJ Library. Verba et al. also state, "We were told that the President avidly followed the polls on the war." Verba et al., "Public Opinion and the War in Vietnam," *Political Science Review* 61.2 (1967): 318.

63. Memo Whitney Shoemaker [Johnson's public correspondence assistant] to President Johnson, 3/29/1968, Mail Summaries, Box 1, LBJ Library.

64. February 1966: A NORC/Stanford University Survey asked, "Would you approve or disapprove of the following in order to continue fighting (in Vietnam) . . . increasing taxes at home?" Thirty-one percent responded they were in favor, 67 percent disapprove, and 3 percent didn't know. March 1966: A Harris Survey asked, "As far as you personally are concerned, if President (Lyndon B.) Johnson said it was necessary to raise taxes to pay for the war in Vietnam, would you favor or oppose raising the income tax?" Forty-four percent responded they were in favor, 49 percent were opposed and 7 percent were not sure. October 1966–July 1967: A Gallup Poll question asked, "The suggestion has been made that income taxes be increased to help pay for the war in Vietnam. Would you favor or oppose an income tax increase for this purpose?" Nineteen percent responded they were in favor, 73 percent oppose, and 8 percent no opinion.

65. In 1965, Verba et al. found that there was a direct correlation between support for the war and willingness to pay for it. Those who favored increasing the war were more likely to be willing to pay the costs of that increase. Conversely, there was a tendency for those who favored de-escalation to oppose the payment of these costs. Verba et al., "Public Opinion and the War in Vietnam," 323–324.

66. Memo, Henry Fowler to President Johnson, 1/13/1967, FI 11, Box 56, WHCF, LBJ Library.

67. Gibbons, *The U.S. Government and the War in Vietnam,* 804–808.

68. Ibid., 806.

69. Ibid., 806.

70. Memo, Arthur Okun to President Johnson, 3/18/1968, "Joint Economic Committee Report," EX FB 11-3, Box 61, WHCF, LBJ Library.

71. Memo, Arthur Okun to President Johnson, 5/27/1968, "Prices and Wages in the First Quarter," EX FG 11-3, Box 61, WHCF, LBJ Library.

72. Memo, Arthur Okun to President Johnson, 5/20/1968, "Added Notes on the Costs of Fiscal Inaction," FI 11, Box 56, WHCF, LBJ Library.

73. Memo, Arthur Okun to President Johnson, 5/20/1968, "Costs of Fiscal Inaction," EX BE 5, Box 25, WHCF, LBJ Library.

74. Letter, Arthur Okun to Chairman Wilbur Mills, 4/8/1968, EX FG 11-3, Box 61, WHCF, LBJ Library. Interestingly, the inflation in 1968 was partly caused by the Federal Reserve's response to its belief that the tax increase would pass. The Fed, expecting that Congress would recognize and act on the need for the surcharge, expanded money supply vigorously in the first half of 1967. See C.E. McLure Jr., "Fiscal Failure: Lessons of the Sixties," *Economic Policy and Inflation in the Sixties*, ed. W. Fellner (Washington, DC: American Enterprise Institute for Public Policy Research, 1972), 56.

75. Memo, Arthur Okun to President Johnson, 5/27/1968, "Prices and Wages in the First Quarter," EX FG 11-3, Box 61, WHCF, LBJ Library.

76. Zelizer, *Taxing America,* 276.

77. The Johnson administration believed that the crisis was directly connected to the failure to pass the surtax. In a memo from Treasury Secretary Fowler to President Johnson on March 4, 1968, he stated that one of four causes of the crisis was "general uncertainty about the international monetary system, caused by worry in Europe among other things over the failure to pass the tax bill." Memo, Henry Fowler to President Johnson,

3/4/1968, "Gold Problems," NSF Agency File, Box 65, WHCF, LBJ Library. See also Memo, Arthur Okun to President Johnson, 5/20/1968, "Costs of Fiscal Inaction," EX BE 5, Box 25, WHCF, LBJ Library.

78. Collins, "The Economic Crisis of 1968," 396.

79. Ibid., 411.

80. *Public Papers of the Presidents of the United States: Lyndon B. Johnson, 1968–69*, vol. 1, entry 170, 469–476 (Washington, DC: Government Printing Office, 1970).

81. Ibid.

82. Zelizer, *Taxing America*, 277.

83. A myriad of authors discuss how the 1966 interest rate increase affected disintermediation and housing. Among these are G.L. Bell, "The Effects of Monetary Policy on Specific Sectors of the Economy," *Journal of Political Economy* 76.4, part 2: Issues in Monetary Research (1968): 818–821; O. Brownlee, "The Effects of Monetary and Credit Policies on the Structure of the Economy," *Journal of Political Economy* 76.4, part 2: Issues in Monetary Research (1968): 786–795; D.I. Fand, "The Impact of Monetary Policy in 1966," *Journal of Political Economy* 74.4 part 2: Issues in Monetary Research (1968): 821–830; S.J. Maisel, "The Effects of Monetary Policy on Expenditures in Specific Sectors of the Economy," *Journal of Political Economy* 76.4, part 2: Issues in Monetary Research (1967): 796–814. See also Memo, Arthur Okun to President Johnson, "The Costs of Fiscal Inaction," 5/20/1968, EX BE 5, Box 25, WHCF, LBJ Library. Memo, Arthur Okun to President Johnson, "Added Notes on the Costs of Fiscal Inaction," 5/20/1968, EX BE 5-2, Box 30, WHCF, LBJ Library.

84. Memo, Gardner Ackley to President Johnson, 5/10/66, "The Case for Higher Taxes," FI 9, Box 55, WHCF, LBJ Library.

85. Report, Fowler to President Johnson, "The Current Economic and Financial Situation," 10/15/1966, EX BE 5, Box 24, WHCF, LBJ Library. In an interview Ackley recounted how many times he warned the president of the Fed's actions. Referring to a time in the spring of 1966, when a White House staffer suggested the president should condemn tight money, Ackley responded, "I went back through my files and pulled out about ten different places in which we had said in so many words, 'If you don't have a tax increase, one of those things you're really going to get is tight money and high interest rates. That is the choice you have to make.' So I said, 'We told you so!'" Hargrove and Samuel, *The President and the Council of Economic Advisers*, 232–233.

86. Letter, Congressman Al Ullman to President Johnson, 6/72/66, BE 5-2, Box 31, WHCF, LBJ Library. Letter, President Johnson to Congressman Al Ullman, 7/7/66, BE 5-2, Box 31, WHCF, LBJ Library.

87. Memo, Gardner Ackley to President Johnson, 8/20/1966, "Conversation with Wilbur Mills," FI 9-Box 55, WHCF, LBJ Library.

88. Robert Solomon, September 12, 1967 at 9:30 am, FOMC Meeting, Washington, DC, Board of Governors of the Federal Reserve System, 29–30.

89. A. Cairncross and B. Eichengreen, *Sterling in Decline: The Devaluations of 1931, 1949, and 1967* (New York: Palgrave Macmillan, 2003).

90. Robert Solomon, December 12, 1967, at 9:30 am, FOMC Meeting, Washington, DC, Board of Governors of the Federal Reserve System, 44–47; Alfred Heyes, December 12, 1967 at 9:30 am, FOMC Meeting, Washington, DC, Board of Governors of the Federal Reserve System, 49.

91. For an in depth discussion of the negative effects of financial disintermediation, see J. Vernon, "Financial Disintermediation in a Macroeconomic Framework: Comment," *Journal of Finance* 28.4 (1973): 1029–1032.

92. William Sherrill, September 12, 1967 at 9:30 am, FOMC Meeting, Washington, DC, Board of Governors of the Federal Reserve System, 43. See also George Clay, Sep-

tember 12, 1967 at 9:30 am, FOMC Meeting, Washington, DC, Board of Governors of the Federal Reserve System, 55.

93. "I believe that we could and should get the Fed on record promising to adjust the monetary policy screws (and especially help to relieve the mortgage famine) in return for a new fiscal program. Congress needs to be reminded that we can have a less restrictive monetary policy, but only by adopting a more restrictive fiscal policy." Memo, Gardner Ackley to President Johnson, 8/9/1966, "An Immediate Tax Program," FI 9, Box 55, WHCF, LBJ Library.

94. Hargrove and Samuel, *The President and the Council of Economic Advisers*, 236, 249. See also Memo, Joseph Barr, Charles Schultze, and Gardner Ackley to President Johnson, "A Second Look at the Economic Outlook and Policy for 1967," 12/14/1966, BE 5, Box 25, WHCF, LBJ Library.

95. Memo, Joseph Barr, Charles Schultze, and Gardner Ackley to President Johnson, "A Second Look at the Economic Outlook and Policy for 1967," 12/14/1966, BE 5, Box 25, WHCF, LBJ Library.

96. In September, Alfred Hayes reported "the money stock had increased at a 9 percent annual rate in the past six months, the fastest for any six months in more than twenty years." Alfred Hayes, December 12, 1967 at 9:30 am, FOMC Meeting, Washington, DC, Board of Governors of the Federal Reserve System, 30–33.

97. Voting FOMC Members present: Chairman William Martin, Vice Chairman Alfred Hayes, Andrew Brimmer, Dewey Daane, Darryl Francis, Sherman Maisel, George Mitchell, J.L. Robertson, Charles Scanlon, William Sherrill, Eliot Swan, and Edward Wayne. A few other members' comments—Vice Chairman Alfred Hayes: 'I would hate to see an excessive rise in interest rates interfere with the vitally needed action on higher taxes.' Member Sherman Maisel: 'It was necessary to do as much as possible to obtain the tax increase, and not to let Congress say, "The Federal Reserve is running the economy. Why should we move?" Member Andrew Brimmer: 'The most important consideration at the moment was the need to encourage fiscal action, which the members of the Committee had favored for some time. In his view any shift toward firming now would lead to rapid reactions in financial markets that would have seriously adverse effects on Congressional attitudes toward the President's program and would jeopardize its enactment.' While he was not at all sure how soon Congress would act and how much of a tax increase would be approved, he thought it would be a serious mistake to reduce the chances of favorable action by firming monetary policy now. Moreover, Chairman Martin was scheduled to testify on the tax increase in hearings before the House Ways and Means Committee this week, and a move toward restraint by the Open Market Committee today, even if it was a modest one, could well complicate the discussion of the relations between fiscal and monetary policy that was likely to develop at those hearings." September 12, 1967 at 9:30 am, FOMC Meeting, Washington, DC, Board of Governors of the Federal Reserve System.

98. "From the standpoint of economic considerations alone, it would have been desirable to adopt a firmer monetary policy a number of months ago. It had been clear then, however, that the overriding need was for a tax increase, and that a firming of monetary policy would make Congressional action on taxes less likely. Now it was clear that any tax increase would come later than it should, and perhaps too late. He certainly had done everything he could to help the administration *persuade* Congress of the need for enactment of a tax increase in this session, but those efforts had been futile. There was no doubt that the System was faced with a serious problem at present. To his mind, the economic statistics for the third quarter demonstrated that the horse of inflation not only was out of the barn but was already well down the road. To pursue the analogy, he did not think the horse could be returned to the barn by monetary policy, but it could be prevented

from trotting too fast." William Martin, December 12, 1967 at 9:30 am, FOMC Meeting, Washington, DC, Board of Governors of the Federal Reserve System, 97–98.

99. "But a more important development since our last meeting has been the demise of any hope for a tax increase during this session of Congress. I cannot help feeling that the prospects for a tax increase in early 1968 are at best dubious. Accentuation of inflationary pressures and a further growth in inflationary psychology appear to be highly likely if excessive demands are piled on top of pre-existing cost pressures. The growth of inflationary attitudes must be checked both in the interest of longer run domestic stability and because of the adverse effects on international confidence in the stability of the dollar. As I said earlier, recent developments have clearly increased the vulnerability of the dollar. The decline in the gold stock announced last week has made this dramatically clear. There is no escaping the fact that our fiscal situation is in sad disarray. It is all the more important that monetary policy behave responsibly. It seems to me that all the fundamentals call for a more restrictive stance, although I am under no illusion that monetary policy can by itself solve all our domestic and international problems. . . . The receding hope of tax action is significant, since we have been inclined to refrain from tightening monetary policy for fear that this might have an adverse effect on the Congressional climate for tax legislation. Unfortunately, the climate was bad enough anyway. The fear of tipping sterling over the devaluation brink was also an inhibiting element." Alfred Heyes, December 12, 1967 at 9:30 am, FOMC Meeting, Washington, DC, Board of Governors of the Federal Reserve System, 49–50.

100. Worsening balance of payments—FOMC Associate Economist Daniel Brill testifying to the FOMC, "Given the problems of inflation and the worsening of our balance of payments situation that have resulted from the excessive pace of activity, there can be no question that fiscal restraint is needed." Daniel Brill, May 28, 1968 at 9:30 am, FOMC Meeting, Washington, DC, Board of Governors of the Federal Reserve System, 58.; Sterling financial crisis—Chairman Martin on Sterling: "If the British were forced onto a floating exchange rate, additional problems would be posed for the United States. Fiscal action in this country would certainly buttress the position of the pound. In fact, one reason the British had delayed drawing on the Fund was that they hoped to be able to tie that action to a change in U.S. fiscal policy." William Martin, May 28, 1968 at 9:30 am, FOMC Meeting, Washington, DC, Board of Governors of the Federal Reserve System, 23; Worsening Disintermediation—Vice Chairman Hayes: "Disintermediation has begun to add pressure on resources available to commercial banks as well as on thrift institutions as rates on money market instruments have moved up." Alfred Hayes, May 28, 1968 at 9:30 am, FOMC Meeting, Washington, DC, Board of Governors of the Federal Reserve System, 69.

101. Vice Chairman Hayes on defense expenditures and a tax increase: "There are, of course, major uncertainties in the budgetary prospects. In the first place, the underlying assumptions of no further escalation in Vietnam and no military involvement in Korea [are uncertain] . . . on balance the budget will remain strongly expansionary unless a sizable tax increase is enacted. The obvious conclusion is that the tax rise is most urgently called for in order to limit the budget's stimulating effects, to make more manageable the Treasury's financing program, and to improve our international position through a demonstration of fiscal responsibility—and, over the longer run, through a strengthening of our competitive position doubt the estimated rise of only $3 billion in cash defense spending." Alfred Hayes, February 6, 1968 at 9:30 am, FOMC Meeting, Washington, DC, Board of Governors of the Federal Reserve System, 55.

102. Quoted in L. Berman, *Lyndon Johnson's War: The Road to Stalemate in Vietnam* (New York: W.W. Norton, 1989), 193.

## CHAPTER 4. BRITAIN AND CURRENCY RESERVES DURING WORLD WAR II AND THE CRIMEAN WAR

1. A number of authors have detailed British domestic financing of World War II, including W.K. Hancock and M.M. Gowing, *British War Economy* (London: His Majesty's Stationery Office, 1949); H.C. Murphy, *The National Debt in War and Transition* (New York: McGraw-Hill, 1950); Sayers, *Financial Policy, 1939–1945*; R. Whiting, *The Labor Party and Taxation: Party Identity and Political Purpose in Twentieth-Century Britain* (Cambridge: Cambridge University Press, 2004), chap. 2.

2. While the British had to borrow various currencies to fight a global war, this chapter focuses solely on the primary source of external war finance with the United States and the need for dollars.

3. While a leader may prefer external war finance in order to avoid negative public support for the war, this chapter is focused primarily on those instances when states have to resort to external war finance even when they prefer not to.

4. For a table of British Empire supplies of munitions from all sources, see Hancock and Gowing, *British War Economy*, 373.

5. For a comparison of British and German war production see Mark Harrison, "The Economics of World War II: An Overview," in *The Economics of War*, ed. Mark Harrison (Cambridge: Cambridge University Press, 1998), table 1.6, 15–16.

6. To understand British external war finance, one must also understand the Sterling Area. The Sterling Area was an informal organization that emerged from the London-centered international market of the nineteenth century. It consisted of all members of the British Commonwealth, apart from Canada, and some nonmembers of the Commonwealth, such as the Irish Republic, Burma, Iceland, Iraq, and Jordan. Before World War II, these countries sold their products for sterling so that they could use the currency either to finance their imports from the United Kingdom or to clear their accounts with third parties. Any member was free to convert their money into dollars (which were kept in London) and draw dollars out as they saw fit. During World War II, when dollars were needed to purchase supplies for the war from the United States, the Sterling Area formalized nonconvertibility. It restricted members from freely converting their balances into dollars at any time and the British Treasury, via the Exchange Equalization Account, was tasked with the responsibility of managing Britain's and the Area's foreign exchange reserve (H. Gaitskell, "The Sterling Area," *International Affairs* [*Royal Institute of Internaitonal Affairs 1944–*] 28.2 [1952]: 170–171).

7. Hancock and Gowing, *British War Economy*, 107. For a discussion of British investments abroad, specifically in the United States, see H. Feis, *Europe: The World's Banker* (New Haven, CT: Yale University Press, 1930); and W.A. Morton, *British Finance, 1930–1940* (Madison: University of Wisconsin Press, 1943).

8. Memo, Department of State to the British Embassy, February 21, 1940, *FRUS, 1940,* 3:97–98.

9. Memo, British Ambassador to the United States Marquees Lothian to Secretary of State Hull, March 1, 1940, *FRUS, 1940,* 3:104.

10. In 1937, the act was amended to include a "cash-and-carry" provision, allowing the sale of materials and supplies to belligerents in Europe as long as they paid cash for goods. Memo, British Ambassador to the United States Marquees Lothian to Secretary of State Hull, March 1, 1940, *FRUS, 1940,* 3:104.

11. Ambassador Joseph Kennedy to Secretary of State Cordell Hull, October 16, 1939, *FRUS, 1939,* 7:222.

12. It should be noted the restriction of imports from the United States angered American officials. The British defended their decision to frustrated American policymakers, explaining that the war would necessitate an increase in expenditures. British ambassador

to the United States, Philip Kerr, wrote to Hull in March 1940, "British consumption of and dollar expenditure on non-essential agricultural products must be increasingly restricted as an imperative condition of financing the war until it reaches a successful conclusion." Memo, British Ambassador (Lothian) to Secretary of State Hull, March 1, 1940, *FRUS, 1940,* 3:104. For an example of US policymakers expressing discontent, see Memorandum of Conversation, by the Secretary of State, January 22, 1940, *FRUS, 1940,* 3, 90. While American policymakers were upset, those at the State Department were sympathetic to Britain's actions. "Of course, we knew the situation in which Great Britain found herself, struggling with all her resources against a powerful foe. The expenses of Britain's war efforts were rising by leaps and bounds. Everything that was not an immediate necessity to life or limb had to be subordinated to the purchase of direct war material. . . . Total British purchases in the United States had risen sharply. Foreign exchange was limited, and every cent of it was being mobilized. . . . Most non-military supplies which could be purchased elsewhere must be sought in alternative markets in order to save Britain's vital dollar exchange." Memorandum of Conversation, by the Chief of the Division of European Affairs [Jay Pierrepont] (Moffat), January 25, 1940, *FRUS, 1940,* 3:91.

13. Ambassador Joseph Kennedy to Secretary of State Cordell Hull, September 3, 1939, *FRUS, 1939,* 7:214.

14. Ambassador Joseph Kennedy to Secretary of State Cordell Hull, September 2, 1939, *FRUS, 1939,* 7:213.

15. Sayers, *Financial Policy 1939–1949,* 241.

16. Ibid., 241.

17. Hancock and Gowing, *British War Economy,* 106.

18. H. D. Hall, *North American Supply* (London: Her Majesty's Stationery Office, 1955), 110–111. For British financing of American factories and the training of American workers to increase plane production, see Hall, *North American Supply,* 289–290; E. R. Stettinius Jr., *Lend-Lease: Weapon for Victory* (New York: Macmillan, 1944), 22.

19. Hall, *North American Supply,* 111.

20. Ibid., 111–112.

21. Ibid.

22. Three times as many orders for planes were placed by the French and British in the first half of 1940 as had been in all of 1939—more than eight thousand planes and thirteen thousand engines (Stettinius Jr., *Lend-Lease,* 22).

23. Aide-Memoire, British Embassy to the Department of State, July 3, 1940, *FRUS, 1940,* 3:43.

24. Memo, British Ambassador (Lothian) to Secretary of State, March 1, 1940, *FRUS, 1940,* 3:101.

25. "As a result of the war United Kingdom purchases in the United States will increase very largely. The pre-war average was about $460 million a year. Present estimates are that purchases will amount to at least $720 million in the first year of the war, and well over $2,000 millions in the first two years of the war. These are only minimum figures; substantial new requirements are bound constantly to arise and are already arising. The increase in purchases will be repeated in the main by aircraft, engineering products and munitions. There will be no equivalent increase in the United States purchases of British goods. . . . If the war goes on for much more than two years the United Kingdom will have transferred to the United States all of its easily negotiable dollar securities, most of its gold and a part of its 'direct' investments in the United States and of its assets in other countries outside the United Kingdom" Memo, British Ambassador (Lothian) to Secretary of State Hull, March 1, 1940, *FRUS, 1940,* 3:106–107.

26. Hall, *North American Supply,* 243.

27. J. Keegan, *The Second World War* (New York: Penguin Books, 1990), 81.

28. Sayers, *Financial Policy 1939–1949,* 133.

29. Ambassador in the United Kingdom (Kennedy) to the Secretary of State, June 12, 1940, *FRUS, 1940,* 3:37.

30. In December, Churchill wrote to Roosevelt, "It takes between three and four years to convert the industries of a modern state to war purposes. Saturation point is reached when the maximum industrial effort that can be spared from civilian needs has been applied to war production. Germany certainly reached this point by the end of 1939. We in the British Empire are now only about half-way through the second year." British Prime Minister (Churchill) to President Roosevelt, December 20, 1940, *FRUS, 1940,* 3:19. For a table comparing the output of principal army weapons by the British and Germans from September 1939 to May 1940, see M.M. Postan, *British War Production* (London: Her Majesty's Stationery Office, 1952), 109, table 12. For a table comparing British war requirements pre- and post-Dunkirk, see ibid., 130, table 13.

31. Stettinius Jr., *Lend-Lease,* 44.

32. A. Weisiger, *Logics of War: Explanations for Limited and Unlimited Conflicts* (Ithaca: Cornell University Press, 2013), 122–123; N.M. Ripsman and S. Levy, "Wishful Thinking or Buying Time: The Logic of British Appeasement in the 1930s," *International Security* 33.2 (2008): 141–181.

33. "His Majesty's Government do not wish to discuss in this *Aide-Memoire* the military consequences of the collapse of France further than to say that the economic and manufacturing resources of almost the whole of Europe are now at the disposal of the Nazi and Fascist Powers for the purposes of attack on Great Britain, now almost the last free country left in Europe. They would only repeat what they have said before, that the immediate sale of destroyers and power boats, aeroplanes and seaplanes, and guns, rifles and ammunition of all kinds is of the upmost importance if the impending attack on Great Britain is to be beaten off before winter sets in . . . if victory over Nazi aggression is to be achieved, they must seek from the United States equipment, supplies of aircraft and other munitions and essential raw materials on an altogether larger scale than hitherto. This is partly because the Nazi successes in Europe have deprived the Allies of many sources of supply to which they have hitherto had access and partly because incessant bombing is likely to reduce their own manufacturing capacity, while intensive submarines and air blockade is likely to reduce the quantity of food-stuffs and materials they can import from abroad." British Embassy to the Department of States, Aide-Memoire, July 5, 1940, *FRUS, 1940,* 3:42–43.

34. Hall, *North American Supply,* 135. The content of the arms surplus order illustrates the extent of Britain's supply disaster and the country's desperation for weapons. For example, the order included 500,000 Enfield rifles, some of them used in World War I, some never used, but all manufactured in 1917 and 1918 and packed away in grease for more than twenty years (Stettinius Jr., *Lend-Lease,* 25). For an account of the American effort to supply reserve stocks to the British, see ibid., 25–28.

35. Prime Minster Churchill wrote to President Roosevelt on June 11, 1940, regarding the specific issue of destroyers. "I already cabled you about aeroplanes including flying boats which are so needful to us in the impeding struggle for the life of Great Britain. But even more pressing is the need for destroyers. Italian outrage makes it necessary for us to cope with much larger number of submarines which may come out into the Atlantic and perhaps be based on Spanish ports. To this the only counter is destroyers. Nothing is so important as for us to have 30 or 40 old destroyers you have already had reconditioned." British Prime Minister (Churchill) to President Roosevelt, June 11, 1940, *FRUS, 1940,* 3:52.

36. "In the face of these dangers, we must try to use the year 1941 to build up such a supply of weapons, particularly aircraft, both by increased output at home in spite

of bombardment, and through ocean borne supplies, as will lay the foundation of victory. . . . Without that reinforcement reaching us is a substantial measure, we shall not achieve the massive preponderance in the air on which we must rely to loosen and disintegrate the German grip on Europe. . . . May I invite you then, Mr. President to give earnest consideration to an immediate order on joint account for a further 2,000 combat aircraft a month?" British Prime Minister (Churchill) to President Roosevelt, December 20, 1940, *FRUS, 1940,* 3:22–24.

37. Stettinius Jr., *Lend-Lease,* 30.

38. Hall, *North American Supply,* 251.

39. British Embassy to the Department of States, Aide-Memoire, July 5, 1940, *FRUS, 1940,* 3:44.

40. Sayers, *Financial Policy 1939–1949,* 367.

41. Hall (*North American Supply,* 256) attributes the origins of Lend-Lease directly to President Roosevelt.

42. Stettinius Jr., *Lend-Lease,* 63.

43. Franklin D. Roosevelt, "Press Conference, December 17, 1940," *The American Presidency Project,* ed. Gerhard Peters and John T. Woolley, http://www.presidency.ucsb.edu/ws/?pid=15913.

44. A copy of the Lend-Lease Act can be found in Stettinius Jr. (*Lend-Lease,* 335–339).

45. In July 1939, a *Fortune* Survey asked the American public, "If England and France go to war against the dictator nations, should we sell them food for cash, credit or not at all?" 69 percent of adults sampled answered cash, whereas only 9 percent answered credit, 15 percent responded not at all and 7 percent responded they did not know. In September 1939, a Gallup Poll asked a sample of Americans, "If the Neutrality Act is changed should England and France be required to pay cash for goods or should we give them credit if they cannot pay?" 87 percent of adults sampled answered cash, whereas only 10 percent responded credit, 3 percent responded no opinion. In October 1939, a *Fortune* Survey asked, "Would you insist on payment in cash or would some form of credit be alright?" 95 percent responded cash, 4 percent responded credit, and 1 percent responded Don't Know. In March 1940, a Gallup Poll asked, "If it appears that Germany is defeating England and France, how far do you think the United States should go in helping England and France? Should we let them buy goods here on credit supplied by our government?" 32 percent of responded Yes and 60 percent responded No, 8 percent responded No Opinion. In April 1940, a Gallup Poll asked, "If during the next year England and France are unable to pay cash for materials bought in this country, should we sell them goods on credit?" 32 percent responded Yes and 62 percent responded No, 6 percent responded No Opinion. In May 1940, a Gallup Poll asked, "If England and France are unable to pay cash for airplanes they buy in this country, do you think we should sell them planes on credit supplied by our government?" 48 percent responded Yes, 46 percent No, 6 percent No Opinion. In November and December 1940, a *Fortune* Survey asked, "Should we sell (supplies to Britain) only for cash or give them credit?" 57 percent responded cash, 36 percent responded credit, and 7 percent responded they did not know. However, once Lend-Lease was introduced to Congress, this figure increased dramatically and by January 1941, 54 percent of Americans believed Congress should pass the Lend-Lease Bill. A Gallup Poll asked, "Do you think Congress should pass the President's Lend-Lease bill?" In January 54 percent of American responded Yes, and in February and March 55 and 54 percent of Americans responded Yes, respectively. All questions can be found at the Roper Center, http://www.ropercenter.uconn.edu/data_access/ipoll/ipoll.html#.TihiaM3qo4g.

46. In regards to British ability to pay back American debt, a *Fortune* Survey carried out by the Roper Organization in November and December 1940, asked a sample of Americans if the US government extended credit to Britain, "What do you think our chances

would be of getting paid [back], good, fair or poor? In November and December, 63 percent of respondents believed that the chance of American's being paid back was poor, 23 percent believed it was fair, and only 5 percent thought the chances of being paid back was good. In both surveys, 10 percent responded that they didn't know. The question was phrased, "If we should give them (Britain) credit, what do you think our chances would be of getting paid—good, fair or poor?" *Fortune* Survey, Lincoln, NE, Roper Center for Public Opinion Research, University of Connecticut. For a discussion of American public opinion and Lend-Lease, see R. F. Kimball, *The Most Unsordid Act: Lend-Lease, 1939–1941* (Baltimore: Johns Hopkins University Press, 1969).

47. W. F. Kimball, "'Begger My Neighbor': American and the British Interim Finance Crisis, 1940–1941," *Journal of Economic History* 29.4 (1969): 761.

48. Hall, *North American Supply*, 267.

49. Kimball, *The Most Unsordid Act*, 159; Sayers, *Financial Policy 1939–1949*, 370–371, 383–384; J. M. Blum, *The Morgenthau Diaries: Years of War, 1941–1945* (Boston: Houghton Mifflin,1967), 220–223.

50. The British Prime Minister (Churchill) to President Roosevelt, December 20, 1940, *FRUS, 1940*, 3:25.

51. Hall, *North American Supply*, 261.

52. Ibid., 263.

53. Kimball, "'Begger My Neighbor,'" 765.

54. D.F. McCurrach, "Britain's U.S. Dollar Problems 1939–45," *Economic Journal* 58.231 (1948): 31.

55. Sayers, *Financial Policy*, 371.

56. Hall, *North American Supply*, 271.

57. Ibid., 276.

58. Franklin D. Roosevelt, "Press Conference, March 11, 1941," *The American Presidency Project*, ed. Gerhard Peters and John T. Woolley, http://www.presidency.ucsb.edu/ws/index.php?pid=16086.

59. A quick note should be said on the Reverse Lend-Lease program. In January 1942, a contingent of American troops arrived to Northern Ireland, marking the beginning of what came to be known as reverse Lend-Lease or reciprocal aid (Stettinius Jr., *Lend-Lease*, 274). That spring, the United States entered into negotiations with the British and the dominions regarding the provision of aid for US armed forces in Europe. The British were happy to supply aid to their ally; however, they were concerned with the details of the financial operations of the British dollar pool as they were still paying cash for preexisting Lend-Lease orders. The British suggested that in order to extend reciprocal Lend-Lease aid, there should be no more transferring of gold or dollar assets to the United States from the Sterling Area. The Reciprocal Aid Agreement with the United Kingdom was signed on September 3, 1942. In regards to financing, it was agreed that the "common articles and services which each Government may authorize to be provided to the other shall be in the form of reciprocal aid so that the need of each Government for the currency of the other may be reduced to a minimum." For negotiations, see Memorandum of Conversation, by the Assistant Secretary of State (Acheson), March 19, 1942, *FRUS, 1942*, 1:537. For British concerns, see Memorandum of Conversation, by the Assistant Secretary of State (Acheson), April 18, 1942, *FRUS, 1942*, 1:544–545. For the entire reciprocal aid agreement and an account of the American effort to supply reserve stocks to the British, see Stettinius Jr., *Lend-Lease*, 334–347.

60. Report of Interdepartmental Committee to President Roosevelt on Policy Decisions Relating to Dollar Position of Lend-Lease Countries, January 1, 1943, *FRUS, 1943*, 3:49.

61. "Judging the total British position at this time, we conclude that the balances now held by the United Kingdom are adequate. In this connection, it will be recalled that in the

Spring of 1941, the British suggested that they should have a 'minimum working balance of $600 million required to meet contingencies everywhere.' It is recommended, in the light of present circumstances, that the United Kingdom's gold and dollar balances should not be permitted to be less than about $600 million nor above about $1 billion." Report of Interdepartmental Committee to President Roosevelt on Policy Decisions Relating to Dollar Position of Lend-Lease Countries, January 1, 1943, *FRUS, 1943*, 3:49.

62. Hull continued, "In addition to the gold and dollar holdings of the British Government, residents of the United Kingdom hold $320 million of private dollar balances and about $1,150 million of long-term investments in the United States." Memorandum to President Roosevelt, 4 January 1944, *FRUS, 1944*, 3:33.

63. "Sir John Anderson stated that the improvement in Britain's dollar balance during 1944 would be almost entirely due to the large expenditures of United States troops within the Empire. In 1944, the British expect to receive $585,000,000 from this source in the United Kingdom and $475,000,000 in the rest of the sterling area, making a total of over a billion dollars. . . . The element in this situation which is most disturbing, Sir John Anderson stated, is the fact that the receipts from United States troops, particularly those in the British Isles, constitute only a temporary source of income." Memorandum of Conversation, by the Under Secretary of State (Stettinius), April 19, 1944, *FRUS, 1944,* 3:49.

64. Memorandum of Conversation, by the Under Secretary of State (Stettinius), April 19, 1944, *FRUS, 1944,* 3:49.

65. The British Chancellor of the Exchequer (Woods) to the Secretary of the Treasury (Morgenthau), September 3, 1943, *FRUS, 1943*, 3:78.

66. The memo continued tying war finance to war outcome: "The recent increase in British liquid assets is thus an essential component in a careful (though nevertheless vulnerable) financial policy by which, though with the most dangerous risks to our postwar position, we have managed to finance a vast war expenditure in India, the Middle East and elsewhere—an expenditure which is, of course, vitally essential to the prosecution of the war. . . . Only if we are left free to pursue our existing policy can we hope successfully to finance our vast and essential commitments outside North America." Memorandum by the British Treasury: The Overseas Assets and Liabilities of the United Kingdom, September 14, 1943, *FRUS, 1943* (Washington, DC: US Government Printing Office), 1943, 3:82–83.

67. The British Chancellor of the Exchequer (Woods) to the Secretary of the Treasury (Morgenthau), September 3, 1943, *FRUS, 1943* (Washington, DC: US Government Printing Office), 1943, 3:79.

68. Memorandum by the British Treasury: The Overseas Assets and Liabilities of the United Kingdom, September 14, 1943, *FRUS, 1943* (Washington, DC: US Government Printing Office), 1943, 3:83.

69. Memorandum by the Assistant Secretary of State (Acheson), November 2, 1943, *FRUS, 1943* (Washington, DC: US Government Printing Office), 1943, 3:98.

70. G.C. Herring Jr., "The United States and British Bankruptcy, 1944–1945: Responsibilities Deferred," *Political Science Quarterly* 86.2 (1971): 264.

71. Ibid., 276.

72. R.G.D. Allen, "Mutual Aid Between the U.S. and the British Empire," in *History of the Second World War*, ed. R.S. Sayers (London: Her Majesty's Stationery Office, 1946), 533.

73. Hancock and Gowing, *British War Economy*, 546.

74. For a summary of events at the start of the war, see N. Rich, *Why the Crimean War? A Cautionary Tale* (New York: McGraw-Hill, 1991).

75. It should be noted that in stark contrast to the geographical scope of World War II, the vast majority of the fighting in the Crimean War took place in the relatively limited area of the Crimea.

76. J. R. T. Hughes, *Fluctuations in Trade, Industry, and Finance* (Oxford: Oxford University Press, 1960), 26. Other estimates of the British cost of the Crimean war are very similar to Hughes's estimate: "Sir George Lewis estimated the total cost of the war at £77,600,000. He arrived at this result by comparing the total expenditure of the three years—1854 to 1856—the last year including also expenditure in the nature of war expenditures—with that of the preceding three years, and assuming that the difference in cost was due to the war. But as Mr. Chisholm points out, only the expenditure on the army and navy should be taken into account . . . this estimate of the cost of war—the total of which is £69,277,000" (S. Buxton, *Finance and Politics: An Historical Study, 1783–1885*, vol. 1 [London: John Murray, 1888], 149); "Total war expenditure may be taken as £69,277,694.2. The net creation of public debt during the war years 1854–7 amounted to £39,715,208. On the other hand the Exchequer balances emerged at the end of the war £7,584,433. Thus net public borrowing amounted to £32,130,775 or 46 per cent of total war expenditure" (O. Anderson, "Loans Versus Taxes: British Financial Policy in the Crimean War," *Economic History Review* 16.2 [1963]: 318); Hirst puts the cost of the Crimean War for England at 74 million sterling (F. W. Hirst, *The Political Economy of War* [London: J. M. Dent & Sons, 1915], 297).

77. While the Crimean War was not the most expensive war the British fought to date, it was the costliest per soldier. Innovations from the Industrial Revolution were integrated into the war effort. The British Army was fighting with the newly developed Minié rifles and new ironclad ships. As a result, the average cost per soldier was £122.1; almost double the cost per soldier than the previous war (Hughes, *Fluctuations*, 26).

78. "On 6 March 1856, when peace negotiations had begun, Earl Grey asserted in the House of Lords that 'somewhere between two-thirds and three-quarters of the whole expenses of the war have been met not by taxation, but by loans'. The government spokesman, Lord Stanley of Alderley, the President of the Board of Trade, agreed to the figure of two-thirds. He took £49,047,522 as the cost of the war to that date, and gave £17,045,030 as the amount raised by taxation and £33,659,000 as that raised by loans. It was only the large extent to which taxation covered the running-down costs of the war in 1856–7 that allowed the proportion of total war expenditure met by borrowing to fall a good deal lower. Total war expenditure may be taken as £69,277,694. The net creation of public debt during the war years 1854–7 amounted to £39,715,208. On the other hand the Exchequer balances emerged at the end of the war £7,584,433. Thus net public borrowing amounted to £32,130,775 or 46 per cent of total war expenditure" (Anderson, "Loans Versus Taxes," 318). For a discussion of Crimean War debt, see O. Anderson, *A Liberal State at War: English Politics and Economics during the Crimean War* (New York: St Martin's Press, 1967), 317; and N. Ferguson, *The House of Rothschild: The World's Banker 1849–1999*, vol. 2 (New York: Penguin Group, 1999), 70–75.

79. Hughes, *Fluctuations*, 4.

80. Ibid., 12.

81. A reserve currency is a currency held by countries as part of their foreign exchange reserves to meet foreign currency payments and manage its trade balance (P. Moles and N. Terry, *The Handbook of International Financial Terms* [Oxford: Oxford University Press, 1997]).

82. When a state has low currency reserves and needs to purchase goods from another country, it will need to purchase more of that currency. These purchases create an additional transaction costs. If a state bills Britain in pounds, it avoids paying this transaction cost in the future.

83. W. Baumgart, *The Crimean War, 1853–1856* (New York: Oxford University Press, 1999), 79.

84. Hughes, *Fluctuations*, 24–25.

85. Ibid., 79.

86. Ibid., 84.

87. Ibid., 141–142.

88. For a detailed list of goods, see *Report of the Board of General Officers, House of Parliament* (London: Her Majesty's Stationery Office, 1856), 358–359.

89. A brief note regarding Britain's ally, France: while France was not as economically well endowed as Britain, the French could afford a larger, better-trained army. Relative to both the British and Russian armies, the French Army was well equipped and trained due to their recent experience fighting in North Africa. The French expeditionary force was by far the largest and made most of the major breakthroughs in the war (Kennedy, *The Rise and Fall of the Great Powers*, 175). Thus the British did not have to support an ally, as they would have to do during World War II. French involvement lowered the cost of war to Britain, decreasing the need to rely on external war finance.

90. Many authors have discussed the state of the British Army at this time, most prominently C. Barnett, *Britain and her Army 1509–1970: A Military, Political, and Social Survey* (New York: William Morrow, 1970), chap. 12; and Baumgart, *The Crimean War*, chap. 8.

91. C. Barnett, *Britain and Her Army*, 280.

92. C.C. Bayley (*Mercenaries for the Crimea: The German, Swiss, and Italian Legions in British Service, 1854–1856* [Montreal: McGill-Queens University Press, 1977], chap. 1) provides a description of British Army recruiting before the Crimean War.

93. Baumgart, *The Crimean War*, 78.

94. Ibid.

95. The war cost the lives of nearly half a million men, a larger total than that of any other European war fought in the hundred years after the congress of Vienna. High-end estimates of Anglo-French losses: "The French lost nearly 100,000 men and the British 60,000. Two-thirds of the total casualties were from disease and hardship, not from battle" (A.J.P. Taylor, *The Struggle for Mastery in Europe, 1848–1918* [Oxford: Oxford University Press, 1954], 81–82). Low-end place British losses near 20,000: "British forces suffered 18,058 fatalities in the Crimean War. Of these casualties only 1,761 were killed by enemy actions, the rest died of wounds or disease" (D. Judd, *The Crimean War* [London: Granada Publishing, 1975], 192).

96. For a table breaking down the cost of the various mercenary forces, see Bayley, *Mercenaries for the Crimea*, 149–150. It should be noted that the cost of hiring mercenaries amounted to less than 1 percent of the entire cost of the war.

97. Bayley, *Mercenaries for the Crimea*, 157–158. For a list of offices of the Swiss Legion by name, see Bayley, *Mercenaries for the Crimea*, 156. The Italian Legion primarily comprised men from Sardinia (Piedmont), but also included men from Lombardy, Parma, Modena, Tuscany, Rome, Hungry, and Naples. It should be noted that the Italian Legion was separate from the Sardinian war effort.

98. A letter from the commissariat officer in Constantinople describes the financial details: "We offer as a substitute for oxen (which is out of our power to supply) an equivalent number of sheep reckoning ten sheep to one ox . . . at the rate of 5*l*. sterling for ten sheep. . . . Should the total stipulated number of sheep not be accepted by the commissariat within two months from the date of the contract, or by such a date as may be fixed therein, the sum of 1*s*. sterling per day for every ten sheep to be paid for their keep, and after the stipulated term all losses by death to be for the account of the Government" (*Report of the Board of General Officers*, 362).

99. Bayley, *Mercenaries for the Crimea*, 100–101.

100. Ibid., 101.

101. H. Hearder, "Claredon, Cavour, and the Intervention of Sardinia in the Crimean War, 1853–1855," *International History Review* 18.4 (1996): 829.

102. Ibid., 834. According to Bayley, interest on the loan was 3 percent. However, both Bayley and Hearder are consistent in that the amount of the loan was £1,000,000 and Britain would furnish troop transports at her own expense to carry the force to Crimea (Bayley, *Mercenaries for the Crimea,* 76).

103. F. Rohrer, "What's a Little Debt Between Friends?" *BBC News* (May 10, 2006).

104. It is interesting to note that Britain was not the only country to receive Lend-Lease aid. Lend-Lease was also extended to countries within the British Empire—Australia, New Zealand, South Africa, and India—as well as the Soviet Union, China, Free France, and other allied nations. However, Britain was the only country that the United States demanded that it strip itself of its gold and dollar assets. Russia, a country with large gold reserves, was never asked to surrender its gold holdings.

105. For a detailed account of Stettinius Jr.'s trips to Britain, see Stettinius Jr., *Lend-Lease,* 240–273.

106. Ibid., 252.

## CHAPTER 5. TAXATION AND CURRENCY RESERVES DURING THE RUSSO-JAPANESE WAR

1. Select works on the origins of the Russo-Japanese War are I. Nish, "Stretching Out to the Yalu: A Contested Frontier, 1900–1903," in *The Russo-Japanese War in Global Perspective*, vol. 1, ed. J.W. Steinberg, B.W. Menning, D. Schimmelpenninck van der Oye, D. Wolff, and S. Yokote (Leiden: Konninklijke Brill, 2005), 45–64; Repington, *The War in the Far East;* D. Schimmelpenninck van der Oye, "The Immediate Origins of the War," in *The Russo-Japanese War in Global Perspective*, vol. 1, ed. J.W. Steinberg, B.W. Menning, D. Schimmelpenninck van der Oye, D. Wolff, and S. Yokote (Leiden: Koninklijke Brill, 2005), 23–44.

2. The previous military conflict of modern Japan was the Sino-Japanese War of 1894–1895. The expenses of the Sino-Japanese War were around ¥200 million, roughly 2.5 times the average budgetary expenditures in the five years preceding the outbreak of war (1889–1983). Half of the war was paid for by government bonds. The remainder was paid for using treasury surplus funds accumulated in the past and by short-term loans from the Bank of Japan (T. Takao, "The Financial Policy of the Meiji Government," *Developing Economies* 3.4 [1965]: 441).

3. N.V. Riasanovsky, *A History of Russia* (Oxford: Oxford University Press, 2000), 422–434.

4. Ibid., 423.

5. C.E. Black et al., *The Modernization of Japan and Russia: A Comparative Study* (New York: Free Press, 1975), 18.

6. It should be noted that Russia's reforms were not one continuous wave of "reforms" in the way that the Meiji Japanese reforms were. It was only with the 1905 rebellion that Nicholas II was forced to consider major political changes (i.e., the creation of a Duma) and a new economic initiative in agriculture (Stolypin's reforms). In addition, there were differences in the reforms. The Japanese pushed for a capitalist class with joint-stock companies. There was justification for corporate wealth and the formation of conglomerates and cartels. Major businessmen became leading spokespersons for this new class of capitalists who combined patriotism with entrepreneurial spirit. Russia's reforms were focused on managing land—including the zemstvos—or on building industry via direct state management and control.

7. Black et al., *The Modernization of Japan and Russia,* 165–166.

8. Ibid.

9. Ibid., 145.

10. Ibid.

11. For a breakdown in the cost of the war see Gotaro Ogawa, *Expenditures of the Russo-Japanese War* (New York: Oxford University Press, 1923). Lower estimates for the cost of the war for Japan: Allen places the cost at ¥1,500 million (G.C. Allen, *A Short Economic History of Modern Japan 1867–1937* [London: George Allen & Unwin, 1972], 48). Takao places the cost of the war at ¥1,730 million (Takao, "The Financial Policy of the Meiji Government," 444).

12. Takao, "The Financial Policy of the Meiji Government," 444.

13. K.B. Pyle, "The Technology of Japanese Nationalism: The Local Improvement Movement, 1900–1918," *Journal of Asian Studies* 33.1 (1973): 56.

14. The Japanese raised a small amount of domestic debt by means of public loans, exchequer bonds, and temporary loans. In order to prevent inflation, the Japanese government attempted to reduce money in circulation and decrease pressure on prices by encouraging decreased spending and increased savings. To ensure saving, regulations were made for the issue of savings loan bonds by the Hypothec Bank of Japan (C. J. C. Hoad, *Commonwealth Military Attache Japanese Army, 1904* (*Russo-Japanese War*) [London: Department of Defence, 1904], 38).

15. For a discussion of the civil bureaucracy during the Tokugawa period, see M. Inoki, "The Civil Bureaucracy: Japan," in *Political Modernization in Japan and Turkey*, ed. R.E. Ward and D.A. Rustow (Princeton, NJ: Princeton University Press, 1964).

16. H.T. Patrick, "External Equilibrium and Internal Convertibility: Financial Policy in Meiji Japan," *Journal of Economic History* 25.2 (1965): 194.

17. R.W. Goldsmith, *The Financial Development of Japan, 1868–1977* (New Haven, CT: Yale University Press, 1983), 5–6.

18. Allen, *A Short Economic History of Modern Japan,* 47.

19. R.M. Bird, "Land Taxation and Economic Development: The Model of Meiji Japan," *Journal of Development Studies* 13.2 (1977): 164.

20. In 1881, the chief financial objectives were the redemption of the inconvertible paper money and the accumulation of a specie reserve, which could serve as a backing for a new issue of convertible notes (Allen, *A Short Economic History of Modern Japan,* 50).

21. For an excellent chart documenting variation of notes in circulation and their decline from 1881 to 1900, see Allen, *A Short Economic History of Modern Japan,* 51.

22. Bird, "Land Taxation and Economic Development," 165. For a discussion of the creation of the land tax, see N. Ike, "Taxation and Landownership in the Westernization of Japan," *Journal of Economic History* 7.2 (1947): 160–182.

23. Allen, *A Short Economic History of Modern Japan,* 42.

24. H. Ishi, "Historical Background of the Japanese Tax System," *Hitotsubashi Journal of Economics* 29.1 (1988): 4.

25. Allen, *A Short Economic History of Modern Japan,* 47.

26. Ibid., 40, 43.

27. Pyle, "The Technology of Japanese Nationalism," 58. The first step in transferring loyalties from hamlets to the administrative towns and villages came in 1901 when Home Ministry officials in the Bureau of Local Affairs began a campaign to encourage the locally elected heads of towns and villages to establish policies for the future development of their units. The second step was to place all communal lands and property under administrative control (ibid., 59). The government also integrated local citizen groups into the state administrative structure so that they might act as mediating links between local government and local society.

28. For an in-depth description of the creation of a rational legal bureaucracy in Meiji Japan, see Inoki, "The Civil Bureaucracy," and B.S. Silberman, "Bureaucratic Development and Bureaucratization: The Case of Japan," *Social Science History* 2.4 (1978): 385–398.

29. Allen, *A Short Economic History of Modern Japan,* 43, 50.
30. Takao, "The Financial Policy of the Meiji Government," 433.
31. S. Sato, "Japan's Fiscal System: An International Comparison," in *Public Finance in Japan*, ed. T. Hayashi and K. Kaizuka (Tokyo: University of Tokyo Press, 1973), 14.
32. Goldsmith, *The Financial Development of Japan,* 34.
33. *Report on the War Finance* (Tokyo: Ministry of Finance, 1906), 25.
34. Pyle, "The Technology of Japanese Nationalism," 56–57.
35. Ibid., 56–57. For a chart detailing the type of tax implemented and the amount received under both schemes, see *Report on the War Finance,* 28.
36. For a detailed account of the location of procurement of warships for the Imperial Japanese Navy from 1869–1945, see H. Jentschura, D. Jung, and P. Mickel, *Warships of the Imperial Japanese Navy, 1869–1945* (Annapolis, MD: Naval Institute Press, 1977).
37. E. Miller, "Japan's Other Victory: Overseas Financing of the War," in *The Russo-Japanese War in Global Perspective: World War Zero*, vol. 2, ed. J.W. Steinberg, B.W. Menning, D. Schimmelpenninck van der Oye, D. Wolff, and S. Yokote (Leiden: Konninklijke Brill, 2005), 467.
38. Miller, "Japan's Other Victory," 469.
39. Ibid., 467.
40. K. Yamamura, "Success Ill-gotten? The Role of Meiji Militarism in Japan's Technological Progress," *Journal of Economic History* 37.1 (1977): 121.
41. Ibid., 126.
42. Ibid., 127.
43. For a history of Japan's iron and steel industry and its need for imports in the 1800s and its move toward self-reliance, see S. Yonekura, *The Japanese Iron and Steel Industry, 1950–1990: Continuity and Discontinuity* (New York: St. Martin's Press, 1994).
44. Takao, *The Financial Policy of the Meiji Government,* 447.
45. Miller, "Japan's Other Victory," 470.
46. Allen, *A Short Economic History of Modern Japan,* 229.
47. Miller, "Japan's Other Victory," 465.
48. Patrick,"External Equilibrium and Internal Convertibility," 189.
49. Miller, "Japan's Other Victory,"468. The indemnity was 1.8 times the cost of the Sino-Japanese War (Takao, *The Financial Policy of the Meiji Government,* 422).
50. Patrick, "External Equilibrium and Internal Convertibility," 207.
51. Takao, *The Financial Policy of the Meiji Government,* 447.
52. Miller, "Japan's Other Victory," 468.
53. Ibid., 471.
54. A.J. Sherman, "German-Jewish Bankers in World Politics: The Financing of the Russo-Japanese War," *Leo Baeck Institute Yearbook* 38.1 (1983): 68.
55. For a detailed account of Takahashi's trip to London and meeting with Schiff, see R.J. Smethurst, *From Foot Soldier to Finance Minister: Takahashi Korekiyo, Japan's Keynes* (Cambridge, MA: Harvard University Asia Center, 2007).
56. Schiff, on numerous occasions, refused to participate in Russian loans and used his influence to prevent the entry of Russia into the money markets of America because of the ill-treatment of the Jews by the Russian government (C. Adler, *Jacob Henry Schiff: A Biological Sketch* [New York: American Jewish Committee, 1921], 16).
57. Miller, "Japan's Other Victory," 474.
58. N. Sussman and Y. Yafeh ("Institutions, Reforms, and Country Risk: Lessons from Japanese Government Debt in the Meiji Era," *Journal of Economic History* 60.2 [2000]: 442–467) argue that Japanese creditworthiness in London was not due to the establishment of modern institutions but to the adoption of the gold standard and military victories over Russia. The study evaluates the effect of major reforms on bond yields using

a data set on sovereign debt traded in London between June 1870 and August 1914. The great majority of Meiji reforms—including the establishment of the Bank of Japan and the introduction of "modern" monetary policy, the promulgation of the Meiji Constitution, and introduction of parliamentary elections—produced no quantitatively significant market response in London.

59. Sherman, "German-Jewish Bankers in World Politics," 68.

60. For a detailed description of each issue, see Miller ("Japan's Other Victory," 475) and *Report on the War Finance* (32–34). For a superb graphical representation of the fluctuation in prices of various Japanese public loans in the London market correlated to military events, see *Report on the War Finance*. For further discussion of the relationship between military success and interest rates and subscription, see Sherman, "German-Jewish Bankers in World Politics," 69.

61. Sherman, "German-Jewish Bankers in World Politics," 69.

62. Miller, "Japan's Other Victory," 472.

63. A.M. Michelson, P.N. Apostol, and M.W. Bernatzky, *Russian Public Finance during the War* (New Haven, CT: Yale University Press, 1928), 68. Ananich places the cost of the war at 6.554 billion rubles. However, this estimate includes the interest on domestic and foreign loans, which amounted to 3.944 billion rubles. When this interest on the debt is excluded, the war cost is 2.610 billion rubles (B. Ananich, "Russian War Financing," in *The Russo-Japanese War in Global Perspecive: World War Zero*, vol. I, ed. J.W. Steinberg, B.W. Menning, D. Schimmelpenninck van der Oye, D. Wolf, and S. Yokote [Leiden: Koninklijke Brill, 2005], 68). Michelson et al. place the cost of the war at 2.295 billion rubles (including 2.113 billion rubles spent in the years 1904–1906 and 182 million rubles spent in the succeeding years) later in the text (Michelson et al., *Russian Public Finance during the War*, 235).

64. J. Long, "Franco-Russian Relations during the Russo-Japanese War," *Slavonic and East European Review* 52.127 (1974): 222.

65. Michelson et al., *Russian Public Finance during the War*, 68. This figure, 5 percent, probably overestimates the amount of the war paid for by tax revenue as it includes both tax revenue and curtailing expenditure. The amount of money raised via curtailing expenditure and raising taxes was 177 million rubles. The curtailment of expenditure, authorized by the Finance Bill of 1904, was effected only after the beginning of the war, by reducing the appropriations by 130 million rubles. The increased rates of taxation were effective from 1905 to 1907 (Michelson et al., *Russian Public Finance during the War*, 68). Russian tax revenue totals in 1904 and 1905 were actually below that of 1903 (R.H. Gorlin, "Problems of Tax Reform in Imperial Russia," *Journal of Modern History* 49.2 [1977]: 247).

66. According to Michelson et al., 81 percent of the war was met by 2.450 billion rubles in loans, and the rest was paid for by the free balance of the Treasury (which amounted in 1904 to 381 million rubles) and several special funds, which amounted to 7.5 million rubles (Michelson et al., *Russian Public Finance during the War*, 68).

67. Tax capacity was so weak in 1905 the Russians began to rereform the tax system. See Gorlin, "Problems of Tax Reform in Imperial Russia."

68. A. Kahan, *Russian Economic History: The Nineteenth Century* (Chicago: Univeristy of Chicago Press, 1989), 64).

69. The personal income tax was drafted in 1905 and sent to the Duma in 1907.

70. Michelson et al., *Russian Public Finance during the War*, 24.

71. Kahan, *Russian Economic History*, 61. The preference for indirect taxes can be explained by the greater ease in collecting such taxes, given the cultural level of both the taxpayers and the bureaucracy, and by the fact that they were less injurious to the wealthier classes (ibid., 61). For the percentage of excise taxes as a percent of total taxes for the years preceding and during the war see ibid., 93.

72. Ibid., 62.

73. Long, "Franco-Russian Relations during the Russo-Japanese War," 214.

74. Y. Kotsonis, "'Face-to-Face': The State, the Individual, and the Citizen in Russian Taxation, 1863–1917," *Slavic Review* 63.2 (2004): 224.

75. Part of this reform was the shifting of a tax system that emphasized estates or collectives to the individual (ibid.).

76. L. Bowman, "Russia's First Income Taxes: The Effects of Modernized Taxes on Commerce and Industry, 1885–1914," *Slavic Review* 52.2 (1993): 257.

77. Ibid., 260–261.

78. In 1885, taxes as a percent of national income were 12.8 percent. This figure increased only slightly in the years preceding the war to 13.2 percent in 1900 (Kahan, *A Russian Economic History,* 93). For a table of the amount of direct and indirect taxes collected by the Russian government from 1861 to 1913 and a table of per capita taxation between 1885 to 1913, see Kahan, *A Russian Economic History,* 62 and 93.

79. Between 1885 and 1887, the annual sum collected was 2.558 million rubles (Bowman, "Russia's First Income Taxes," 262).

80. Ibid., 263; Kotsonis, "Face-to-Face," 227.

81. Bowman, "Russia's First Income Taxes," 263.

82. Kotsonis, "Face-to-Face," 227.

83. Kahan, *A Russian Economic History,* 62

84. Bowman, "Russia's First Income Taxes," 264. The records of the Moscow finance office and the Moscow Municipal Duma show that verification of all data except for business licenses was very superficial. Sections where information about turnover and profits should have been recorded frequently remained empty. While inspectors were given wide discretionary powers, they often remained ignorant of how to define "net income," "turnover," or "productivity." Moscow finance office records also indicate that, initially, only about 22 of a sample of 1000 taxpayers even provided statements and only two of these provided the required information about turnover (Bowman, "Russia's First Income Taxes," 265).

85. Ibid., 259.

86. Ibid., 259.

87. Ibid., 262.

88. Ibid., 262–263.

89. For a discussion of the effect of unstable currency on Russia's economy in the latter half of the nineteenth century and the government's various attempts to stabilize it, see O. Crisp, "Russian Financial Policy and the Gold Standard at the End of the Nineteenth Century," *Economic History Review* 6.2 (1953): 156–172.

90. During the earlier part of the period, prior to 1897, the prevailing monetary unit, called the *credit ruble*, represented a nonconvertible paper currency, defined in terms of quantity of silver that it was supposed to represent. The credit ruble was made convertible during a short period of the early 1860s, but as a result of the loss of foreign exchange and precious metals, the attempt was aborted. Thus the credit ruble was not supported by a fixed amount of reserve of precious metals; its exchange rate abroad fluctuated (Kahan, *A Russian Economic History,* 50).

91. Crisp notes, "The maintenance of this large gold reserve was a luxury, especially in view of Russia's position as a debtor state, but was felt to be necessary for purposes of elasticity and to sustain foreign confidence" (Crisp, "Russian Financial Policy and the Gold Standard," 168).

92. Kahan, *A Russian Economic History,* 51.

93. In February 1904, the tsarist treasury had 905.8 million rubles in gold on hand and 680 million rubles of paper currency in circulation. According to the law of 1897, the State Bank could still print another 200 million. In March 1904, the Finance Committee

calculated that more than 700 million rubles could be mobilized, enough for war until January 1905 at the cost of 2 million rubles a day. But in the case of military defeats or protracted war, the government would be bankrupt by early 1905 (Ananich, "Russian War Financing," 452).

94. Long, "Franco-Russian Relations during the Russo-Japanese War," 214–215.

95. Ibid., 222.

96. Although the Franco-Russian Alliance became official in 1894, the creditor-debtor financial relationship had been developing since 1890 (Long, "Franco-Russian Relations during the Russo-Japanese War," 213). The Franco-Russian Alliance did not require France to support Russia against Japan unless England attacked Russia. However, the Russian government believed it was France's duty to extend its abundant financial resources (Long, "Russian Manipulation of the French Press, 1904–1906," *Slavic Review* 31.2 [1972]: 344). While the French government was not in favor of the war, it willingly loaned money to Russia. For a discussion of the extension of French credit abroad, see Feis, *Europe*.

97. Ananich, "Russian War Financing," 453.

98. Ibid., 453; Long, "Franco-Russian Relations during the Russo-Japanese War," 216.

99. Ananich, "Russian War Financing," 453. Long states that the interest on this debt was at 5 percent not 6.5 percent (Long, "Franco-Russian Relations during the Russo-Japanese War," 217).

100. Long, "Franco-Russian Relations during the Russo-Japanese War," 218.

101. Ananich, "Russian War Financing," 454.

102. Long, "Franco-Russian Relations during the Russo-Japanese War," 224.

103. Ananich, "Russian War Financing," 454–455.

104. J. Acton, *The Cambridge Modern History*, vol. 12 (New York: MacMillan, 1910). 598.

105. R.A. Esthus, "Nicholas II and the Russo-Japanese War," *Russian Review* 40.4 (1981): 400.

106. Ibid.

107. For a detailed account of the events leading up to the massacre, see W. Sablinsky, *The Road to Bloody Sunday* (Princeton: Princeton University Press, 1976); G. D. Surh, *1905 in St. Petersburg: Labor, Society, and Revolution* (Stanford, CA: Stanford University Press, 1989).

108. Sablinsky, *The Road to Bloody Sunday*," 275.

109. J. Long, "Organized Protest against the 1906 Russian Loan," *Cahiers du Monde Russe et Sovietique* 13.1 (1972): 23–39.

110. Long, "Russian Manipulation of the French Press," 344.

111. Long, "Franco-Russian Relations during the Russo-Japanese War," 228.

112. Ibid., 230.

113. Ibid., 231.

114. Ananich, "Russian War Financing," 457.

115. Ibid.

## CHAPTER 6. CONFRONTING THE COSTS OF WAR, 1823–2003

1. A notable work is Gustavo A. Flores-Macías and Sarah E. Kreps, "Political Parties at War: A Study of American War Finance," *American Political Science Review* 107.4 (2013): 833–848, although their work is limited to American war finance, specifically war taxation.

2. For example see Organski and Kugler, *The War Ledger*, and Kugler and Domke, "Comparing the Strength of Nations.

3. E.g., Rasler and Thompson, "Global Wars, Public Debts, and the Long Cycle."

4. D. J. Singer, S. Bremer, and J. Stuckey, "Capability Distribution, Uncertainty, and Major Power War, 1820–1965," In *Peace, War, and Numbers*, ed. B. Russett (Beverly Hills,

CA: Sage, 1972), 19–48; "SIPRI Military Expenditure Database" (Solna, Sweden: SIPRI Research Institute, 2012), http://milexdata.sipri.org.

5. I draw from the Correlates of War Project (COW) v4.0. As discussed earlier in the book, war duration affects war finance. Longer wars have an inherently different dynamic than short wars, as shorter wars have different revenue needs and limit the state's war finance tool kit. Thus I use six months as the cutoff point because data limitations militate against going under six months. There are few "long wars" in COW as the average war is about four months long. Thus, to ensure a significant number of observations, I include wars over 180 days.

6. T. Fazal, P. Fortna, J. Stanton, and A. Weisiger, *War Initation and Termination (WIT) Coding Instrument and Data Set: Columbia University*. https://qdr.syr.edu/discover/projectdescriptionsfazal.

7. According to COW, other participants in the Korean War included Thailand, the Philippines, Turkey, Australia, Greece, France, Belgium, the Netherlands, the United Kingdom, Columbia, and Canada.

8. Seligman, "The Cost of War and How it was Met," 739–770.

9. There are nine African, six Middle Eastern, twelve Central and South American, and eighteen Asian countries in the data set.

10. The concept of triangulation is borrowed from I. S. Lustick, "History, Historiography, and Political Science: Multiple Historical Records and the Problem of Selection Bias," *American Political Science Review* 90.3 (1996): 605–618. Triangulation is the construction of a background narrative of a historical event through the identification of claims made by different historians, despite their approach from difficult archival sources and/or implicit theoretic or political angles. Of the ninety-five observations, I have information for 82 percent of the cases.

11. The accompanying codebook for the data set (providing an in-depth analysis of coding rules, coding decisions, and data sources) as well as the list of all cases included can be found at sites.bu.edu/cappella/confronting-the-cost-of-war-data/.

12. "Monetary Commercial English News," *Commercial and Financial Chronical* 26 (April 27, 1878): 407. For secondary sources on borrowing to finance Russia's war with Turkey, see Crisp, "Russian Financial Policy and the Gold Standard"; J. Karel, *An English View of Russian Finance* (Washington, DC: US Bureau of Foreign Commerce, 1896); M. F. Maurice, *The Russo-Turkish War 1877: A Strategical Sketch* (London: Swan Sonnenschein, 1905), 244–245.

13. Karel, *An English View of Russian Finance,* 38.

14. S. J. Shaw and E. K. Shaw, *History of the Ottoman Empire and Modern Turkey: Reform, Revolution, and Republic*, vol. 2, *The Rise of Modern Turkey 1808–1975* (Cambridge: Cambridge University Press, 1977), 185.

15. Hozier, *The Russo Turksish War,* 605.

16. Ibid., 605.

17. Maurice, *The Russo-Turkish War 1877,* 14.

18. Hozier, *The Russo Turkish War,* 605.

19. Shaw and Shaw, *History of the Ottoman Empire and Modern Turkey,* 222. Turkey also did not pay her troops and repudiated her debt to aid in the war effort: "The Turkish troops had during the twenty months received no regular pay: they were merely lodged and fed by the State, and got, but at the rarest intervals, a few piastres: yet they continued to fight with undiminished zeal, and desertions and insubordination were never heard of amongst the regular troops" (Hozier, *The Russo Turkish War*, 604); "Some partial explanation of the mystery was afforded by the fact that the Government was not paying official salaries (ibid., 605); . . . that the payment of the foreign debt was left in abeyance" (ibid., 605).

20. Another example of coding difficulty is Cambodia during the Vietnamese-Cambodian War. During this war, there was no Cambodian currency. Market prices were established by supply and demand in Vietnamese Dong, Thai Baht, gold, and rice (R.R. Ross, *Cambodia: A Country Study* (Washington, DC: Library of Congress for the Department of the Army, 1987); M. Vickery, *Kampuchea: Politics, Economics, and Society* (London: Frances Printer, 1986). However, there are data on how the war was financed overall. We know that a small percentage of the Cambodian war effort was financed by domestic taxation while the rest of the war was financed via external funding, primarily from the Chinese. For data on domestic taxation and rice production, see C.H. Twining, "The Economy," in *Cambodia 1975–1978: Rendezvous with Death*, ed. K.D. Jackson (Princeton, NJ: Princeton University Press, 1989). For data on Chinese military aid, see T.S. An, "Turmoil in Indochina: The Vietnam-Cambodia Conflict," *Asian Affairs* 5.4 (1978): 283; K.D. Jackson, "Cambodia 1978: War, Pillage, and Purge in Democratic Kampuchea," *Asian Survey* 19.1, A Survey of Asia in 1978: Part I (1978): 80; S.J. Morris, *Why Vietnam Invaded Cambodia: Political Culture and the Causes of War* (Stanford, CA: Stanford University Press, 1999), 76; D. Pike, *Vietnam Cambodia Conflict,* Report Prepared by the Congressional Research Service for the House Subcommittee on Asian and Pacific Affairs, October 4, 1978 (Washington, DC: GPO, 1978), 11–15; R.S. Ross, *Cambodia*, 107–109; A. Weisinger, "From Small Wars to Armageddon: Explaining Variation in Interstate War Duration and Severity," Ph.D diss., Columbia University, 2008; Central Intelligence Agency, "Sino-Soviet Competition in Indochina," *Interagency Intelligence Memorandum*, 1978.

21. For the Republic of Korea, see Cole and Park, *Financial Development in Korea*; Manson et al., *The Economic and Social Modernization of the Republic of Korea*; for the Republic of Vietnam, see D. C. Dacy, *Foreign Aid, War and Economic Development: South Vietnam, 1955–1975* (Cambridge: Cambridge University Press, 1986). A note of caution here: detecting the presence of printing can be difficult. Not all cases are obvious. The US financing of the Vietnam War is an example. How much the United States "printed" is debatable, as it is hard to discern how much debt was monetized versus nonmonetized. "The gross debt of the United States rose $53 billion (FY1964 to FY1968). Even though the combined deficits on GNP accounting amounted to $19.7 billion. The $19.7 billion represents the excess of federal expenditures over current receipts, ignoring various forms of asset transactions. Our question is how much of this was absorbed by borrowing from the non-bank public and how much was money created. Clearly, the government issued new debt worth far more than the deficit defined by NIPA (national income and product accounts) principles. Of the $53 billion of new debt, the public absorbed $16.3 billion, close to the NIPA deficit, but the Federal Reserve absorbed $17.4 billion in federal securities in the same period, which certainly has some causal relationship with the burgeoning money supply. Thus, the question of how much of this was absorbed by borrowing from the non-bank public and how much was money creation appears over determined and possibly unsolvable. Employing a quarterly model of the macro economy with Federal Reserve policy partially endogenous for the year 1953–1976, W.D. McMillan and T.R. Beard, 'The Short Run Impact of Fiscal Policy on the Money Supply,' *Southern Economic Journal* 47 (1980): 122–135, estimated that around 17 percent of any increase in the deficit was monetized; M.J. Hamburger and B. Zwick, 'Deficits, Money and Inflation,' *Journal of Monetary Economies* 7 (1981): 141–150, estimated that between 20 percent and 25 percent of any increase in the deficit was monetized" (Edelstein, "War and the American Economy," 379–380).

22. For difficulty in implementing the capital tax, see D. Rock, *Argentina, 1516–1987: From Spanish Colonization to Alfonsin* (Berkeley: University of California Press, 1987), 61. For the impact of land rents, see R. Alemann, *Breve historia de la politica económica argentina, 1500–1989* (Buenos Aires: Editorial Claridad, 1989), 99.

23. A. Haimann, "Did Argentina Have a Currency Board in the Mid-1880s?" *Studies in Applied Economics* 4.1 (2013): 2.

24. V.B. Reber, "A Case of Total War: Paraguay, 1864–1870," *Journal of Iberian and Latin America Studies* 5.1 (1999): 23.

25. Weathering troops abroad—armies surviving off of foreign lands or plunder—was a prominent method of war finance before the twentieth century and the rise of the modern state. It was too expensive for states to maintain standing armies both during and after wartime. Thus states promoted their armies to stay abroad and let the host country pay the bill. See Brewer, *The Sinews of Power: War, Money, and the English State, 1688–1783* (New York: Alfred A. Knopf, 1989); M. Howard, *War in European History* (New York: Oxford University Press, 2009).

26. Nick Svendsen, *The First Schleswig-Holstein War 1848–50* (Solihull, West Midlands, UK: Helion, 2007), 152.

27. Ibid., 67–68.

28. Sicotte, Richard, Catalina Vizcarra, and Kirsten Wandschneider, "The Fiscal Impact of the War of the Pacific," *Cliometrica* 3 (2009): 97–121.

29. The seven participants in which there was no evidence of borrowing: Germany in the First Schleswig-Holstein; Russia in the Estonian and Latvian Wars of Liberation 1918–1920 as well as in the Russo-Polish War of 1919–1920; the United States in the Korean War, 1950–1953; Libya during the War over the Aouzou Strip; and Iraq during the Gulf War.

30. For further discussion of each of these cases, see the codebook.

31. The fourth case is Brazil during the La Plata War from 1851–1852.

32. These ten belligerents are: Brail and Paraguay during the Lopez War, Peru and Chile during the Pacific War, Russia during the Russo-Japanese War, Bolivia during the Chaco War, Germany during World War II, the Republic of Korea during the Korea War, and the Republic of Vietnam during the Vietnamese War.

33. I document cost of war in the codebook where possible.

34. E.g., Shultz and Weingast, "The Democratic Advantage"; Paul Poast, "Central Banks at War," *International Organization* 69.1 (2015): 63–95.

35. Matthew DiGiuseppe and Patrick E. Shea ("Sovereign Credit and the Fate of Leaders: Revisiting the 'Democratic Advantage," *International Studies Quarterly* forthcoming) find that the "democratic advantage" literature overstates the potential political backlash from credit downgrades in democracies and ignores the importance of sovereign credit to nondemocratic leaders.

36. See Michael A. Allen and Matthew DiGiuseppe, "Tightening the Belt: Sovereign Debt and Alliance Formation," *International Studies Quarterly* 57.4 (2013): 647–659.

37. See Rosella Cappella Zielinski and Paul Poast, "Financial Intervention and Conflict: Explaining Sovereign-to-Sovereign Loans to War Belligerents," Working Paper (2015).

38. See Rosella Cappella Zielinski, "War Finance and Military Effectiveness," Working Paper (2015).

39. For example, see Jonathan D. Caverley, *Democratic Militarism: Voting, Wealth and War* (Cambridge: Cambridge University Press, 2014); Cappella Zielinski, "War Finance and Military Effectiveness."

40. Branislav L. Slantchev ("Borrowed Power: Debt Finance and the Resort to Arms," *Political Science Review* 106.4 [November 2012]: 787–809) explores this question via the effect of wars paid for by debt.

41. See Fujihira, "Conscripting Money"; Jeff Carter and Glenn Palmer, "Regime Type and Interstate War Finance," *Foreign Policy Analysis* forthcoming.

# Bibliography


Acton, J. *The Cambridge Modern History.* Vol. 12. New York: MacMillan, 1910.

Adler, C. *Jacob Henry Schiff: A Biological Sketch.* New York: American Jewish Committee, 1921.

Akerlof, G.A. "The Missing Motivation in Macroeconomics." *American Economic Review* 97.1 (2007): 5–36.

Alemann, R. *Breve historia de la política económica argentina, 1500–1989.* Buenos Aires: Editorial Claridad, 1989.

Allen, G.C. *A Short Economic History of Modern Japan 1867–1937.* 3rd rev. ed. London: George Allen & Unwin, 1972.

Allen, M.A., and Matthew DiGuiseppe. "Tightening the Belt: Sovereign Debt and Alliance Formation." *International Studies Quarterly* 57.4 (2013): 647–659.

Allen, R.G.D. "Mutual Aid between the U.S. and the British Empire" In *History of the Second World War,* edited by R.S. Sayers, 518–556. London: Her Majesty's Stationery Office, 1946.

An, T.S. "Turmoil in Indochina: The Vietnam-Cambodia Conflict." *Asian Affairs* 5.4 (1978): 245–256.

Ananich, B. "Russian War Financing." In *The Russo-Japanese War in Global Perspecive: World War Zero,* Vol. 1, edited by J.W. Steinberg, B.W. Menning, D. Schimmelpenninck van der Oye, D. Wolf, and S. Yokote, 449–464. Leiden: Brill, 2005.

Anderson, O. "Loans Versus Taxes: British Financial Policy in the Crimean War." *Economic History Review* 16.2 (1963): 314–327.

——. *A Liberal State at War: English Politics and Economics during the Crimean War.* New York: St Martin's Press, 1967.

Ardant, Gabriel. "Financial Policy and Economic Infrastructure of Modern States and Nations." In *Formation of the National State in Western Europe,* edited by Charles Tilly, 164–242. Princeton, NJ: Princeton University Press, 1975.

Ashworth, J., and B. Heyndels. "Politicans' Preferences on Local Tax Rates: An Empirical Analysis." *European Journal of Political Economy* 13 (1997): 479–502.

Austin, D. Andrew. "Overview of the Federal Public Debt." *Congressional Research Service.* 2001. http://cnsnews.com/sites/default/files/documents/OVERVIEW%20OF%20THE%20FEDERAL%20DEBT-CRS-05-11-11.pdf.

Bailey, M.J. "The Welfare Cost of Inflationary Finance." *Journal of Political Economy* 64.2 (1956): 93–110.

Balderson, T. "War Finance and Inflation in Britian and Germany, 1914–1918." *Economic History Review* 42.2 (1989): 222–244.

Bank, S.A., J.S. Kirk, and J.J. Thorndike. *War and Taxes.* Washington, DC: Urban Institute Press, 2008.

Barnett, A. D. *China and the Major Powers in East Asia.* Washington, DC: Brookings Institution, 1977.

Barnett, C. *Britian and Her Army, 1509–1970: A Military, Political, and Social Survey.* New York: William Morrow, 1970.

Barnett, M.N. *Confronting the Costs of War: Military Power, State, and Society in Egypt and Israel*. Princeton, NJ: Princeton University Press, 1992.
Barro, R.J. "On the Determination of Public Debt." *Journal of Political Economy* 87 (1979): 940–971.
——. "Inflation and Economic Growth." *Annals of Economics and Finance* 14.1 (2013): 85–109.
Bates, R.H. "A Political Scientist Looks at Tax Reform." In *Tax Reform in Developing Countries*, edited by M. Gillis, 473–491. Durham, NC: Duke University Press, 1989.
Baumgart, W. *The Crimean War, 1853–1856*. New York: Oxford University Press, 1999.
Bayley, C.C. *Mercenaries for the Crimea: The German, Swiss, and Italian Legions in British Service, 1854–1856*. Montreal: McGill-Queen's University Press, 1977.
Belasco, A. *The Cost of Iraq, Afghanistan, and Other Global War on Terror Operations since 9/11*. Washington, DC: Congressional Research Service, 2011.
Bell, G.L. "The Effects of Monetary Policy on Specific Sectors of the Economy." *Journal of Political Economy* 76.4, Part 2: Issues in Monetary Research (1968): 818–821.
Bensel, R.F. *Yankee Leviathan: The Origins of Central State Authority in America, 1859–1877*. New York: Cambridge University Press, 1990.
Berglas, E. "Defense and the Economy." In *The Israeli Economy: Maturing through Crises*, edited by Y. Ben-Porath, 173–191. Cambridge, MA: Harvard University Press, 1986.
Berman, L. *Lyndon Johnson's War: The Road to Stalemate in Vietnam*. New York: W.W. Norton, 1989.
Birati, A., and A. Cukierman. "The Redistributive Effects of Inflation and of the Introduction of a Real Tax System in the U.S. Bond Market." *Journal of Public Ecnomics* 12 (1979): 125–139.
Bird, R.M. "Land Taxation and Economic Development: The Model of Meiji Japan." *Journal of Development Studies* 13.2 (1977): 162–174.
Black, C.E., M.B. Jansen, H.S. Levine, M.J. Levy Jr., H. Rosovsky, G. Rozman, et al. *The Modernization of Japan and Russia: A Comparative Study*. New York: Free Press, 1975.
Blackburn, R. *Mercenaries and Lyndon Johnson's "More Flags": The Hiring of Korean, Filipino, and Thai Soldiers in the Vietnam War*. Jefferson, NC: Mcfarland, 1994.
Blainey, G. *The Causes of War*. New York: Free Press, 1973.
Blair, C. *The Forgotten War: American in Korea, 1950–1953*. New York: Times Books, 1987.
Blum, J.M. *From the Morgenthau Diaries: Years of War, 1941–1945*. Boston: Houghton Mifflin, 1967.
Bogart, E.L. *Direct and Indirect Costs of the Great World War*. 2nd rev. ed. New York: Oxford University Press, 1920.
——. *War Costs and Their Financing*. New York: D. Appleton, 1921.
Bowman, L. "Russia's First Income Taxes: The Effects of Modernized Taxes on Commerce and Industry, 1885–1914." *Slavic Review* 52.2 (1993): 256–282.
Brewer, J. *The Sinews of Power: War, Money, and the English State, 1688–1783*. New York: Alfred A. Knopf, 1989.
Brownlee, O. "The Effects of Monetary and Credit Policies on the Structure of the Economy." *Journal of Political Economy* 76.4, Part 2: Issues in Monetary Reserach (1968): 786–795.
Buchanan, J.M. *The Collected Works of James M. Buchanan*. Vol. 2. *Public Principles of Public Debt: A Defense and Restatement*. Indianapolis: Liberty Fund, 1999.

——. *The Collected Works of James M. Buchanan*. Vol. 4. *Public Finance in Democratic Process: Fiscal Institutions and Individual Choice*. 1967; reprint Indianapolis: Liberty Fund, 1999.
Budd, E.C., and D.F. Seiders. "The Impact of Inflation on the Distribution of Income and Wealth." *American Economic Review, Papers and Proceedings* 61.May (1971): 128–138.
Bueno de Mesquita, B., and R.M. Siverson. "War and the Survival of Political Leaders: A Comparative Study of Regime Types and Political Accountability." *American Political Science Review* 89.4 (1995): 841–855.
Bueno de Mesquita, B., A. Smith, R.M. Siverson, and J. Morrow. *The Logic of Political Survival*. Cambridge, MA: MIT Press, 2003.
Burdekin, R., A. Denzau, M. Keil, T. Sitthiyot, and T. Willett. "When Does Inflation Hurt Economic Growth? Different Nonlinearities for Different Economies." *Journal of Macroeconomics* 26 (2004): 519–532.
Buxton, S. *Finance and Politics: An Historical Study, 1783–1885*. Vol. 1. London: John Murray, 1888.
Cairncross, A., and B. Eichengreen. *Sterling in Decline: The Devauluations of 1931, 1949 and 1967*. 2nd ed. New York: Palgrave Macmillan, 2003.
Campbell, J.T., L.S. Cain, A. Rapoport, and P.E. Converse. "Public Opinion and the Outbreak of War." *Journal of Conflcit Resolution* 9.3 (1965): 318–333.
Cappella Zielinski, Rosella. "War Finance and Military Effectiveness." Working Paper, Boston University, 2015.
Cappella Zielinski, Rosella, and Paul Poast. "Financial Intervention and Conflict: Explaining Sovereign-to-Sovereign Loans to War Belligerents." Working Paper, Boston University, 2015.
Carpenter, D.P. *The Forging of Bureaucratic Autonomy: Reputations, Networks, and Policy Innovation in Executive Agencies, 1862–1928*. Princeton, NJ: Princeton University Press, 2001.
Carter, Jeff, and Glenn Palmer. "Regime Type and Insterstate War Finance." *Foreign Policy Analysis* (Forthcoming).
Caverley, Jonathan D. *Democratic Militarism: Voting, Wealth, and War*. Cambridge: Cambridge University Press, 2014.
Centeno, M.A. *Blood and Debt: War and the Nation-State in Latin America*. University Park: Pennsylvania State University Press, 2002.
Central Intelligence Agency. "The Eastern Arab World." *National Intelligence Estimate*, number 36–66 (February 17, 1966).
——. "Arms Shipment to Jordan." *Intelligence Memorandum* (January 17, 1967).
——. Directorate of Intelligence. "Jordan's Armed Forces." *Intelligence Memorandum* (January 17, 1967).
——. "Probable Soviet Objectives in Rearming Arab States." *Special National Intelligence Estimate*, number 11-13-67 (July 20, 1967).
——. "Sino-Soviet Competition in Indochina." *Interagency Intelligence Memorandum*, 1978.
Cheibub, J.A. "Political Regimes and the Extractive Capacity of Governments: Taxation in Democracies and Dictatorships." *World Politics* 50 (April 1998): 349–376.
Chesney, F.R. *The Russo-Turkish Campaigns of 1828 and 1829, 1854*. New York: Redfield, 1854.
Chetty, R., A. Looney, and K. Kroft. "Salience and Taxation: Theory and Evidence." *American Economic Review* 99.4 (2009): 1145–1177.
Chiozza, G., and H.E. Goemans. "Peace through Insecurity: Tensure and International Conflict." *Journal of Conflict Resolution* 47.4 (2003): 443–467.

Colaresi, M. "When Doves Cry: International Rivalry, Unreciprocated Cooperation, and Leadership Turnover." *American Journal of Political Science* 48.3 (2004): 555–570.

Cole, D. C., and Y. C. Park. *Financial Development in Korea 1945–1978*. Cambridge, MA: Harvard University Press, 1983.

Collins, R. M. "The Economic Crisis of 1968 and the Waning of the 'American Century.'" *American Historical Review* 101.2 (1996): 396–422.

Condit, D. M. "The Test of War 1950–1953." *History of the Office of the Secretary of Defense*. Vol. 2. Washington, DC: Historical Office, Office of the Secretary of Defense, 1998.

Cordesman, A. H. *Jordanian Arms and the Middle East Balance*. Washington, DC: Middle East Institute, 1983.

Crisp, O. "Russian Financial Policy and the Gold Standard at the End of the Nineteenth Century." *Economic History Review* 6.2 (1953): 156–172.

Cummings, J. W. *Towards Modern Public Finance: The American War with Mexico, 1846–1848*. London: Pickering & Chatto, 2009.

Dacy, D. C. *Foreign Aid, War and Economic Development: South Vietnam, 1955–1975*. Cambridge: Cambridge University Press, 1986.

Daggett, S. *Costs of Major U.S. Wars*. Washington, DC: Congressional Reserach Service, 2010.

Detzer, K. *The Army Reader*. New York: The Bobbs-Merrill, 1943.

Dickson, P. G. M. *The Financial Revolution in England. A Study in the Development of Public Credit, 1688–1756*. London: Macmillan, 1967.

DiGuiseppe, Matthew, and Patrick E. Shea. "Sovereign Credit and the Fate of Leaders: Revisiting the 'Democratic Advantage.'" *International Studies Quarterly*. Forthcoming.

Downing, B. M. *The Military Revolution and Political Change: Origins of Democracy and Autocracy in Early Modern Europe*. Princeton, NJ: Princeton University Press, 1992.

Downs, A. *An Economic Theory of Democracy*. New York: Harper and Row, 1957.

——. "An Economic Theory of Political Action in a Democracy." *The Journal of Political Economy* 65.2 (1957): 135–150.

——. "How Smart and Tough Are Democracies? Reassessing Theories of Democratic Victory in War." *International Security* 33.4 (2009): 9–51.

Dudley, L., and P. Passell. "The War in Vietnam and the United States Balance of Payments." *Review of Economics and Statistics* 50.4 (1968): 437–442.

*The Economic and Political Hazards of an Inflationary Defense Economy*. Washington DC: Joint Committee on the Economic Report, 1951.

"Economic Effect of Vietnam Spending." *Hearings Before the Joint Committee, Congress of the United States, Ninetieth Congress, First Session, April 24–27, 1967*, Vol. 1. Washington, DC: Government Printing Office, 1967.

*An Economist's Statement on Anti-Inflationary Measures*. Washington, DC: Joint Committee on the Economic Report, 1950.

Edelstein, M. "War and the American Economy in the Twentieth Century." In *The Cambridge Economic History of the United States: The Twentieth Century*, edited by S. L. Engerman and R. E. Gallman, 329–406. Cambridge: Cambridge University Press, 2000.

Eichengreen, B. *Globalizing Capital: A History of the International Monetary System*. Princeton, NJ: Princeton University Press, 1996.

Ertman, T. *Birth of the Leviathan: Building States and Regimes in Medieval and Early Modern Europe*. Cambridge: Cambridge University Press, 1997.

Esthus, R.A. "Nicholas II and the Russo-Japanese War." *Russian Review* 40.4 (1981): 396–411.
Fairchild, F.R. "German War Finance–A Review." In *War Finance*, Vol. 3, edited by L. Neal, 106–121. 1922; reprint Brookfield, VT: Edward Elgar Publishing, 1994.
Fand, D.I. "The Impact of Monetary Policy in 1966." *Journal of Political Economy* 74.4 Part 2: Issues in Monetary Reserach (1968): 821–830.
Farrar-Hockley, A. *The British Part in the Korean War.* Vol. 2. London: HMSO, 1995.
Fazal, T., P. Fortna, J. Stanton, and A. Weisiger. *War Initiation and Termination (WIT) Coding Instrument and Data Set: Columbia University.* https://qdr.syr.edu/discover/projectdescriptionsfazal.
Feis, H. *Europe: The World's Banker, 1870–1914.* New Haven: Yale University Press, 1930.
Feldman, G.D. *The Great Disorder: Politics, Economics, and Society in the German Inflation 1914–1924.* Oxford: Oxford University Press, 1997.
Feldstein, M. "The Welfare Cost of Permanent Inflation and Optimal Short Run Economic Policy." *Journal of Political Economy* 87.4 (1979): 749–768.
——. "The Costs and Benefits of Going from Low Inflation to Price Stability." In *Reducing Inflation: Motiviation and Strategy*, edited by C.D. Romer and D.H. Romer 123–156. Chicago: Chicago University Press, 1997.
——. "Capital Income Taxes and the Benefit of Price Stability." In *The Costs and Benefits of Price Stability*, edited by M. Feldstein, 9–39. Chicago: University of Chicago Press, 1999.
Ferguson, N. *The House of Rothschild: The World's Banker 1849–1999.* Vol. 2. New York: Penguin Group, 1999.
Filson, Darren, and Suzanne Werner. "A Bargaining Model of War and Peace: Anticipating the Onset, Duration, and Outcome of War." *American Journal of Political Science* 46.4 (2002): 819–838.
Finkelstein, A. "E-ZTax: Tax Salience and Tax Rates." *Quarterly Journal of Economics* 124.3 (2009): 969–1010.
Flores-Macias, Gustavo A., and Sarah E. Kreps. "Political Parties at War: A Study of American War Finance." *American Political Science Review* 107.4 (2013): 833–848.
Fordham, Benjamin O. *Building a Cold War Consensus: The Political Economy of U.S. National Security, 1949–1951.* Ann Arbor, MI: The University of Michigan Press, 1998.
Fujihira, S. "Conscripting Money: Total War and Fiscal Revolution in the Twentieth Century." Ph.D. diss., Princeton University, 2000.
Gabbay, Y. "Israel's Fiscal Policy, 1948–1982." In *Economic and Social Policy in Israel: The First Generation*, edited by M. Sanbar, 85–112. Lanham, MD: University Press of America; Jerusalem Center for Public Affairs/Center for Jewish Community Studies, 1990.
Gaitskell, H. "The Sterling Area." *International Affairs* (*Royal Institute of International Affairs 1944–*) 28.2 (1952): 170–176.
Gartner, S.S., and G.M. Segura. "War, Casualties, and Public Opinion." *Journal of Conflict Resolution* 42 (1998): 278–300.
Gartner, S.S., G.M. Segura, and M. Wilkening. "All Politics are Local: Local Losses and Individual Attitudes Towards the Vietnam War." *Journal of Conflict Resolution* 41 (1997): 669–694.
Gasiorowski, M.J. "Economic Crisis and Political Regime Change: An Event History Analysis." *American Political Science Review* 89.4 (1995): 882–897.
Gibbons, W.C. *The U.S. Government and the Vietnam War: Executive and Legislative Roles and Relationships*, Vol. 4. *July 1965–January 1968.* Princeton, NJ: Princeton University Press, 1995.

Giffen, S. R. *Economic Inquiries and Studies*. Vol. 1. London: George Bell and Sons, 1904.
Gillman, M., and M. Kejak. "Contrasting Models of the Effect of Inflation on Growth." *Journal of Economic Surveys* 19.1 (2005): 113–136.
Gilpin, R. *War and Change in World Politics*. Cambridge: Cambridge University Press, 1981.
Goemans, H. E. *War and Punishment*. Illustrated ed. Princeton, NJ: Princeton University Press, 2000.
Goldsmith, R. W. *The Financial Development of Japan, 1868–1977*. New Haven: Yale University Press, 1983.
Gorlin, R. H. "Problems of Tax Reform in Imperial Russia." *Journal of Modern History* 49.2 (1977): 246–265.
Gourevitch, Peter. "The Second Image Reversed: The International Sources of Domestic Politics." *International Organization* 32 (1978): 881–912.
Grey, J. *The Commonwealth Armies and the Korean War*. Manchester: Manchester University Press, 1988.
Gross, B. M., and J. P. Lewis. "The President's Economic Staff during the Truman Administration." *American Political Science Review* 48.1 (1954): 114–130.
Haimann, A. "Did Argentina Have a Currency Board in the Mid-1880s?" *Studies in Applied Economics* 4.1 (2013): 1–9.
Halberstam, D. *The Best and the Brightest*. New York: Random House, 1972.
Hall, H. D. *North American Supply*. London: Her Majesty's Stationery Office, 1955.
Hamburger, M. J., and B. Zwick. "Deficits, Money and Inflation." *Journal of Monetary Economies* 7 (1981): 141–150.
Hamby, Alonzo L. "The Vital Center, the Fair Deal, and the Quest for a Liberal Political Economy." *American Historical Review* 77.3 (June 1973): 653–678.
Hamilton, A. "First Report on the Public Credit (Communicated to the House of Representatives, January 14, 1790)." In *The Works of Alexander Hamilton*, Vol. 2, edited by H. C. Lodge, 227–290. New York: Knickerbocker Press, 1904.
Hammond, P. L. *LBJ and the Presidential Management of Foreign Relations*. Austin: University of Texas Press, 1992.
Hancock, W. K., and M. M. Gowing. *British War Economy*. London: His Majesty's Stationery Office, 1949.
Hanson, Jonathan K. "Forging then Taming Leviathan: State Capacity, Constraints on Rules, and Development." *International Studies Quarterly* 58.2 (2004): 380–392
Hargrove, E. C., and M. A. Samuel, eds. *The President and the Council of Economic Advisers: Interviews with CEA Chairman*. Boulder, CO: Westview Press, 1984.
Harries, M., and S. Harries. *Soldiers of the Sun: The Rise and Fall of the Imperial Japanese Army*. New York: Random House, 1994.
Harrison, Mark. "The Economics of World War II: An Overview." In *The Economics of World War II*, edited by Mark Harrison, 1–42. Cambridge: Cambridge University Press, 1998.
Hearder, H. "Claredon, Cavour, and the Intervention of Sardinia in the Crimean War, 1853–1855." *International History Review* 18.4 (1996): 819–836.
Helleiner, E. *States and the Reemergence of Global Finance*. Ithaca, NY: Cornell University Press, 1994.
Heller, W. *New Dimensions of Political Economy*. Cambridge, MA: Harvard University Press, 1966.
Helsing, J. W. *Johnson's War/Johnson's Great Society: The Guns and Butter Trap*. Wesport: Praeger, 2000.
Herring, G. C., Jr. "The United States and British Bankruptcy, 1944–1945: Responsibilities Deferred." *Political Science Quarterly* 86.2 (1971): 260–280.

Hickman, B.G. *The Korean War and United States Economic Activity*. New York: National Bureau of Economic Research, 1955.
Hirst, F.W. *The Political Economy of War*. London: J. M. Dent & Sons, 1915.
Hoad, C.J.C. *Commonwealth Military Attache Japanese Army, 1904 (Russo-Japanese War)*. London: Department of Defence, 1904.
Hood, C. "The Tax State in the Information Age." In *The Nation-State in Question*, edited by T.V. Paul, G.J. Ikenberry, and J.A. Hall, 213–227. Princeton, NJ: Princeton University Press, 2003.
Houben, A. *The Evolution of Monetary Policy Strategies in Europe*. Boston: Kluwer Academic, 2000.
Howard, M. *War in European History*. Updated ed. New York: Oxford University Press, 2009.
Hozier, H.M. *The Russo Turkish War*. Vol. 4. 1878; reprint London: Elibron Classics (William Mackenzie), 2005.
Huber, J.D., and N. McCarty. "Bureaucratic Capacity, Delegation, and Political Reform." *American Political Science Review* 98.3 (2004): 481–494.
Hughes, J.R.T. *Fluctuations in Trade, Industry, and Finance*. Oxford: Oxford University Press, 1960.
Hume, D. *Essays, Moral, Political, Literary*. 1742; reprint Indianapolis: Liberty Fund, 1987.
Huntington, S.P. *Political Order in Changing Societies*. New Haven: Yale University Press, 1968.
Ike, N. "Taxation and Landownership in the Westernization of Japan." *Journal of Economic History* 7.2 (1947): 160–182.
*Inflation and Communism*. Washington, DC: Joint Committee on the Economic Report, 1951.
Inoki, M. "The Civil Bureaucracy: Japan." In *Political Modernization in Japan and Turkey*, edited by R.E. Ward and D.A. Rustow, 283–300. Princeton, NJ: Princeton University Press, 1964.
*IRS Historical Fact Book: A Chronology 1646–1992*. Washington DC: US Department of the Treasury, Internal Revenue Service, 1993.
Ishi, H. "Historical Background of the Japanese Tax System." *Hitotsubashi Journal of Economics* 29.1 (1988): 1–20.
Jackson, K.D. "Cambodia 1978: War, Pillage, and Purge in Democratic Kampuchea." *Asian Survey* 19.1, A Survey of Asia in 1978: Part I (1978): 72–84.
Jentschura, H., D. Jung, and P. Mickel. *Warships of the Imperial Japanese Navy, 1869–1945*. Annapolis, MD: Naval Institute Press, 1977.
Judd, D. *The Crimean War*. London: Granada, 1975.
Kahan, A. *Russian Economic History: The Nineteenth Century*. Chicago: University of Chicago Press, 1989.
Kanovsky, E. "The Economic Aftermath of the Six Day War: UAR, Jordan and Syria, Part 2." *Middle East Journal* 22.3 (1968): 278–296.
——. *The Economic Impact of the Six-Day War: Israel, The Occupied Territories, Egypt, Jordan*. New York: Praeger, 1970.
——. *The Economy of Jordan*. Tel Aviv: University Publishing Projects, 1976.
Karel, J. *An English View of Russian Finance*. Washington, DC: US Bureau of Foreign Commerce, 1896.
Katznelson, Ira, and Martin Shefter, eds. *Shaped by War and Trade: International Influences on American Political Development*. Princeton, NJ: Princeton University Press, 2003.
Keegan, J. *The Second World War*. New York: Penguin Books, 1990.

Keith, E.G. "The Excess Profits Tax Act of 1950." *National Tax Journal* 4.3 (1951): 193–207.

Kennedy, P. *The Rise and Fall of the Great Powers: Economic Change and Military Conflict from 1500 to 2000*. New York: Random House, 1987.

Ketchum, R.M. *Saratoga: Turning Points of America's Revolutionary War*. New York: Henry Holt, 1997.

Keynes, J.M. *Essays in Persuasion*. New York,: Harcourt, 1932.

——. *How to Pay for the War: A Radical Plan for the Chancellor of the Exchequer*. New York: Harcourt, 1940.

Khan, M., and A. Senhadji. "Threshold Effects in the Relationship Between Inflation and Growth." *IMF Staff Papers* 48.1 (2001): 1–21.

Kimball, W.F. "'Begger My Neighbor': America and the British Interim Finance Crisis, 1940–1941." *Journal of Economic History* 29.4 (1969): 758–772.

——. *The Most Unsordid Act: Lend-Lease, 1939–1941*. Baltimore: Johns Hopkins Press, 1969.

Kipp, J.W. "M. Kh. Reutern on the Russian State and Economy: A Liberal Bureaucrat during the Crimean Era, 1854–60." *Journal of Modern History* 47.3 (1975): 437–459.

Knorr, K. *The Power of Nations: The Political Economy of International Relations*. New York: Basic Books, 1975.

Kotsonis, Y. "'Face-to-Face': The State, the Individual, and the Citizen in Russian Taxation, 1863–1917." *Slavic Review* 63.2 (2004): 221–246.

Kramer, G.H. "Short-Term Fluctuations in U.S. Voting Behavior, 1896–1964." *American Political Science Review* 65.1 (171): 131–143.

Krooss, H.E. *American Economic Development*. Englewood Cliffs, NJ: Prentice-Hall, 1955.

Kugler, J., and W. Domke. "Comparing the Strength of Nations." *Comparative Political Studies* 19.1 (1986): 39–69.

"Lack of Funds May End Balkan War." *Wall Street Journal*, July 8, 1913.

Lamborn, A.C. "Power and the Politics of Extraction." *International Studies Quarterly* 27 (1983): 125–146.

Landon, S., and L.D. Ryan. "The Political Costs of Taxes and Government Spending." *Canadian Journal of Economics* 30.1 (1997): 85–111.

Lawson, F.H. *Why Syria Goes to War: Thirty Years of Confrontation*. Ithaca, NY: Cornell University Press, 1996.

Lee, J.W. "The Impact of the Korean War on the Korean Economy." *International Journal of Korean Studies* 5.1 (2001): 97–118.

Leland, A., and M.J. Oboroceanu. *American War and Military Operation Casualties: Lists and Statistics*. Washington, DC: Congressional Research Service, 2010.

Levi, M. *Of Rule and Revenue*. Berkeley: University of California Press, 1988.

Lewis-Beck, M.S., and M. Stegmaier. "Economic Determinants of Electoral Outcomes." *Annual Review of Political Science* 3 (2000): 183–219.

Lieberman, E.S. "Taxation Data as Indicators of State-Society Relations: Possibilities and Pitfalls in Cross-National Reserach." *Studies in Comparative International Development* 36.4 (2002): 89–115.

——. *Race and Regionalism in the Politics of Taxation in Brazil and South Africa*. Cambridge: Cambridge University Press, 2003.

Lobell, Steven E., Norrin M. Ripsman, and Jeffrey W. Taliaferro, eds. *Neoclassical Realism, the State, and Foreign Policy*. Cambridge: Cambridge University Press, 2009.

Long, J. "Organized Protest against the 1906 Russian Loan." *Cahiers du Monde Russe et Sovietique* 13.1 (1972): 23–39.

——. "Russian Manipulation of the French Press, 1904–1906." *Slavic Review* 31.2 (1972): 343–354.
——. "Franco-Russian Relations during the Russo-Japanese War." *Slavonic and East European Review* 52.127 (1974): 213–33.
López-Villavicencio, Antonia, and Valérie Mignon. "On the Impact of Inflation on Output Growth: Does the Level of Inflation Matter?" *Journal of Macroeconomics* 33 (2011): 455–464.
Lorrell, M., C. Kelly Jr., and D. Hensler. *Casualties, Public Opinion, and Presidential Policy During the Vietnam War*. Santa Monica, CA: Rand—Project Air Force, 1985.
Lounge, D. E., and R. J. Sweeney. "Inflation and Real Growth: Some Empirical Results." *Journal of Money, Credit, and Banking* 13 (1981): 497–501.
Lucas, R. E., and N. Stokey. "Optimal Fiscal and Monetary Policy in an Economy without Capital." *Journal of Monetary Economics* 12 (1983): 55–93.
Lustick, I. S. "History, Historiography, and Political Science: Multiple Historical Records and the Problem of Selection Bias." *American Political Science Review* 90.3 (1996): 605–618.
Maisel, S. J. "The Effects of Monetary Policy on Expenditures in Specific Sectors of the Economy." *Journal of Political Economy* 76.4, Part 2: Issues in Monetary Research (1967): 796–814.
Manson, E. S., M. J. Kim, D. H. Perkins, K. S. Kim, and D. C. Cole. *The Economic and Social Modernization of the Republic of Korea*. Cambridge, MA: Harvard University Press, 1980.
Ma'oz, M. *Syria and Israel: From War to Peace-Making*. New York: Oxford University Press, 1995.
Mastanduno, M., D. A. Lake, and G. J. Ikenberry. "Toward a Realist Theory of State Action." *International Studies Quarterly* 33 (1989): 457–474.
Maurice, M. F. *The Russo-Turkish War 1877: A Strategical Sketch*. London: Swan Sonnenschein, 1905.
Mazower, M. *Greece and the Inter-War Economic Crisis*. Oxford: Oxford Unversity Press, 1991.
McCurrach, D. F. "Britian's U.S. Dollar Problems, 1939–45." *Economic Journal* 58.231 (1948): 356–372.
McLure, C. E., Jr. "Fiscal Failure: Lessons of the Sixties." In *Economic Policy and Inflation in the Sixties*, edited by W. Fellner, 7–87. Washington, DC: American Enterprise Institute for Public Policy Research, 1972.
McMillan, W. D., and T. R. Beard. "The Short Run Impact of Fiscal Policy on the Money Supply." *Southern Economic Journal* 47 (1980): 122–135.
Meltzer, A. *A History of the Federal Reserve, Volume 1: 1913–1951*. Chicago: University of Chicago Press, 2003.
Michelson, A.M., P.N. Apostol, and M.W. Bernatzky. *Russian Public Finance During the War*. New Haven: Yale University Press, 1928.
Mill, J. S. *Principles of Political Economy*. 7th ed. 1848; reprint London: Longmans, Green, 1909.
Miller, E. "War, Taxation, and the English Economy in the Late Thirteenth and Early Fourteenth Centuries." In *War and Economic Development: Essays in Memory of David Joslin*, edited by J. M. Winters, 11–32. Cambridge: Cambridge University Press, 1975.
Miller, E. S. "Japan's Other Victory: Overseas Financing of the War." In *The Russo-Japanese War in Global Perspective: World War Zero, Vol. 2*, edited by J. W. Steinberg, B. W. Menning, D. Schimmelpenninck van der Oye, D. Wolff, and S. Yokote, 466–478. Leiden, The Netherlands: Brill, 2005.

Millet, A. R. *The War for Korea, 1950–1951: They Came from the North*. Lawrence: University Press of Kansas, 2010.

Modigliani, F. "Long-Run Implications of Alternative Fiscal Policies and the Burden of the National Debt." *Economic Journal* 71.284 (1961): 730–755.

Moles, P., and N. Terry. *The Handbook of International Financial Terms*. Oxford: Oxford University Press, 1997.

"Monetary Commercial English News." *Commercial and Financial Chronical* 26 (April 27, 1878): 407.

Morozov, B. "The Outbreak of the June 1967 War in Light of Soviet Documentation." In *The Soviet Union and the June 1967 Six Day War*, edited by Y. Ro'i and B. Morozov, 42–64. Washington, DC: Woodrow Wilson Center for Scholars, 2008.

Morris, S. J. *Why Vietnam Invaded Cambodia: Political Culture and the Causes of War*. Stanford, CA: Stanford University Press, 1999.

Morton, W. A. *British Finance, 1930–1940*. Madison: University of Wisconsin Press, 1943.

Mueller, J. E. "Trends in Popular Support for the Wars in Korea and Vietnam." *American Political Science Review* 65.2 (June 1971): 358–375.

——. *War, Presidents, and Public Opinion*. New York: Wiley, 1973.

Murphy, H. C. *The National Debt in War and Transition*. New York: McGraw-Hill, 1950.

Nish, I. "Stretching Out to the Yalu: A Contested Frontier, 1900–1903." In *The Russo-Japanese War in Global Perspective, Vol. 1*, edited by J. W. Steinberg, B. W. Menning, D. Schimmelpenninck van der Oye, D. Wolff and S. Yokote, 45–64. Leiden: Konninklijke Brill, 2005.

Nordhaus, W. D. "The Effects of Inflation on the Distribution of Economic Welfare." *Journal of Money, Credit, and Banking* 5 (173): 465–508.

Ogawa, Gotaro. *Expenditures of the Russo-Japanese War*. New York: Oxford University Press, 1923.

Ohanian, L. E. "The Macroeconomic Effects of War Finance in the United States: World War II and the Korean War." *American Economic Review* 87.1 (1997): 23–40.

——. *The Macroeconomic Effects of War Finance in the United States: Taxes, Inflation, and Deficit Finance*. New York: Garland, 1998.

Okamoto, S. *The Japanese Oligarchy and the Russo-Japanese War*. New York: Columbia University Press, 1970.

Organski, A. F. K., and J. Kugler. *The War Ledger*. Chicago: University of Chicago Press, 1980.

Ott, A. F., and P. Hughes-Cromwick. "The War on Poverty: Two Decades Later." In *Lyndon Baines Johnson and the Uses of Power*, edited by B. J. Firestone and R. C. Vogt, 51–75. New York: Greenwood Press, 1988.

"Ownership of Federal Securities." *Federal Security Bulletin* (December 2010): 50–52.

Parks, R. W. "Inflation and Relative Price Variability." *Journal of Political Economy* 86.1 (1978): 79–95.

Patrick, H. T. "External Equilibrium and Internal Convertibility: Financial Policy in Meiji Japan." *Journal of Economic History* 25.2 (1965): 187–213.

Patterson, J. T. *Grand Expectations: The United States, 1945–1974*. Oxford: Oxford University Press, 1996.

Peltzman, S. "How Efficient is the Voting Market." *Journal of Law and Economics* 33.1 (1990): 27–63.

Pickens, D. K. "LBJ, the Council of Economic Advisors, and the Burden of New Deal Liberalism." In *Lyndon Baines Johnson and the Uses of Power*, edited by B. J. Firestone and R. C. Vogt, 191–204. New York: Greenwood Press, 1988.

Pigou, A. C. *The Economy and Finance of War: Being A Discussion of the Real Costs of the War and the Way in Which They Should be Met*. London: J. M. Dent & Sons, 1916.

Pike, D. *Vietnam Cambodia Conflict*. Report Prepared by the Congressional Research Service for the House Subcommittee on Asian and Pacific Affairs, October 4, 1978 (Washington, DC: GPO, 1978), 17–18.
Pintner, W. M. "Inflation in Russia during the Crimean War Period." *American Slavic and East European Review* 18.1 (1959): 81–87.
Plessner, Y. *The Political Economy of Israel from Ideology to Stagnation*. SUNY Series in Israeli Studies. Albany: State University of New York Press, 1994.
Poast, Paul. "Central Banks at War." *International Organization* 69.1 (2015): 63–95.
Polk, James K. "Third Annual Message, December 7, 1847." *The American Presidency Project*. Online by Gerhard Peters and John T. Woolley. Retrieved from http://www.presidency.ucsb.edu/ws/?pid=29488.
Pollack, S. D. *War, Revenue, and State Building: Financing the Development of the American State*. Ithaca, NY: Cornell University Press, 2009.
Postan, M. M. *British War Production*. London: Her Majesty's Stationary Office, 1952.
Powell, R. "Bargaining and Learning while Fighting." *American Journal of Political Science* 48.2 (2004): 344–361.
Pratt, E. E. "Our Change in the Near East: Tariff Duties Which Destroy the Basis of Exchange by Export and Import Endanger a Valuable Commerce-War and Politics Hinder Reconstruction in Asia Minor and the Balkans." *Our World 1* (April 1922).
*Public Papers of the Presidents of the United States: Lyndon B. Johnson, 1967*. Vol. 1, entry 3, 2–14. Washington, DC: Government Printing Office, 1968.
Putnam, Robert D. "Diplomacy and Domestic Politics: The Logic of Two-Level Games." *International Organization* 42.3 (spring 1988): 427–460.
Pyle, K. B. "The Technology of Japanese Nationalism: The Local Improvement Movement, 1900–1918." *Journal of Asian Studies* 33.1 (1973): 51–65.
Rasler, K. A., and W. R. Thompson. "Global Wars, Public Debts, and the Long Cycle." *World Politics* 35.4 (1983): 489–516.
——. *War and State Making: The Shaping of the Global Powers*. Boston: Unwin Hyman, 1989.
Reber, V. B. "A Case of Total War: Paraguay, 1864–1870." *Journal of Iberian and Latin America Studies* 5.1 (1999): 15–40.
Reeve, W. D. *The Republic of Korea: A Political and Economic Study*. London: Oxford University Press, 1963.
Reinhart, C. M., and K. S. Rogoff. *This Time is Different: Eight Centuries of Financial Folly*. Princeton, NJ: Princeton University Press, 2009.
Repington, Charles a Court. *The War in the Far East, 1904–1905 (By the Military Correspondent of The Times)*. New York: E. P. Dutton, 1905.
*Report of the Board of General Officers, House of Parliament*. London: Her Majesty's Statonery Office, 1856.
*Report on the War Finance*. Tokyo: Ministry of Finance(Ōkurashō), 1906.
Riasanovsky, N. V. *A History of Russia*. 6th ed. Oxford: Oxford University Press, 2000.
Ricardo, D. "Chapter XVII: Taxes on Other Commodities than Raw Produce." In *The Works of David Ricardo*, edited by J. R. McCulloch, 146–154. 1846; reprint London: John Murray, 1888.
——. "Essay on the Funding System." In *The Works of David Ricardo*, edited by J. R. McCulloch, 513–548. 1846; reprint London: John Murray, 1888.
Rich, N. *Why the Crimean War? A Cautionary Tale*. New York: McGraw–Hill, 1991.
Riddell, T. *A Political Economy of the American War in Indo-China: Its Costs and Consequences*. Washington, DC: American University, 1975.

——. "The Vietnam War and Inflation Revisited." In *Lyndon Bains Johnson and the Uses of Power*, edited by B. J. Firestone and R. C. Vogt, 217–232. New York: Greenwood Press, 1988.
Ripsman, N. M., and S. Levy. "Wishful Thinking or Buying Time? The Logic of British Appeasement in the 1930s." *International Security* 33.2 (2008): 141–181.
Rivlin, P. *The Israeli Economy*. Boulder, CO: Westview Press, 1992.
Rock, D. *Argentina, 1516–1987: From Spanish Colonization to Alfonsin*. Berkeley: University of California Press, 1987.
Rockoff, Hugh. "From Plowshares to Swords: The American Economy in World War II." *NBER Working Paper Series on Historical Factors in Long Run Growth*. Historical Paper 77. Cambridge, MA: NBER, 1995.
Rohrer, F. "What's a Little Debt Between Friends?" *BBC News* (May 10, 2006).
Roosevelt, Franklin D. "Press Conference, December 17, 1940." *The American Presidency Project*. Online by Gerhard Peters and John T. Woolley. http://www.presidency.ucsb.edu/ws/?pid=15913.
——. "Press Conference, March 11, 1941." *The American Presidency Project*. Online by Gerhard Peters and John T. Woolley. http://www.presidency.ucsb.edu/ws/?pid=16086.
Ross, R. R. *Cambodia: A Country Study*. 3rd ed. Washington, DC: Library of Congress for the Department of the Army, 1987.
Ryan, M. A., D. M. Finkelstein, and M. A. McDevitt. *Chinese Warfighting: The PLA Experience Since 1949*: Armonk, NY: M. E. Sharpe, 2003.
Sablinsky, W. *The Road to Bloody Sunday*. Princeton, NJ: Princeton University Press, 1976.
Sandler, S., ed. *The Korean War: An Encyclopedia*. New York: Routledge, 1995.
Sarkees, M. R., and F. Wayman. *Resort to War: 1816–2007*. Washington, DC: CQ Press, 2010.
Sartori, G. "Concept Misformation in Comparative Politics." *American Political Science Review* 64.4 (1970): 1033–1053.
Sato, S. "Japan's Fiscal System: An International Comparison." In *Public Finance in Japan*, edited by T. Hayashi and K. Kaizuka, 3–26. Tokyo: Universitiy of Tokyo Press, 1973.
Sayers, R. S. *Financial Policy, 1939–1945*. London: Her Majesty's Stationery Office, 1956.
Scheve, K., and D. Stasavage. "The Conscription of Wealth: Mass Warfare and the Demand for Progressive Taxation." *International Organization* 64 (fall 2010): 529–561.
——. "Democracy, War, and Wealth: Evidence from Two Centuries of Inheritance Taxation." *American Political Science Review* 106.1 (2012): 81–102.
Schimmelpenninck van der Oye, D. "The Immediate Origins of the War." In *The Russo-Japanese War in Global Perspective, Vol. 1*, edited by J. W. Steinberg, B. W. Menning, D. Schimmelpenninck van der Oye, D. Wolff and S. Yokote, 23–44. Leiden: Koninklijke Brill, 2005.
Schuessler, J. M., "Democracy, Deception, and IR Theory." *International Security Studies Forum Roundtable* 5.4 (2012): 45–47.
Schultz, K. A., and B. R. Weingast. "The Democratic Advantage: Institutional Foundations of Financial Power in International Competition." *International Organization* 57 (winter 2003): 3–42.
Seabrooke, L. *The Social Sources of Financial Power: Domestic Legitimacy and International Financial Orders*. Ithaca, NY: Cornell University Press, 2006.
Seligman, E. R. A. "The Cost of The War and How it was Met." *American Economic Review* 9 (December 1919): 739–770.

Shaw, S.J., and E.K. Shaw. *History of the Ottoman Empire and Modern Turkey: Reform, Revolution, and Republic; The Rise of Modern Turkey 1808–1975*. Vol. 2. Cambridge: Cambridge University Press, 1977.
Sherman, A.J. "German-Jewish Bankers in World Politics: The Financing of the Russo-Japanese War." *Leo Baeck Institute Yearbook* 38.1 (1983): 59–73.
Sicotte, Richard, Catalina Vizcarra, and Kirsten Wandschneider. "The Fiscal Impact of the War of the Pacific." *Cliometrica* 3 (2009): 97–121.
Silberman, B.S. "Bureaucratic Development and Bureaucratization: The Case of Japan." *Social Science History* 2.4 (1978): 385–398.
Simpson, P.M. "Lyndon B. Johnson and the 1964–1968 Revenue Acts: Congressional Politics and 'Fiscal Chickens Coming Home to Roost.'" In *Lyndon Baines Johnson and the Uses of Power*, edited by B.J. Firestone and R.C. Vogt, 205–216. New York: Greenwood Press, 1988.
Singer, D.J., S. Bremer, and J. Stuckey. "Capability Distribution, Uncertainty, and Major Power War, 1820–1965." In *Peace, War, and Numbers*, edited by B. Russett, 19–48. Beverly Hills, CA: Sage, 1972.
"SIPRI Military Expenditure Database." Solna, Sweden: Spiri Research Institute, 2012.
Slantchev, Branislav L. "Borrowed Power: Debt Finance and the Resort to Arms." *Political Science Review* 106.4 (November 2012): 787–809.
Sloan, J. "President Johnson, The Council of Economic Advisors, and the Failure to Raise Taxes in 1966 and 1967." *Presidential Studies Quarterly* 15.1 (1985): 89–98.
Smethurst, R.J. *From Foot Soldier to Finance Minister: Takahashi Korekiyo, Japan's Keynes*. Cambridge, MA: Harvard University Asia Center, 2007.
Smith, A. *An Inquiry into the Nature and Causes of the Wealth of Nations*. 5th ed. Vol. 2. 1776; reprint Indianapolis: Liberty Fund, 1981.
Sprague, O.M.W. "Loans and Taxes in War Finance." *American Economic Review* 7.1 (1917): 199–213.
Steinmo, S. *Taxation and Democracy: Swedish, British, and American Approaches to Financing the Modern State*. New Haven, CT: Yale University, 1993.
Stettinius, E.R., Jr. *Lend-Lease: Weapon for Victory*. New York: Macmillan, 1944.
Stevens, R.W. *Vain Hopes, Grim Realities: The Economic Consequences of the Vietnam War*. New York: New Viewpoints, 1976.
Stiglitz, J.E., and L.J. Bilmes. *The Three Trillion Dollar War: The True Cost of the Iraq Conflict*. New York: W. W. Norton, 2008.
Studenski, P., and H.E. Krooss. *Financial History of the United States*. New York: McGraw-Hill, 1952.
Surh, G.D. *1905 in St. Petersburg: Labor, Society, and Revolution*. Stanford, CA: Stanford University Press, 1989.
Sussman, N., and Y. Yafeh. "Institutions, Reforms, and Country Risk: Lessons from Japanese Government Debt in the Meiji Era." *Journal of Economic History* 60.2 (2000): 442–467.
Svendsen, Nick. *The First Schleswig-Holstein War 1848–50*. Solihull, West Midlands, UK: Helion, 2007.
Takao, T. "The Financial Policy of the Meiji Government." *Developing Economies* 3.4 (1965): 427–449.
Taylor, A.J.P. *The Struggle for Mastery in Europe, 1848–1918*. Oxford: Oxford University Press, 1954.
Tignor, R.L. *Capitalism and Nationalism at the End of Empire: State and Business in Colonizing Egypt, Nigeria, and Kenya, 1945–1963*. Princeton, NJ: Princeton University Press, 1998.

Tilly, C. ed. *The Formation of National States in Western Europe*. Princeton, NJ: Princeton University Press, 1975.

——. "War Making and State Making as Organized Crime." In *Bringing the State Back In*, edited by P. Evans, D. Rueschemeyer, and T. Skocpol, 169–187. Cambridge: Cambridge University Press, 1985.

——. *Coercion, Capital, and European states, AD 990–1990*. Cambridge, MA: B. Blackwell, 1990.

Tomz, M. *Reputation and International Cooperation: Soverign Debt across Three Centuries*. Princeton, NJ: Princeton University Press, 2007.

Tooze, A. *The Wages of Destruction: The Making and Breaking of the Nazi Economy*. New York: Viking, 2007.

Truman, Harry S. "Annual Message to the Congress on the State of the Union, January 5, 1949." *The American Presidency Project.* Online by Gerhard Peters and John T. Woolley. http://www.presidency.ucsb.edu/ws/?pid=13293.

——. "Special Message to the Congress Reporting on the Situation in Korea, July 19, 1950." *The American President Project.* Online by Gerhard Peters and John T. Woolley. http://www.presidency.ucsb.edu/ws/?pid=13293.

Tuan, N.A. *South Vietnam Trial and Experience: A Challenge for Development*. Athens, OH: Center for International Studies, Ohio University, 1987.

Twining, C.H. "The Economy." In *Cambodia 1975–1978: Rendezvous with Death*, edited by K.D. Jackson, 109–150. Princeton, NJ: Princeton University Press, 1989.

United States. Department of Defense. "Conduct of the Persian Gulf War: Final Report to Congress." Washington, DC: Department of Defense, 1992.

Verba, S., R.A. Brody, E.B. Parker, N.H. Nie, N.W. Polsby, P. Ekman et al. "Public Opinion and the War in Vietnam." *American Political Science Review* 61.2 (1967): 317–333.

Vernon, J. "Financial Disintermediation in a Macroeconomic Framework: Comment." *Journal of Finance* 28.4 (1973): 1029–1032.

Vernon, J. R. "World War II Fiscal Policies and the End of the Great Depression." *Journal of Economic History* 54.4 (1994): 850–868.

Vickery, M. *Kampuchea: Politics, Economics, and Society*. London: Frances Printer, 1986.

Wagner, R. Harrison. "Bargaining and War." *American Journal of Political Science* 44.3 (2000): 469–484.

Walder, D. *The Short Victorious War: The Russo-Japanese Conflict*. New York: Harper & Row, 1974.

Walters, R., Jr. *Albert Gallatin: Jeffersonian Financier and Diplomat*. New York: The Macmillan Company, 1957.

Waterbury, J. *The Egypt of Nasser and Sadat: The Political Economy of Two Regimes*. Princeton, NJ: Princeton University Press, 1983.

Weisiger, A. *Logic of War: Explanations for Limited and Unlimited Conflicts*. Ithaca, NY: Cornell University Press, 2013.

Whiting, R. *The Labor Party and Taxation: Party Identity and Political Purpose in Twentieth-Century Britain*. Cambridge: Cambridge University Press, 2004.

Wilkenfeld, H.C. *Taxes and People in Israel*. Cambridge, MA: Harvard University Press, 1973.

Wilson, R.A. *Personal Exemptions and Individual Income Tax Rates, 1913–2002*. Washington, DC: Internal Revenue Service, 2008. Retrieved from http://www.irs.gov/pub/irs-soi/02inpetr.pdf.

Witte, J.F. *The Politics and Development of the Federal Income Tax*. Madison: The University of Wisconsin Press, 1985.

Wolff, E. "The Distributional Effects of the 1969–75 Inflation on Holdings of Household Wealth in the United States." *Review of Income and Wealth* 25 (1979): 195–207.
Yamamura, K. "Success Ill-gotten? The Role of Meiji Militarism in Japan's Technological Progress." *Journal of Economic History* 37.1 (1977): 113–135.
Yonekura, S. *The Japanese Iron and Steel Industry, 1950–1990: Continuity and Discontinuity*. New York: St. Martin's Press, 1994.
Young, A.N. *China's Wartime Finance and Inflation, 1937–1945*. Cambridge, MA: Harvard University Press, 1965.
Zelizer, J.E. *Taxing America: Wilbur D. Mills, Congress, and the State, 1945–1975*. Cambridge: Cambridge University Press, 1998.

# Index

www.ingramcontent.com/pod-product-compliance
Lightning Source LLC
Chambersburg PA
CBHW032047100926
51263CB00013B/267/J
* 9 7 8 1 5 0 1 7 0 2 4 9 5 *